In the Ether

A Memoir of Holding Space

Colleen Hildebrand

Le Bovier Publishing

First Edition Release. September 2022

Cover design by: Colleen Hildebrand
Digital design by: Jenna Hildebrand

ISBN: 979-8-9865571-0-6

"The most beautiful people we have known are those who have known defeat, known suffering, known struggle, known loss, and have found their way out of the depths. These persons have an appreciation, a sensitivity, and an understanding of life that fills them with compassion, gentleness, and a deep loving concern.

Beautiful people do not just happen."

~Elisabeth Kubler-Ross

Contents

Chapter 1. Listen.. 1

Chapter 2. Magical Motherfucker... 8

Chapter 3. Let's Talk about Sex... 15

Chapter 4. Three Rules... 23

Chapter 5. Bearing Children.. 30

Chapter 6. Rules, not Wishes.. 37

Chapter 7. Feral Boys 41

Chapter 8. Southern Comfort.. 48

Chapter 9. Strays... 56

Chapter 10. Behavioral Evolution.. 63

Chapter 11. All In 68

Chapter 12. Spilling Ink 74

Chapter 13. Interior Landscapes.. 78

Chapter 14. Christmas Parties and Greek Mythology............... 83

Chapter 15. Risk Assessment... 87

Chapter 16. Bound in a Nutshell.. 92

Chapter 17. Revelation I... 97

Chapter 18. Truth, Consequences, and Nietzsche.................... 101

Chapter 19. Character Witness.. 104

Chapter 20. Calumny as Spectator Sport 110

Chapter 21. Batshit Crazy 115

Chapter 22. Nice Jugs... 121

Chapter 23. Cosmic Jokes 126

Chapter 24. Caught in the Spin 131

Chapter 25. Image Rehearsal Therapy 136

Chapter 26. An Agnostic, Insomniac, and Dyslexic Walk into a Bar .. 142

Chapter 27. Farsighted 146

Chapter 28. Collective Magic 153

Chapter 29. Snakes 161

Chapter 30. Saying I Love You 169

Chapter 31. Empath 176

Chapter 32. Clerical Error 182

Chapter 33. On Being Asked What Advice I'd Give a Son 194

Chapter 34. Hard Decisions 203

Chapter 35. Prisms 207

Chapter 36. Doves 215

Chapter 37. Revelation II 225

Chapter 38. Cosmic Irony 234

Chapter 39. Things You Can't Tell by Looking 240

Chapter 40. Cleaving 245

Afterword 248

Acknowledgements 251

About the Author 252

For Ryan and Abby,

You already know.

Author's Note

This is a story I am honored to tell for many reasons. Though I have combined multiple events into single occasions for economy, changed a detail or two for anonymity, and have likely fallen victim to the subjectivity of memory, I have presented the years from late 2015 to 2021 as we lived them. Additionally, I have changed the names of all characters other than Abby, Ryan, Scott, Jenna, Peter Blair, Ashlyn, and Dion.

In truth, this memoir has a very specific audience: my daughter, Abby, and her former boyfriend, Ryan. I wrote it for them as each searched for meaning in events that began to unfold in November of 2016. I thought I could help them make sense of it all, help them find themselves and—if I am being honest—help them find each other again. That was my hope.

I began writing *In the Ether* in May 2017. By then, I knew I was witnessing something uncommon and meaningful. Without realizing it, I was already several thousand words into a draft because of the emails and letters Ryan and I exchanged up to that point. When I finally chose the title in 2019, after a phone conversation he and I had about "all these crazy coincidences," which neither of us believed were coincidental, I certainly didn't anticipate its current relevance, which still confounds me. The body of text from the first to final chapter exists as it did when I completed the manuscript on July 5, 2020, the night of a full Buck moon on which I spoke to both Abby and Ryan, each calling me concerned about the other. This note and the afterword are newer, written little more than a month after an accident proved the first sentence of chapter one unfathomably true. For just a moment, I believed I knew how this story would end. I think we all did. The events of July 2021, however, kept my writing honest.

This book tells Ryan's story, but only as it became known to me through my relationship with him—and that began when he met my daughter, Abby. Their connection, perhaps star-crossed and eternal, invited me to write these pages. This book, most accurately, is our story.

Chapter 1

Listen

Listen, I'd like to tell you a story, but you should know before it begins, I don't know how it ends. You could argue that it isn't really mine to tell. It's Abby and Ryan's—or Abby's and Ryan's. That detail makes a difference. I guess it's the version I experienced. But, I think theirs would be pretty close. The situation is messy. It isn't one I would have imagined involving me or anyone I know, but Abby always had a knack for the unexpected. When she was three years old, my father died, and with her being so little, we didn't bring her to the burial. As my husband and I were leaving, I bent down to kiss her goodbye and was met with crossed arms and a scowl. "What's wrong?" I asked. Too quickly she shot back, "I never get to bury Pawpaw!" That comment, rather than the sadness and beauty of the service, is what I remember best about the day of my dad's funeral.

He passed away unexpectedly—to us anyway—of a massive heart attack. I say "to us" because he knew he was going to die. Easter Sunday had been the week before, and our whole family was together for dinner. When my mom invited us to dinner again the following week, I found it unusual, but Daddy wanted everyone to come over for barbeque. So, we put the girls in their car seats and made the hour-long drive to my parents' house, had a nice time, and said our I-love-you's and goodbyes, just like the week before. The

1

next day, Daddy died.

I got the call while I was at work, during first period. My principal stood at my classroom door and quietly called me outside, saying to bring my things. A quiet panic rose in me. When I was close enough to hear him just above a whisper, he said, "There's been an accident." My eyes filled. I thought Scott or Jenna or Abby, but before I could speak, Mr. Brauner said, "Your dad has had a heart-attack. Scott is waiting on the phone in the office for you." I knew immediately he was gone.

Scott said the EMT had taken him to the hospital with my mom, and that my sister, Ella, was on her way. But I knew. When I got off the phone, Mr. Brauner asked if I'd like someone to drive me home, but I told him I'd be fine. The forty-minute drive gave me time. I could think, remember, talk to him in that strange way that the living try to engage the dead. And I did. During that drive I had the sensation that he was with me, lingering as some say souls do. I spoke to him, aloud, as crazy as that sounds. I guess that's just human, really. But what's actually crazy is that I heard him speak back—not audibly, but through an inner voice. He told me what you'd expect, I guess, that he loved me and that he had to go. He had tied the loose ends here and now had to fix things with Zeke, my brother. Zeke had died more than a decade before—drowned on his twenty-fourth birthday. He and my dad had fought just before. It was the last time they saw each other.

Daddy was a wild man of sorts for some of his life. Of course, he had settled by the time I was born. I only saw his past through stories and occasional flashes of anger that scared me so deeply into myself, letting even my voice escape seemed a risk. Despite his explosive temper and alternate reticence, I know he loved me, though he didn't say it until tragedy drew the words from him. I heard my Dad's first "I love you" when I was nineteen, standing on our front lawn hoping that my brother's body would be found alive. It wasn't.

Driving home the day Daddy died was strange. The conversation I had with him felt so real that I am not sure whether I experienced the power of the mind to create its own reality in response to stress or the peace of other-worldly contact. It wasn't the first time I faced that wonder. After Zeke died, I had a "visitation" dream. It was about two weeks after his funeral, and I had fallen asleep on the sofa. I dreamed I saw myself sleeping there, but then, in the dream, I woke when Zeke shook my shoulder. "Colleen, wake up. Are you up?" he said. I remember my confusion, knowing he was gone, but there in the grey and blue flannel shirt he wore too often, he bent over me beside the floral sofa in my parents' den. I sat up. "Tell Mom and Dad, I'm okay. Everything's good." That was all. I remember wanting to speak to him, beginning to say something, but then I awoke, sitting up just as I was in the dream.

I guess it was a dream.

Part of me wants to believe, maybe does believe, that it was real. Another part just marvels at the power of our brains. Either way, I felt better about Zeke, about his soul, about the fight.

The day of that fight, over thirty years ago, should be a blur of memory, but it is as clear as the air before me and equally laden with motes of the other lives, other influences, which led to it. I suppose there is no such thing as an isolated incident. It was a Thursday. I had come home from college knowing the rear passenger-side tire on my car was going flat. Maybe if I had stopped to fix it, tempers and blame and confusion wouldn't have combined into tragedy. The tire initiated the whole episode: Why couldn't any of us take care of the things we had? Why were we so irresponsible? Did we know money didn't grow on trees? When Zeke, who had just come in from work, spoke up saying the tire wasn't a big deal and that he would fix it, Daddy, who was just getting ready to leave for work, a night shift, told him to mind his "own fucking business." Ella, my sister, was there and said something in Zeke's defense. Daddy told her to shut up and get out, that she didn't live there anymore. I had heard my dad speak crassly before, but never to us. The argument evolved into something else: a battle of wills—not between a father and son, but between two men who never shared a perspective.

The result was ugly, violent.

When my dad reached for Zeke's shotgun on the rack in the corner of the den, Zeke grabbed him. My father looked at him with an expression I had never seen before, a combination of rage, frustration, and sadness. Zeke didn't wrestle the gun away from Daddy, though. He didn't have to. Inexplicably, my dad just stopped. He put the gun down on the kitchen counter and walked out of the room. I didn't see him again until too early that Saturday morning, when Scott brought me home from what would become our first full weekend spent together. Funny, I just realized my father and my then-future husband said, "I love you," to me for the first time on the same day.

Sometimes emotion, good or bad, has to boil within us before we allow it to bubble over and escape from our lips. In the weeks following my dad's death, my family—my mom, sister, and uncles—talked more about Zeke's. It was as if we were searching for a connection that would allow us to make sense of separate tragedies, of how we got from there to here in what seemed less than the thirteen years it had been. Sometimes, I think nothing is separate at all. Zeke's death, Daddy's death—everything bleeds into everything else. I look for the connections. Sometimes, I find them. Occasionally, they burst in demanding attention. But usually, to most, the universe is quiet.

So are we.

Too often we only talk, truly express ourselves, in crisis, with past and present moments spilling down our cheeks. I wish I knew a better way into the future, one that leaves the pain of the past uninvited. How can we keep the wisdom gained from tragedies and wrongs and walk forward uninjured? How can we make sense of life? Sometimes, survival seems to be denial, selective and focused, a purging. But I find that difficult to accept. Reflection, introspection, and searching benefit us far more. We have to choose it, though. My dad taught me that. After Zeke's death, he changed. He sank into himself and found meaning in loss, in letting go, which must have been unimaginably hard to do given the circumstances. He began healing by reading. He started with the Bible, the book of Ezekiel.

I didn't have a visitation dream about my father. I guess the conversation I had in the car the day he died took its place. When I got home from school that morning, Scott met me at the door, saying we had to hurry. I told him, no, Daddy was already gone. "When? Did your mom or Ella call school?" he asked. I said no. I just knew. Scott said we couldn't be sure yet, and we left with the girls, whom he had picked up from school, strapped into their car seats just like the day before, except this time, we dropped them off at our babysitter's home. We made the hour-long drive again, and when we arrived at the hospital, my brother-in-law met us at the door saying, "They couldn't resuscitate him."

Like Zeke, Daddy had a two-day wake and funeral, and like Zeke's, it was packed. The morning of the funeral started with a church service, and when a St. Michael the Archangel school bus pulled into the parking lot and unloaded my entire senior class, I struggled to contain my tears. During the homily, Father John spoke of life being a book, and I hoped my students thought of Donne's "Meditation 17," the literature we were studying when Mr. Brauner came to my classroom with the news that day. Donne says, at death, a life is not torn from the volume, but "translated into a better language." How appropriate, I thought, Thank you, Daddy. The church service, which Jenna and Abby attended, ended, and then we brought them to my sister's in-laws' home while everyone else continued to the cemetery. That's when Abby said she never gets to bury Pawpaw.

Jenna was absolutely no help in preparing me to raise her little sister. Four years older, Jenna is completely different. She never slept as a baby. Midnight car rides and late-night vacuuming were regular parts of our routine in the first several months. Those were the only things that kept her from crying sometimes. Jenna was a difficult baby. Since then, my girls have changed roles. Abby was a difficult teenager. Where Jenna has never given me a reason, in twenty-six years, to doubt or mistrust her, Abby rained a deluge of reasons over the past twenty-two to make up for all the tears she didn't cry as an infant. High school was a trial, not so much academically—she's very smart—but socially. She's my wild child, my unprovoked rebel.

Often I'd ask Abby if there were some memory or resentment lodged in her mind causing her to act in ways one might expect of a girl raised in different circumstances—less fortunate ones, dysfunctional ones. She always said no, that Scott and I were never the cause, that she wasn't rebellious. She was curious, adventurous.

To me, she was inscrutable.

Her thirst for adventure terrified me—her, too, at least on one occasion. In high school, she wrote a prize-winning essay about it. I was exceedingly proud of her accomplishment, but a bit embarrassed by her unabashed disclosure. I've saved it, the essay, and reread it from time to time.

Of Kittens and Curiosity

I am three years old; I am in the chicken coop at Camp. I have a ragged towel as my armor, and I intend to use it for one purpose: kitten-wrangling. Although the summer sun steadily approaches the horizon and the mosquitoes become more vicious, I refuse to go inside for dinner until I am accompanied by a furry little feline, which will probably not be too happy about being swaddled in the towel. Finally, I hear a very faint "mew" coming from the corner of the coop. I slowly creep towards the nearly imperceptible sound and peek behind the last chicken box; I spy a terrified, tiny, black kitten with blurry blue eyes. Immediately, I scoop her up into the towel and try to console her while protecting my hands from her frantic scratches. She looks at me with mistrust in her eyes, and I am wondering, why is she doing this? How doesn't she see that I am trying to keep her safe? Why won't she just let me protect her? For the next twelve years, I would ask myself these questions every time a kitten strayed from me and allowed its curiosity to lead it into danger, which was always present in the form of blood-thirsty raccoons or speed limitless country roads.

I am eight years old and holding one of three new kittens which recently appeared at Camp. My determination to keep them safe is strong. Over the years, too many sweet babies have disappeared into the country night. Every morning, I wake up and head to the barn to check on them. I open the tack room door, praying that all three are still in the crate. I see only two. How could one have escaped? The box is so tall. Why would one escape? Although I make sure they have food, water, and what I think is a safe environment every evening, it isn't enough. They are growing stronger and more agile, causing me to grow more frustrated with my inability to keep up with their energy and curiosity. Each time I carry them back to their safe haven in the crate, they become rambunctious, wanting to roam more widely. I am eight years old, and my only concerns are the kittens' safety and happiness, yet I am failing them; I need help.

Confused, I ask my mom, "Momma, why don't they want to stay in the tack room when I'm not there? Why do they still want to be out where bad things can hurt them? They just don't know how dangerous it is!"

"Well sweetie," my mom responds, "you're right; they don't understand. God made them curious, and they want to explore and discover things on their own. No matter how much you love them, you can't stop them from being kittens."

I know she is right; they need more independence, more room to grow, so I give them access to the whole barn again. They seem thrilled as they jump from saddle to saddle in the tack room, stalking each other. Unfortunately, those happy few days end in greater tragedy than we have experienced before. Upon going to feed them one morning, I discover another kitten has vanished.

Crying and frustrated, I trekked back to the kitchen to tell my mom the awful news. Although she did not seem surprised, she listened patiently as I pleaded to take the remaining kitten home, to let it live in the house where I could care for it and know it would be safe. To my surprise, she agreed.

Years later, my mom shared the truth of the two kittens' disappearances with me, a revelation that also explained her soft-heartedness toward the little survivor. Unknown to me, she would go down to the barn early to feed the horses and check on the kittens before I woke. On one morning, she walked into the feed room to discover a raccoon scurrying out through a small opening where the concrete floor met the corrugated metal wall. Also, that morning, she swept up the four tiny paws and vertebrae, for raccoons will devour anything, except another animal's feet and spine. Despite my efforts, I could not protect them from the laws of nature, for I could hardly protect myself.

I am seventeen years old; it is a Saturday morning, and I just stepped out of the shower. Something isn't right; I feel distant from the world around me, and my heart begins to race. My vision seems blurry; sound is muffled. I fall onto my bed, faintly calling for my mom. She rushes to me, and one of the last images I see is the fear in her eyes when she looks into mine. She asks me what happened, and I attempt to answer, then all goes black. She wraps me in a towel and holds me. I hear her, as if through water, ask if we need to call 911, but I say no. I just need to eat—I haven't eaten since noon yesterday. Hesitant to let me go, she rushes to the kitchen. As I lie on my bed, weak and alone, I understand. I understand what is really happening to me. My curious and defiant nature has led me to this moment; my body is having a reaction induced by substances that have no business being in my system, yet they are there. I have chosen to use them. In that moment, I understand. I understand her seventeen years of worry and warning. I understand her powerlessness to control what happens to me. In that moment, I understand her. She is me, and in that moment, I realize, I am a kitten.

Seems like an epiphany, doesn't it? I hoped it would be, but from ages seventeen to twenty, there were times when I thought she might be lost to the night.

Learning, like letting go, comes slowly. I suppose her risk-taking spirit was critical to bringing us here, but still, as much as Abby can make the most ordinary thing interesting, sometimes ordinary would be nice. With Jenna's being so untroubled, I could have easily forgotten how wrong life can go, even vainly forgotten my own failures in light of successful parenting. I consider Abby the child who has kept me human, who's kept me humble. She has been struggling against me as often as she's been nestled in my arms, crying over some self-inflicted disappointment, mother and child cleaving together. Now, though, she is twenty-two years old and has moved on, attempting to save lives far greater than those of kittens. And I'm still trying to save everyone, though I know too well that people can only save themselves. I know I have to let go.

I'm not sure whether I should consider myself fortunate to have learned early that life is an exercise in release, but I am certain of that truth. Loss through death, disappointment, error, neglect, or choice is inevitable, but understanding that does not make accepting it any easier. There is a lifetime of difference between knowing something and feeling its truth. Learning to continue through great pain—to find a reason to smile through it, a noble cause to encourage you forward—is a lesson I thought I understood absolutely. Yet, I continue to listen and learn. I marvel at what others have encountered and have survived—are surviving. I suppose my quiet life always had an inner intensity that readied me for the tasks to come, and I wanted to help him. I wanted to help Abby help him.

Chapter 2

Magical Motherfucker

"Can he stay with us?" she asked after calling me up to her room. The question seemed outrageous, but coming from Abby—a fledgling nestled into the white down comforter of her bed—it shouldn't have surprised me.

She had known him less than six months, had only seen him in person over a brief week in December, and now, in March, she really expected me to say "yes." I had never met him, this Marine who had become her most recent future plan. His story—his need—was compelling.

He had a home near the river, the banks of which had recently flooded with the unprecedented spring rains. The house—already in disrepair—had taken in water. His father had just passed away—the day after Abby's birthday—and he was coming home from Camp Pendleton to handle the funeral arrangements.

"I'm sure he has friends he can stay with, love," I told her, eying her phone lying screen-lit-up on the comforter. Ryan Freeman, shirtless with his dog, smirked at me.

Abby responded, "But, we live closer than most of them, and the actual close ones flooded, too, and besides, I want him to be somewhere comfortable, where he can feel taken care of instead of having to take care of everybody else."

I leaned against her dresser to brace myself for what I knew would be a persuasive argument, but still trying to deflect, I said, "Abby, don't be so dramatic. He must have family or someone."

Her voice rose an octave as she scooted to the edge of her bed and sat cross-legged. "Mama, you don't understand. The people he has don't have anything. His brother is living out of his car right now because of the house. His sister just had a baby and lives with her boyfriend's family. His grandparents' house still has a foot of sludge in it—that I'm sure he's gonna be the one to clean up—and that doesn't even count the stacks of magazines his grandma's collected for thirty years. Which are now soaked," she rambled.

"Sweetie, I get it. He has it rough. But you have to understand most sane people don't invite twenty-two-year-old strangers who have romantic interests in their freshly-eighteen-year-old daughters into their homes. You don't even really know this boy—man!" I corrected. My common sense was trying hard to outweigh my compassion.

At still a notch higher, she said, "Mom," dragging the word out into two syllables, "I've talked to him every day since Christmas! Aren't you the one who says good relationships aren't based on physical contact? Well, he's in California. All we can do is talk!" She punctuated her justification by throwing herself backward onto the mattress.

Sitting down next to her, my hand patting her knee, I said, "Abby, this is just a lot. I have so many hesitations. All I can promise is that I'll think about it and talk to Dad, but what you've told me about the situation doesn't make me feel great. I mean, we'd have to be crazy."

What Abby had told me about Ryan Freeman's situation was horrific, truly a mother's nightmare. He came from hardship: a broken, struggling home complete with various types of dysfunctions. She said his mom died when he was fifteen, a possible suicide or the result of domestic violence. The details were fuzzy. Though officially ruled a suicide, no one in the family accepted it, with good reason. There was a boyfriend, a turbulent relationship, an intense argument. Ryan and his younger brother found her in the kitchen, shotgun on the ground.

Now, his father was gone, too.

Ryan had called Abby on Friday morning. She was in her first-period class, calculus, and he knew that, so she found his timing odd. Abby asked permission to step outside to answer and, later told me, all he said was, "I'm going home." Misunderstanding, she told him that was good; he could catch up on sleep after working all night. Then he said, "No, I mean coming home. I'm coming home. Daddy's dead." Then, she said his voice cracked and he sobbed.

That day was only the second time in my career as a teacher that my life outside of the classroom flowed uncontrollably in. Abby came immediately to my room, seeking the comfort she could not offer Ryan, calling me into the breezeway to tell me what happened. Abby had friends, or people she thought were friends, in my class. As I tried to console her just outside the door, I imagined what they might have been saying inside. Some had already expressed harsh opinions of Ryan, asking her if she were insane—talking to a guy like "that." *That* may have meant promiscuous or older or poor or any number of other things that would seem foreign to a gaggle of suburban girls. The real problem, as I saw it, was that Abby had ventured from the crowd. She wanted nothing to do with high school boys and it became a problem.

Adolescence was a tough time for Abby, and in hindsight, I have some regrets about my choices for her then. She had always been curious about life, which was wonderful when it led her to research the life cycle of the periodic cicada, but it wasn't so great when, at the age of eleven, she told me she was having "sexual urges". I can assure you, sexual urges are two words that no mother wants to hear from her child. But there they were. At least she was secure enough in our relationship to be honest with me although, for a time, that would change, too. The span from eleven to sixteen hijacked Abby, replacing my preciously feisty child with her wily doppelganger, an exchange of ginger tea for vinegar. I've never been mistaken for being older than I am, at least not until recently, as I can no longer outrun the consequences of the sun, but Abby looked thirteen at eleven, fifteen at thirteen, and, well, you get the idea. Her face was just as young and sweet as you can imagine, all doe-brown eyes above a splash of the lightest freckles. But from the neck down, she had suddenly become Jessica Rabbit. She was drawn that way, but she wasn't bad—yet.

I suppose Scott and I were a bit blind to her no longer looking like a little girl, but others weren't, and she enjoyed the attention more than we realized, something social media certainly facilitated. Her Facebook friends became too numerous for me to keep up with, though I tried to monitor things. In fact, although I had no clue at the time, my eighth-grade Abby had "friended" an older high school student named Ryan Freeman (though five more years would pass before she ever saw him in person). I suppose Abby did no more than most typical kids—experimenting with different combinations of friends, alcohol, and drugs throughout her teens.

The problem was that I had hoped my daughters would not be typical.

Parenting requires such a delicate balance—no wonder some parents go far off course. Imperfect people are bound to raise imperfect kids, but I think all parents hope their children are somehow improved versions of themselves. Maybe some don't. It's possible, I suppose, that some parents aren't really up for the commitment or the challenge, and the resentment or confusion or guilt over it, over their own lack, overwhelms them, exploding outward like shots from a pneumatic rifle—not with enough force to kill, but enough for the target to feel the impact. Parents—people—don't have to be maladjusted to aim and fire words, though. We have all wished to recapture some bullet once it has left the barrel.

I know I have.

Often, I feel I have never gotten parenting right, not that I wasn't ready for the commitment. Both Jenna and Abby were well-planned babies, yet I've suffered the work-motherhood dilemma as much as those with more prestigious careers. I was the one who couldn't chaperone the class field trips because I had my own class to attend, the one who sent crappy Valentines for the first-grade exchange, thinking a card was enough when other moms found time to make thirty gift bags filled with treasures. And socially, I've always been a bit off-center, a little too in my mind, too soft and hopeful. That idealism spilled into my parenting, making me especially bad at discipline, thinking that thinking about what was wrong and discussing it was better than punishment.

Abby and I talked about consequences quite seriously when she was about sixteen, after failed attempts to reform her habits through typical discipline. I acknowledged that imposed consequences—taking her phone away, suspending privileges, requiring extra "chores"—would only encourage her sneakiness and resentfulness. She agreed. So, we talked about natural consequences, about what would be worth the risk, and about how sometimes the realization of what is worth it happens too late, and how tragic that can be. After all, Zeke had not planned to drown himself, only his sadness. I wish, still, I could convey to her how much his death hurt everyone, the devastation it brought to friends, to my dad, to all of us. Some risks are not worth the likely results.

The belief in the invincibility of youth is quite a spectacle to see. Rarely, if ever, can neophyte risk-takers discern adaptive from maladaptive risks; and rarely are they aware of the long-term consequences of the latter—of the lasting impressions they leave deeply embedded in the primal soil of the amygdala. Some experiences would be better if forgotten, but the body cannot forget, though the conscious mind may appear to free itself from the burden from time to time.

Sometimes I think Abby has pushed certain memories down so deep she can no longer connect cause to effect. When she was nearly fifteen, she had her first boyfriend, a nice enough kid, who was a year older than she. He was a student in my sophomore class, and I did my best not to mingle being his teacher with being his girlfriend's mother.

The non-mingling was pointless. As young romance often does, the relationship ended abruptly with the requisite drama, but my presence between the two of them seemed to create a negative association in Abby's brain between me and her first heartbreak. Where mothers are typically the source of comfort, I somehow seemed to worsen her pain. The situation between them was typical enough; there was a party, attended by both of them (though not together), and to Abby's horror, through a bedroom door left ajar, she caught a glimpse of him with some other girl, venturing into places she had not dared to go. They broke up. She did her best to avoid him, but I saw him every morning in second period. I suppose my knowing him in a context that did not include Abby caused her to resent me.

This first romance ended painfully, full of unasked and unanswered questions, self-doubt, confusion. Even seeing his name atop a stack of papers on the kitchen table as I did my weekend grading pained her, and I wonder if, somewhere in that still-developing adolescent brain, she grew angry at me for seeing him Monday through Friday and for reading what he wrote and responding—for still having a "relationship" with him. Of course, the logic twisted like the coils of a broken clock, but the emotions were as real as the passage of time. My relationship with Abby suffered. She challenged more of my motherly advice, became reticent, and seemed to resent me for a long while.

Tension filled the next years as Abby defined herself among her peers as the outlier who would willingly test the boundaries, skirting along the margins of expected decorum, allowing others to develop better ideas of what was and was not acceptable through their observations of her and the reactions she elicited—namely, the gossip. I think she, however, mixed up the messages, embracing the scandalous behavior instead of avoiding it. Somehow, she came away from her first romantic relationship believing she had to become "that kind of girl" to hold a boy's attention. And become her, she did. The next boyfriend acquainted her with indulgent, wild nights and morning after pills. I found out, of course—that's when we had that conversation about imposed punishment. I don't think I grounded Abby again, yet she did begin to notice the consequences, the kind life brings of its own accord. But, Abby is a slow learner, for all her potential brilliance. I suppose if Abby had not created herself in her own image, she never would have met Ryan. God knows if she had embraced an image closer to mine, the forest of red flags would have driven her back, kept her from rushing headlong toward risk.

Instead, she gathered those flags like daisies.

Abby and Ryan met through Instagram, and, you could say, their mutual admiration for well-proportioned physiques. Ryan had no clue that @itsyaqurlabby (her Instagram account) and "Abby Hildebrand" on Facebook were the same person. I suppose Abby Hildebrand was just an obsessed little girl to him—if he noticed that they were friends at all. "Itsyaqurl," well, she was something else. He commented on a post as he was coming home from deployment, and she commented back. They exchanged DMs. They texted. They met at a local gym and went on a date—a sushi restaurant. She had given me a tidy description of him back then: joined the Marines to create more opportunities for himself; was very driven and responsible, super smart; and although he came from nothing, was determined to make something of himself. All of that was great, but a quick perusal of his social media accounts, none of which were private, showed a few other qualities.

Ryan did seem to be most of what Abby had claimed, but I could see that he, too, was a wild one. His Instagram was interesting: waterfalls and hiking; a close up of his eye, very blue; a meme reading "The amount of alcohol I would need to sleep with you would actually kill me. #handorregret;" a number of selfies; various tattoos; him on a beach wearing only a guitar; him beside his mother's grave; Marine shenanigans; and alcohol, lots of it. How many pictures included bottles and bottles of Jack Daniels? And what was last Halloween's outfit? Daisy Dukes, cowboy boots and hat, and a tie-dye crop-top reading "magical motherfucker." This was the young man my child wanted to invite into our home.

Ok, it was funny. Well, in fact, many of his hashtags were out-rightly hilarious, but not in a daughter's-romantic-interest-acceptable way, more of a this-is-funny-so-I'm-gonna-say-it way, which, I suppose, demands a certain kind of respect. Maybe. Anyway, while I was more amused than horrified, I was also saddened, and more than a little cautious, especially when, sometime in February, I learned that, back in December, Abby and Ryan had gotten to know each other better than I had realized. I couldn't believe she had already slept with him. She hardly knew him. Was this whom I had raised? Had she at least used protection? Was she aware of diseases? I asked all these questions, and naturally she swayed between defensiveness and guilt. I don't remember what happened next. She probably cried. Abby is a strange combination of audacious and fragile, like, well, like an angry kitten.

Now it was mid-March, just after her eighteenth birthday, and she wanted him to stay in our home. As it turns out, I was casual friends with a teacher at Ryan's former high school. I had no idea of whether she knew him, or knew of him, but I needed a more reliable reference than Abby. I called Donna one afternoon.

"Hey, Donna. It's Colleen Hildebrand."

"Hey, girl, how is that *Time* article going over in your 101?" she asked, talking shop.

"It's confusing them, but it isn't terrible. But listen, I'm calling about something personal," I explained, probably confusing her, because, although we were friendly at professional events, we weren't close friends.

"Oh? What's going on?"

"Well, my youngest, Abby, has met someone a bit older who went to Park, and I was wondering if you knew him. His name is Ryan Freeman."

"Oh my God! Yes."

Here it was: confirmation that no mother in her right mind would invite this womanizing, hard-living, foul-mouthed, pretty-boy Marine to stay under the same roof as her daughter.

I was unprepared for what came next.

"You will never meet someone with such a huge reason to hate the world but who loves life so much. Ryan was one of my favorite students. He was in my English III class, and he was awesome. So smart, but from a really bad family situation. One of the sweetest boys..."

Ryan Freeman was, indeed, a magical motherfucker.

Donna, a teacher not known for her fondness of students, simply gushed over him for a solid five minutes, and all the while, I was thinking, great, exactly what I was hoping to hear. I can't deny, though, that all along, a small voice within me had been saying similar things, not so much because I had surmised them from my investigation of Ryan, but because I had begun to see a change in Abby. She was becoming herself again, regaining perspective and compassion and respect.

Donna was able to elaborate on some of what Abby had already told me about Ryan: his mother's death, the suspicions, Ryan's role in caring for his siblings, who were close in age but clearly looked to him for support. She told me that he had been homeless for a time, slept in the school parking lot in his car at one point, yet never seemed to spend a minute feeling sorry for himself. After a few days of researching and deliberating, I finally brought Abby's outrageous request to Scott, although I had already made up my mind.

I, of course, acknowledged how ridiculous it was to consider but countered the logic with compassion. We arrived at a compromise of who would sleep where and spoke to Abby, who listened more attentively and patiently than she had in months, maybe years. When Scott and I finished speaking, Abby hesitantly confirmed, "So, he can stay with us?"

We nodded our assent. We were crazy.

Chapter 3

Let's Talk about Sex

The ten days Ryan would be in town happened to fall over spring break and Easter, which came early in 2016, so, thankfully, I didn't have to worry about Abby skipping school to stay home with him. He wanted her to pick him up from the airport, which I thought was odd given the reason for his homecoming. Surely, his brother or sister or the close friend he would stay with when he wasn't here would be a better choice. But no, Abby braved the airport traffic a bit nervously then brought him home to 9317 Kismet Circle. Jenna had a trip with her boyfriend, Michael, planned over that week, so my firstborn would not be home, and although Ryan could have stayed in our extra room upstairs, we decided separate floors were best. He would sleep in Abby's room and Abby would sleep downstairs on the sofa. I knew the futility of the arrangement, really, but Scott and I had to convey our expectations that this visit would not be conjugal. It was. In fact, I distinctly remember going on a fifteen-minute run and noticing the open blinds of Abby's bedroom window as I got home—keeping a lookout, no doubt.

What a losing battle it is to try to prevent young, curious, hungry bodies from satisfying themselves. Sex is such an enigma. I suppose that's because there are as many meanings, purposes for sex, as there are people who have sex. When I taught at St. Michael's years ago, I somehow won the job of speaking at various events—at the senior retreat, the honor society induction, and a True Love Waits assembly. Teaching at an all-boys Catholic school was sometimes a study in hypocrisy. I mean, to be sure, all of them knew what the Church said, what it wanted them to say, but what it said and they did were seldom aligned. I remember how I began the TLW's talk, probably a little shocking for the priests, who had been the ones to decide that a married, not-too-unpleasant-looking woman might engage the students' attention more than one of them would. I momentarily, silently questioned whether they were using me in some offensive way when Father Mike first asked, but then I decided I had something to say and accepted the task of telling seventy-eight eleventh grade boys that everything their bodies were telling them was wrong.

Walking into the chapel—where God could see us close up—I had the chorus of Salt-N-Pepa's "Let's Talk about Sex" in my head. I wondered if I should open by bursting into song. I didn't. Instead, I asked questions: "So, is anyone here, besides me, married?" No hands went up, of course. "No, huh? What about kids? Anyone have kids, I mean, that you know of?" That got an irreverent laugh from the braver boys. Father looked slightly peeved at what may have seemed like the opening of a stand-up routine. I continued, "Ok, then, no one here is married and starting a family, except me. I guess that means it's safe to say I'm the only one in the room having sex." The looks on their faces ranged from amused to confused to horrified. Whether they were horrified because I was a grown-up teacher who just admitted to being fully human or because I was a relatively young woman who did not acknowledge them as sexual beings, I couldn't tell, but I capitalized on their disbelief.

"Well, I can tell my last statement surprised some of you. But why? We'll talk about that, but before we really get into this, I'm going to need a few healthy volunteers." As I said this, I picked up a short stack of paper cups from behind the podium, so you can imagine the uncomfortable tension that developed as everyone wondered what role a collection of ten disposable cups at a sex talk might play. I explained, "I'd like to give these out to those of you who are willing to participate in an illustration, sort of a social experiment. And don't worry, you won't have to do anything with the cup other than spit in it, but if you are a guy who might enjoy the company of a young woman, please consider playing along." With that appeal to masculinity, hands shot up. I handed out the cups and told the boys to hold on to them for a bit.

I returned to my planned discussion by assuring them that I was not going to preach words like "no" and "don't" and "wait" at them. They had had enough of that, and I was sure it was working wonderfully. Instead, I was going to give them a few practical things to think about. I asked them to consider their reactions to my revelation that I was a sexually active person, and then discussed some of the stereotypes associated with sex: sexism, ageism, lookism. I asked which of the "isms" held them guiltiest. We talked about the inherent value of life, consent, double standards, reputations, and unanticipated consequences. Turns out there was a father among us, but the baby had been adopted by a couple in another state. The birth mother received updates—he did not. We talked about equality and responsibility working both ways. Finally, I told them a story about Amy, a lovely cardboard cutout of a "good" girl. Amy met Jared, my first volunteer sitting front and center, at the age of fourteen. They dated well into sophomore year, when hormones raged in a way that could no longer be ignored. She initiated the idea of sex. They were in love, and she wanted to prove it to him.

At this point, I told Jared he had a decision to make: would he or would he not have sex with Amy? The room smirked in anticipation. If he would, I told him to spit in the cup discreetly as he walked over to the table at the back of the room, where he would leave it. He did just that, not exactly discreetly. Believe me: I know how disgusting this is, but I can assure you that sixteen-year-old boys will enthusiastically, theatrically spit into paper cups or anywhere else, especially if they think it implies something about their virility. So, back to Amy. She and Jared continued dating throughout junior and most of senior year and it was great, but then graduation, separate colleges, and the freedom of it all brought the relationship to its natural but painful, amicable end. Jared and Amy went their separate ways.

Amy had brief relationship with volunteer number two several months later, and although he could have had sex with her one night after she passed out at his apartment, he did not spit in the cup, unlike many of the other guys she met and liked between her sophomore and senior years at State. Volunteers three through six spit, spit, spit, and spit. Number seven was different: a really good guy, a finance major, not just a hook-up. They were together almost a year, but then he graduated, received job offers and, soon enough, was going to New York to work as an investment banker. He hoped she understood. It was just too great an opportunity to pass up. Maybe, if they were both still single in a few years, fate would put them back together. Number eight was a rebound: spit. Nine was her first post-college relationship, and she loved him, but she wasn't ready to become a mother to his two kids. Nonetheless, the spit had been spat. So, there was Amy, having lived her life as she pleased and having defied the odds of becoming a one-in-three-statistic, which we also discussed. Now, at age twenty-five, she is back in her hometown, single, and alone at the farmer's market when who happens to be buying a jar of local honey, but Jared, after all those years.

She's happy to see him. He compliments her. They talk. There's still a spark. They have coffee. They have dinner. They'll soon have breakfast, so they have a really honest conversation about who they have been and become over the past seven years. As I say all this, I walk to the back of the chapel, where all those biohazard spit cups are. I'm also putting on latex gloves as I walk, a feat of coordination I surprised myself in accomplishing. The students watch, some cringing a little, wondering what will come next.

When I arrive at the table, I continue to narrate Amy and Jared's discussion of their dating lives post-each other as I pour, with my gloved hands, each spit cup into a larger, single glass. It was disgusting. As I conclude, I walk over to Jared and say that Amy has been honest with him, telling him that his past doesn't bother her, but she's wondering how he feels about hers. She's had sex with several other men, so aptly represented by the DNA—and whatever may be attached to it—contained in the glass. Then she looks at him and says, "This"—and here I raise the glass, thick with the remnants of experience, to which he was the first contributor— "is part of who I am." Does he want her?

I know the metaphor is imperfect, but it's visceral and memorable. In fact, Father got one or two parent phone calls over it because some thought it went too far, but I can guarantee those boys thought about the implications of sex beyond its physical pleasure that day. I hope they also learned something about hypocrisy. That was my point, I think. STDs aside, sex can't be divorced from meaning. Oxytocin and vasopressin assure that, and often the meaning is not equal for both parties. People treat sex as if it is recreation or an enhanced handshake to acknowledge attraction until love arrives, at which point it is supposed to mean something about commitment and value, a flipped switch. It's the difference between Monopoly and Wall Street. That's a problem.

So, yes, I'm fairly certain that Ryan was the racecar and Abby was the Scottie dog and they were all over the board despite my best attempts to raise Abby not to be Amy, though her choices are not uncommon. I wanted my daughters to see sex as a bond, not recreation. And like all things, what began as a game evolved. Actually, it transmuted entirely. You know the ticking that you hear on a rollercoaster as it begins to pick up speed or ascend its inclines? Well, that crescendo and the subsequent rush of its fall and the loops of its resolution have been the background music to the wild ride of their relationship.

When Abby and Ryan walked through the front door, only I was home, so we were all spared the tension Scott—who had, indeed, agreed to the arrangement, though reluctantly—would bring home with him. Ryan immediately introduced himself and thanked me for allowing him to stay. I expressed my condolences and suggested that Abby help him with his things, really just a duffel bag, and show him up to her room. They were down quickly enough and sat at the counter while I washed the few dishes in the sink, mostly just to be doing something that looked purposeful. Abby asked where Scott was, feeling a little anxious about Ryan's meeting him. He was at the gym, a very alpha place to be, but not as bad, I suppose, as out back cleaning his gun, which—by the way—doesn't exist.

Scott Hildebrand is a piece of work. He was the football star, ladies' man, life of the party in college, before me. How we fell in love so quickly and have lasted so long is a bit mysterious, but all these years later, I'm still smiling about it. He's a rare man, the kind who is strong enough to love without hesitation, to admit when he's wrong, and to forgive fully. He's not much like my own father was, except in his generosity, perhaps. But, he has none of the temper. I believe I love him most because of that—because he could be dangerous—his size makes that clear, but he chooses to be safe, which might just be the most noble thing I can imagine. Yes, I think that's why I love him. I feel safe and valued and content with him. Of course, he'd rather hear that it's because he's so attractive, which he is, but looks aren't enough to make a relationship last. We have lasted over thirty-one years, twenty-eight of which have been wonderful. If you add up all the times that we've second guessed ourselves, grew angry with each other, or were just in a bad place for whatever reason, three years of struggle would be about right, which doesn't sound so bad to me. Having gone through it makes me sure I am where I want to be. Despite the mythology around it—the madness, the rush, the crush, the falling—love really is a choice. When problems arise, there is only one of two options in every relationship, no matter how new or old: you either choose to work through it or give up on each other. People are either worth the effort or they're not. Scott and I have had our trying moments. We've chosen to get through them. We've chosen each other every time.

When he walked in that afternoon, sweaty shirt nearly dripping, post workout pump still going strong, I wanted to tell him there was no need for so much testosterone. Nonetheless, he shook Ryan's hand, quite firmly I'm sure, and introduced himself as Scott, not "Mr. Scott or Mr. Hildebrand." Being a polite southern boy, though, Ryan "mistered" him immediately, saying, "Thank you for having me, Mr. Scott. You don't know how much I appreciate it." Satisfied that his scent had marked the territory sufficiently, Scott told Ryan that he looked forward to talking with him but was going to take a quick shower right now. Ryan, standing at ease, said "yes sir," and that Abby was going to take him to his grandmother's soon to discuss arrangements for his father's service, but he looked forward to it when they got back. The reminder of Ryan's purpose in being home seemed to send a wave of conviction through Scott, as if he realized the posturing was not necessary. His demeanor softened as he expressed his condolences. Both Scott and I had lost our fathers; the difference, though, was that Scott's is still living.

Ryan stayed with us for about six of the ten days he was in town, breaking up the time with nights at friends' places and his own damaged home. During his time with us, I talked with him about nothing too intrusive, though he was quite willing to reveal some uncomfortable bits of his past. Upon each revelation, he'd offer a smile—his smile! I'll have to come back to that—and a bit of wisdom he'd gleaned from the experience and some wild tale of past adventures that sounded like lies. They weren't. Every time, there was Instagram or Facebook, or a picture on his camera roll to offer proof of the impossible. A thirteen-foot alligator in your backyard? "Well, yes, ma'am, would you like to see it?" And there was the picture. Shot in the leg by your brother? Picture. Baptized in the Jourdan River? Yep, on deployment. Picture. A flip off a thirty-foot cliff? Video. As I spoke with him, I thought, this boy's life is the stuff of fiction. I also thought he had a serious problem with taking risks. I understand the thrill of an adrenaline rush, but he seemed to have a bet with fate. We all know fate wins in the end, so why was he so eager to race towards it? There's an answer to that question, a long, complex one that has not begun to unravel yet.

Ryan was a storyteller, someone who saw making others smile as his job, his gift. But his disregard for his own safety, so well documented in images, was troubling. He, too, was clearly a dangerous man, but in a different way from Scott. I knew Abby really didn't need a like-minded soul with whom to run the ragged edges of life. I hoped she'd find someone who could lure her to a more centered, grounded place, but nothing indicated Ryan Freeman would be that someone. In him was a capacity for mayhem. He was the kind of person you just can't imagine, even if you try. He was electric in a room, so much so that it might just go up in flames—that he'd somehow extinguish. He was warm and consoling, despite the knives in his back. He was authentic yet contradictory, a lush velvety suede, one color when brushed in one direction, several shades darker in the other, and the underside: the toughest leather deeply grooved with pathways of memories beyond words, despite all the stories. Over the next three years, that is what I would come to understand and respect about Ryan Freeman, despite the turn of events that would lead me to knowing him so much better.

Abby and Ryan attended his father's funeral later that week, and true to Mr. Freeman's wishes, the event was more a celebration of his life than a mourning of his death. She dressed in a sky-blue romper with deep purple paisley accents that complemented Ryan's grey suit and blue eyes. They were a beautiful couple, a picture of possibility. Abby told me that after the pastor said a few ceremonious words, Ryan, losing patience with the impersonal nature of the ceremony, spoke up, asking the pastor to excuse his ungodly language and proceeded to call "bullshit" on the service. Then he played Lynyrd Skynyrd's "Free Bird," the thirteen-minute rendition, because that's what his father would want. He was finally free from what must have been a painful life.

The oldest poets, mystics, and sages tell us that life is suffering, and people try to ease their pain through all manner of avoidance or excuse or distraction—pick an addiction, any addiction. But hiding from the problem isn't really living, despite the thrill of the risk or the short-lived pleasure. I grasp why people gamble with life or hide from it. But if they mask the pain too long, they create future complexities, harder to untangle—maybe even for the next generation. Instead of protecting, the mask prescribes. Instead of just deceiving the audience, it directs the performer, and when the mask deludes the one who wears it, something has gone horribly awry. I think that's what happened to Ryan's dad. He took his own life. I guess he tried to run from pain so much that the escape rather than the pain killed him. He was only forty-seven. No one welcomes pain. But we can't get away from anything by ignoring it or hiding it under something else—drugs, sex, anything.

After the service and burial, everyone went back to Ryan's grandmother's property along the river, dotted with mobile homes and campers belonging to extended family and friends. There, they remembered the good times, Abby said, over gumbo, boudin, and rivers of whiskey. That night, Ryan stayed at his own home, sleeping on a damp mattress on the floor, surrounded by friends who gathered, some for the occasion, some for the spectacle of what it might become in the later hours. Abby came home in the early morning light without him, seeming more moved by the events of the prior day and night than she had been by anything that had ever occurred in her own family. In her memory, it was the first funeral she had ever attended, the first irrevocable loss she had witnessed, the first faint sting of truth.

Ryan had dinner with us one last time before his leave ended. He did his best to keep the conversation polite but interesting as he entertained us with the story of his tooth, or more appropriately, its absence—remember that smile I promised to come back to? Ryan was missing a front tooth because, he explained, "You see, my buddy had just got this pit-bull-mix puppy from his cousin, but it was about five months old, so it wasn't real little, but I'll tell you, it was a tough little mutt. What was his name? Something from mythology. Severus?"

"That's Snape's name from Harry Potter, unless you mean the Roman emperor. But it isn't mythological," Abby corrected.

Ryan shot her a look and said, "That ain't it anyway." Then he smiled, trying hard to keep his lips closed.

"Cerberus," I offered.

"Yeah! Uh, yes, ma'am, that was it. Cerberus. He was all black with this one crazy ass half blue, half brown eye. Anyhow, so Kyle, my friend, was bragging on how much power a pit bull's got in its jaws, like, saying as much as an alligator or some sh-stuff, so I said there was no way, 'cause alligators exert like 3,500 pounds of pressure when they clamp down on some poor sonnova—s.o.b. Anyway, I made the mistake of saying I bet I could bite pound for pound as hard as that puppy. Well, let me tell you, that was real stupid of me. So, Kyle, he gets this idea that me and the dog should have a tug-o-war with this old, nasty rawhide chew toy, and I mean it's fu-reaking disgusting. Probably didn't help that I was a little lit—aw, shit, I shoulda left that out. I'm sorry. Sorry for saying shit, too. Anyhow..." Ryan was cracking himself up and absolutely not caring about his hugely gapped-toothed grin, which was a change from the self-conscious, closed-lip smiling I had seen all week.

Seeing him lose himself in the memory of his missing tooth and simultaneously attempt to censor himself made us all smile so hard our cheeks hurt. He went on saying, "I grabbed the rawhide, got down on all fours, like this," and here began the re-enactment, "and I put it in my mouth and growled and barked like a dog wanting to play. Then here comes the little fu—sucker wanting his chew toy, so he, like, grabs the other end and starts jerking the piss out of it and trying to shake it, you know, like dogs do. Man, he clean ripped it and my tooth right out. My mouth was bleeding all over. We never found my tooth. I think the dog ate it." As Ryan stood up, he reached for his phone.

"Wanna see a picture?"

Chapter 4

Three Rules

The first pregnancy scare came about three months later. Abby had talked for months about the possibility of taking a gap-year between high school graduation and college, even getting a passport for a possible opportunity to work on a farm in New Zealand from August to January. Upon meeting Ryan, however, her interest in sheep faded. Wolves, half-domesticated and missing an incisor, were more to her liking. So instead, she lobbied for a graduation trip to California, in particular, Oceanside, where Ryan was stationed. I can't explain why—maybe because she was, at eighteen, a legal adult, maybe because she had saved her money diligently, maybe because she had a gift for logical persuasion, or maybe the previous four years had just sapped all the fight out of us—but we let her go. I know that seems terrible, allowing a young woman to travel to a military base two thousand miles away alone. Saying it out loud makes it sound so bad. I marvel that she returned home unscathed, well mostly, except for the pregnancy scare, which scared me more than Abby.

Before her trip, I did my homework. I knew the hotel on base required her to register with an enlisted sponsor, and she would be unable to walk around base unaccompanied, which was some consolation. I looked up every rule regarding visitors on base I could find. I made sure her birth control prescription was filled. I also spoke to Ryan.

That was interesting.

I have always been a shy person, not one to initiate contact. In fact, I'm certain my childhood silence would today be diagnosed as social anxiety disorder. More than anything else, motherhood has pushed me beyond the comfortable silences and familiar I'll-figure-it-out-myself endeavors that comprised my first twenty-five years of life. Hardly combative and preferably non-confrontational, I still hesitate to ask for help when I can't find the herbs de Provence on the spice aisle. Believe me, I know how ridiculous that is. Half of the time, the store doesn't even have herbs de Provence.

Even more than teaching, being a mother has forced me to face the discomfort of having to impose my will simply because it is my will, not because I have the greater authority of a school board behind me. You might imagine that the authority of God, of ancient stories and of modern statistics—of evidence, of consequences—would be enough to bolster my demands for caution and responsibility, but somehow it hasn't been. Being Abby's mother—far more than being Jenna's—has challenged me. It has tested my resolve and made me cautious around anyone associated with her—coaches, friends and their parents, and even with bosses she's had. I have wondered whether they think of me as a clueless pushover or, worse, as a "cool mom" who condones the discord Abby trails behind her.

I am neither.

Confounded by the force of sheer will required to keep a child safe, I chose to resist the instinct to protect and instead gave her the freedom to be brave in her experience, hoping she would be courageous enough to learn from all the inevitable mistakes. Nonetheless, I attempted to measure the potential harm she faced against the innumerable factors that might mitigate—or even justify—it in deciding what to allow or advise against.

I did not fool myself into thinking I had control. I still don't.

A mother's desire to protect her children, as any hen can show you, far exceeds her will to defend herself. Still, though, something feels unnatural in exerting authority over another equally human being, especially when that being is my legally-adult daughter. It's like snow telling rain how to fall. California might just fall into the ocean while Abby's there, but I decided that there was no catastrophe uncommon to man awaiting her. Nonetheless, I would attempt to ward off a few of the common pitfalls as best I could by making my minimal expectations known to Ryan.

I prefaced the call to him with a text. I found my footing, my comfort, in the humor I saw in a small complaint Abby had about his texting. So far, the one aspect of Ryan Freeman that was notably imperfect—other than the missing tooth—was his grammar. He must have believed, at first, that I was quite intrusive, and, later, hysterically funny. Lord knows I thought I was. This is what the text said:

Hey Ryan, this is Abby's mom. I hate to bother you, but she has brought something to my attention that I just can't ignore. I know this will be uncomfortable to hear from me, but letting it go without addressing the situation simply opposes everything on which I have established my values and those I hope to convey to Abby. I hope you understand, but I simply cannot tolerate certain behaviors. This misuse of your/you're must end. It is truly the difference between knowing your shit and knowing you're shit. I hope you recognize the consequence of this important issue. Hahaha. I hope ____ (a. your b. you're) doing well. When you have a minute, I would like to talk to you about Abby's visit. Let me know when you can chat.

Not long after I sent that, Ryan texted back saying that he'd be happy to call me after work that evening around 9:00 p.m., accounting for the two-hour time difference. I told him that although nine was way past my bedtime, it would be fine, and promptly at 9:00 p.m. my phone rang.

I answered, "Hi, Ryan. Thanks for calling."

"Oh, yes, ma'am." Ryan was a big yes ma'ammer. "No problem at all. I've gotta tell you, when I first got your text, I didn't know what you were gonna say! I was kinda scared! But then I nearly pissed myself I laughed so hard. I will indeed correct that error."

"Well, good! I'm glad you got a kick out of it. I really did want to chat with you about June, though," I replied.

"Yes, ma'am. I understand why you'd be nervous," he said.

I added, "Yeah, she's never flown alone before. In fact, she's only flown once. And I imagine that Los Angeles is a little busier than our airport, so that has me concerned."

"I understand. And it is, but I'll get there at least forty-five minutes before her flight lands, so she won't be waiting alone or anything. Then I'll check her into the hotel, and she can't really be off the hotel grounds on base without me, so while I'm at work, she'll hopefully bring a book or something. I promise I'll take good care of her."

"I appreciate that, Ryan. I know Abby plays the Miss Independent role pretty well, but she still has parents who worry to death about her. Ten days feels like a really long time. Do you have plans to go off base?"

"Yes, ma'am. We do! I have a couple of hikes planned for us and we'll probably go to the zoo, too, definitely the beach."

"That sounds great. I'm glad she'll get to see a bit of California. We've never been out that way even though Scott's dad lives outside LA. So, let's see: you'll pick her up at LAX, make sure she gets to and stays at the hotel safely, and usually be with her when you aren't working, right?" I asked.

"Yes, ma'am. That's the plan."

"That sounds good. Ok, so one last thing, Ryan."

"Oh, Lord! Why am I nervous?"

"Probably because you have some idea of what I'm about to say. Alright, I have a list of three rules for y'all to follow. Here goes: One: Abby may not come back physically altered. No tattoos, no new piercings."

"Yes, ma'am. I will do my best to enforce that."

"Two: She may not come back injured, physically or emotionally."

"Lordy, I sure hope not!" he exclaimed.

"And three, which is the most important: She may absolutely not come home pregnant, no babies."

"Oh my lord, I agree two hundred percent with you about that! I'm not tryna be a dad yet!"

"Ok, just please be sure to recall how babies happen, Ryan. And that babies happen to lots of people who aren't really trying to create them, so don't practice too well."

"Yes, ma'am. I understand what you're saying, and I appreciate your being honest with me and still trusting me enough to let Abby come out to visit. I promise I'll follow all the rules and make sure she does, too."

"Thank you, Ryan, and I do hope y'all have a great time, but to say I'm not a little worried would be a lie. Just be smart and safe, ok."

"We will."

"Well, thank you for calling and for the reassurance, Ryan. I'll let you get back to your night now. Take care of yourself. Good night."

"Yes ma'am. You have a good night, too."

With that, we said goodbye. Ryan was difficult to decipher in some ways. For as open as he was, I knew there was more to him. After all, he was—and is—a person, so he's quite complex, as we all are. Both Scott and I understand people pretty well, especially young people, having taught for over twenty-five years, and Scott's explanation of Ryan was "he's a good-looking young guy and takes advantage of that." Maybe the implied lifestyle bothered me. I know it did. I was unsure of how much I trusted him. Yet, my skepticism focused on aspects of his personality inconsequential to me—those with which Abby would have to contend. In what I had directly seen and heard in him, I found little to be objectionable–but that was just the problem. I wondered how much of him was genuine and how much was smart enough to tell me what I wanted to hear.

I cannot deny that I liked him. Scott did, too, but the proper balance of protection and freedom in parenting Abby always challenged me. Ryan and all that came with him posed an even greater test of the scale. We were certainly not planning her engagement, but we did oppose her going such distances for a boy who would be little more than a fling. In fact, I am inherently opposed to flings altogether, as you may recall. True love may not wait until marriage, but it shouldn't rush across the country to jump into bed, either. Or maybe it does. I am still trying to figure that out.

I wanted so badly for Abby to act responsibly rather than impulsively. I wondered about Ryan's feelings for her. He and Abby had been talking since December, with much greater regularity and familiarity since March, and she was uninterested in any other boys. No matter what she believed or how she behaved, I did not think Ryan was being completely genuine with her regarding his own social habits. While she was interested in no one else, I doubted the same was true of him. Perhaps I wasn't giving him enough credit, but he seemed to be, as Scott suggested, a young man who—let's just say—loved the company of women. While I understood and agreed that an exclusive relationship over such long distances was impractical, I also registered worry over everything seeming to move so fast. Abby was proclaiming her undying love for a young man who may have seen her, at the time, as no more than an obsessed little girl from back home with the means to travel and without inhibition.

While having an eighteen-year-old daughter lovesick over a twenty-two-year-old Marine presented concerns, it also had its benefits. Abby had calmed down. She no longer seemed to be seeking an escape from her life, to be embracing the riotous discord she mistook for freedom. She was more respectful to us, even thankful for us, having seen the alternative life might offer. She was more focused, far less apt to entertain the advances of local boys. In some ways, Ryan's appearance in Abby's life nudged her toward self-assumed responsibility, leaving her earthed in a possibility that seemed worth the sacrifice of instant gratification in favor of the future's uncertain promises. She became grounded and purposeful for the first time. The difference evinced itself in the details of her daily life: her demeanor was more settled; her grades improved; she washed dishes without being asked. Regardless of what Ryan was doing, Abby was doing well, so part of me was thankful for Ryan's influence, no matter how wayward he was. The other part of me wondered whether Abby would be irreparably disappointed to discover that she had simply made herself the most convenient among the many possible companions Ryan might have had. Was she worth more than any one of them to him?

Within three weeks of my conversation with Ryan, Abby graduated from high school, went to the beach on our almost-annual family vacation, and departed for California. At eighteen, she was far braver than I was. Flying alone is something I still find daunting, but she found her courage in her longing for Ryan. When Scott and I brought her to the airport, we were both thinking, Why are we crazy? What are we doing? We didn't say it, though. I still don't know what else we could have done. She would have found a way to Ryan even if it meant leaving in secrecy. I'd rather know. In my career, I have seen far too many "mama's angels" lie, cheat, and bully their way to their goals, academic and social, and I have cringed when colleagues praise those students as exemplars. If people only knew the forked tongues behind the smiles, they might avoid the toxic entanglements that ruin them. So many people are just snakes, venomous ones. Having encountered an adder or two over the years, I certainly did not want to raise one. I prefer to know my girls as honest and flawed than to be deceived, thinking they are perfect. The cost of such knowledge, however, can be painful. I recall tearful conversations attesting to that, and there were more to come.

The immediate future, however, was full of youthful optimism and California sun. While Abby was in Oceanside, both she and Ryan stayed in touch with me. There were "just landed" and "just left LAX with Ry" texts from her, and from Ryan, "got her luggage, waiting on her now." Of course, there were selfies both sent through texts and Instagrammed by Abby. Ryan's social media remained relatively quiet except for one collage, a tiny square of which contained an image of him and Abby under a waterfall. I noted the absence of any claims of fondness for her on his part, but I also noted that he offered no objection to the abundance of photographic evidence of their togetherness she displayed. Abby's social media was nearly an hour-by-hour account of her trip. Ryan was tagged in every photo. I wondered if it meant anything at all.

Though she texted every day, Abby called me only twice over the ten days she was gone. The first was the morning after she arrived, when she assured me that she had checked in successfully, and yes, Ry—she had taken to calling him by a single syllable—had stayed with her. He had just left for work—or duty? I'm not sure which is correct, but he was off to fix helicopters.

Shortly after becoming aware of Abby's interest in Ryan, which was sometime in mid-January, I heard from a former student of mine named Brian. He was also a former Marine. He gave me advice that I didn't fully understand at first. He said to find out what Ryan's MOS was, and if it began with 03, I should do everything in my power to prevent the relationship from going anywhere. So, I asked, first what an MOS was, and then I asked what his was. Brian's MOS was 0351, assaultman, and he explained how even a year out, he still had trouble being kind to those who loved him. The experience had changed him, and I could see small signs of that even in our brief conversation. No longer was he the wry conversationalist he had been after class. He was direct and alert—very alert.

Naturally, Brian's warning concerned me. I asked Abby if she knew Ryan's MOS. She responded, "What's an MOS?" I explained. She did not know. In fact, at that point she had no idea of what Ryan did and assumed that he was infantry since he had just returned from deployment. I told her what Brian said to me, and I could see that it bothered her. When she next spoke to

Ryan, she asked, and happily reported that there was no need to thwart her efforts to establish a relationship. His MOS was 6072, which confirmed that he was not infantry and that he was a smart kid, which did not surprise me. As an aviation mechanic, his ASVAB line score had to be above average, which makes his and a college scholarship recipient's seeming inability to abide by three simple rules even more perplexing.

I think they misunderstood them as a wish list.

Chapter 5

Bearing Children

The second call I received from Abby was quite different, not an obligatory run-down of the logistics of her safety, but more of a heartfelt outpouring—the saccharine kind—that can come only from a girl in love. I tried to reserve judgment.

"Mom," she said, more as a statement than as a greeting when I answered her call.

I responded with my typical, "Hi, sweetie. How is everything?"

"So good. Ry is so amazing, Mama. I mean he's just—I love him, Mama."

"Well, that's a big statement, love. What have you gotten to know about him? What makes him amazing?" I asked.

"I don't even know. It's just the way he is with people. I mean, he walks in and people just respect him, like they know something about him, but they don't always. Like the other night we went to a bonfire on the beach, and this guy he didn't really know had a four-wheeler there, and after Ry talked to him for a minute, the guy asked him if he wanted to borrow it so we could go explore a little. It was so awesome. And then, another thing happened when it seemed like these dudes were gonna get into a fight, and Ry just sort of walked over and stood there. Like he didn't do or say a thing, the guys just stopped. And he's been so sweet to me." She finally stopped to breathe.

"Did you expect him not to be?" I asked, a little too incredulously.

"No! He's always sweet, but I mean, we've talked more about what we want in life, and we just get each other so much. I know I want to do life with him. We just understand each other. We, like, play off each other. He challenges me, and he makes me laugh, and we love just to pick up and go. And I'm so happy with him." Her voice trailed off slightly at the end.

"I'm happy to hear that you're happy, but why do I feel like a 'but' is hidden in there somewhere?"

"I guess there is. I mean, we aren't exclusively dating, officially, but we are. I'm not interested in anyone else. Ever again. I'd marry him tomorrow."

"Oh, Abby. Believe me, I understand how fast love can happen, but you've spent a total of what, twelve days of your life in his physical presence? Don't you think planning forever is a little premature? Does the fact that he doesn't even like the stuff you post on Facebook or Instagram mean anything? Or is he just not on it much?"

"He said he doesn't want to start an official relationship until he's discharged. And definitely not before his next deployment. He said that his commanding officer told them to be careful about what they do on social media before they get deployed because they don't want terrorists to find out stuff about their personal lives because it can be used against them."

"Well, I don't know how the military works, but not even acknowledging you? Sounds a little suspect to me. It sounds like something a smart guy might say to a naive girl who also knows nothing of military operations."

"Mom, why are you always so skeptical of everybody? I don't think he's making things up. Besides, he'll be out in a little over a year. You'll see."

"Abby, I'm not trying to discredit him or destroy your dreams. I really am happy for you, and I like Ryan. I just want you to be grounded, to have your own plans. This is a new relationship, and although it seems to be moving right along, you have to remember that things can change suddenly. Life is like that."

"Oh, Mom, don't get all morbid. I know it can change and that's why I want to enjoy it right now, with Ry."

"I know, love. I just don't want you to get hurt."

"Mama, I'm a big girl. I can manage whatever comes."

We talked for a few more minutes, changing the subject to their next excursion, a hike to Potato Chip Rock in Poway. I really was glad for her, and I was thrilled that she was enjoying the outdoor life California offers, especially when my worst fears had her primarily in a hotel room "practicing" too often. Of course, there was obviously plenty of time for that, too.

Abby came home sun-kissed, encouraged, committed. Ryan could apparently fly, and by association, she floated a little above the masses. Abby, for the amazing talent that she has, had never quite found the ambition to call it forth fully, so while idling above average had been the norm all through high school, she was quite happy to have any boost in status that required little effort on her part. Association would do just fine. That association grew more complex in the weeks to come.

About two days after her return, I caught sight of something disturbing: a clover tattoo on her left butt cheek, visible as she lounged immodestly in her too-short pajama shorts and fuzzy socks.

"Abby Glynne Hildebrand! What is that!"

"What?"

"That! That lucky charms graffiti on your ass!"

"Mom! Language! And I got that in California. It's a clover."

"Clearly, I can see it's a clover. I apologize for not being precise in my question. Let me rephrase: Why did you get a tattoo in California when I specifically asked you not to?"

"Mama, really? You know I wanted another one anyway. I mean why does it matter if I get it here or in Cali? It's more of a fun story there anyway. I can show my grandkids how Grandpa and Grandma got tattoos together when we were young."

"Ok, first of all, how many grandkids want to see their grandma's withered clover ass-tat? That's disturbing. And second, he watched you get this?"

"Yep."

"But the rules! Oh my gosh. Don't tell me he got one, too?"

"Yep, well, no, not a clover. He got another bandy thing on his forearm. It means something, but I can't remember what."

"I am so upset right now."

In retrospect, the tattoo was nothing. She already had a peacock feather and has continued adding ink over the years. I was much more upset about the empty "yes, ma'am's" I'd gotten from Ryan.

I would be more upset in the coming weeks. In early July, she told me that her period was late—about two-and-a-half weeks late. I had to ask: Did she take her pills regularly? Did they use protection? Did he actually ejaculate inside of her? No, no, and yes. I couldn't believe what I was hearing. Didn't I talk to her honestly, clearly, about sex? More clearly than about the tattoo? Didn't I talk to him? Didn't they understand biological reproduction? I was so angry. I didn't understand at all. I needed an explanation. Why would someone starting college in the fall or someone about to be deployed to the Middle East—anyone who has all the intelligence and means to prevent the chaos of an unplanned pregnancy—intentionally take a chance like this? I needed an explanation, and with my child's penchant for honesty no matter how graphic, I was likely to get one.

It was awful.

Phrases such as "caught up in the moment," "realized too late," and "he tried not to come"—which she actually said to me—collided with retorts of "adult responsibility," "it's called expecting for a reason," and "evidently arrived" as we "discussed" the situation. After the initial shock of what Abby was telling me began to wear off, I asked if she had taken a pregnancy test yet. She had taken a home test, she said, and it was negative, but at over two weeks late, we both doubted its accuracy. Then I asked if she had told Ryan. She had. He had known for a week already. This really exasperated me because it implied the magnitude of the situation escaped them, that our wishes—Scott's and mine—were not even a consideration. The inconvenience and expense to our already stretched lives was specifically why I had spoken to both Abby and Ryan so plainly.

Youth can rarely see past itself.

They had already discussed plans. They would get married when the semester was over, right before he deployed again, which would be in either March or June, which meant he would deploy at a higher pay. She would eventually finish school using his GI bill, which he had said is allowed, if maintaining her GPA to keep a scholarship became too hard with taking care of a baby. He would send money for childcare. They would make it work.

My head was spinning. I was simultaneously relieved that he took the responsibility on himself and irritated because some part of what I was hearing sounded premeditated, which would make everything they had previously said regarding their futures a lie. I was also upset because she had not considered how difficult life would be for us all. With Ryan overseas, there would be no sense in her moving to California, so the obvious solution would be for her to live at home and commute to school instead of getting an apartment next semester. We would all share the little burden of joy, financial and otherwise. How could I tell Scott this? He would be devastated—his great fear as a father realized. I managed not to cry. I told Abby I wanted to speak to Ryan, but I could wait until after her ob-gyn appointment to do that, and that she could wait until then to tell Scott. We would wait for confirmation from a doctor that there was a reason to worry.

I sat in the waiting room of the doctor's office expecting the worst, so I had already begun bargaining with myself about the "unanticipated blessing." The extra room could become a nursery. We could even put a little refrigerator and microwave—the ones from Jenna's old dorm room—up there to give Abby some sense of autonomy. She could schedule evening classes when possible so we could juggle childcare without anyone spending a fortune. She would go to school. That was non-negotiable.

I planned and ordered my thoughts as best I could to cope with the potential outcome, but somewhere in my twisted musings was something I hate to admit, something selfish: if she had a baby, she would finally understand. It would be worth the chaos. She would realize the sacrifice required of motherhood, the pain of it, the selflessness of it, and worst of all, the constant fight against the resentment of it. That's an ugly truth. It doesn't accompany all mother-child relationships, I imagine. But, when a mother spends the child's lifetime acting out the values she hopes the child adopts as her own only to see that child embrace every opposite value, the struggle not to feel personally affronted—not to feel indignant, rejected, discredited, disgraced—is real. That bitterness haunted me throughout Abby's teens with every lie I'd discover, at first, then, later, with every disclosure she'd make.

Parenting is hard.

Sometimes I think the biblical story of Eve's punishment of pain in childbearing is wrongly reduced to the simple, physical pain of giving birth. The reality, the true pain, arrives later, when the little being to whom you have first sacrificed your body—then your sleep, your time, your comfort, and sometimes your sanity—shows no regard for you: for the tangle of love and fear, rules and forgiveness, hope and exasperation, tenacity and surrender that makes you her mother. You feel reduced to an option, one to be rejected like antiquated technology. Regardless of how useful you believe yourself, your capacities are never enough.

Most mothers feel little resentment over the incessant cries of a hungry, wet, or frustrated infant who, herself, must be struggling mightily to make sense of the world. When understanding seeps slowly in, though, mothers begin to have expectations, fantasies of acknowledgement and appreciation. Sometimes, in the early years, they come true in the form of a picked flower offered on a playground or of a hand-crafted card that was not coerced by a well-meaning teacher. Sometimes the later years bring behaviors and conversations that convey thanks. Sometimes gratitude goes too often unexpressed, or worse, it is expressed in words made hollow by their lack of counterpart in action. Giving up expectations becomes just "giving up," and you find yourself sitting in a doctor's waiting room contemplating your failures in motherhood, nursing morose daydreams that your wayward child's vision of you will suddenly snap into focus. *Maybe she will miraculously comprehend the magnitude of my love for her when she holds her own child in her arms for the first time.* That's what I was thinking, anyway.

Not until I became a mother did I understand my mother's love. Though I was always certain of it, felt secure within it, I did not fathom its depth until I held Jenna against me after a long, difficult delivery. And after Abby, I understood that love is unlimited. For all the wrong reasons, I hoped Abby, who had ventured so far from my hopes for her, would have a similar revelation. She wouldn't. Not yet anyway, but I couldn't tell immediately. She emerged from the cool, grey hallway looking rather stoic. I stood and walked toward her, quietly asking, "Well?"

She met me near the door of the waiting area and smiled faintly before saying, no, she was not pregnant. The doctor could not account for why she was so late, but there would be no baby in the next nine months. I reached out and took her hand, squeezed it, and offered a tight-lipped smile meant to convey more than it probably did. I was thankful not only because she wasn't pregnant but also because I would have time to change my thinking, to do better. Having a baby should not come with echoes of "I told you so." I was relieved. She was relieved. We were also sad in some strange way. I hugged her before we got into the car, and we drove home in silence.

After the fact, I told Scott the whole ordeal, and he was thankful to have dodged the stress of its unfolding. Abby told Ryan she was not pregnant, and as she told me about their conversation, I could hear sorrow in her voice.

"It's a good thing that I'm not. I know that," she said.

"Then why do you seem disappointed?" I asked.

"I don't know. Well, no. I do know. I think because I could see our lives. I mean, I know it would have been hard, and hard for you and Dad and even Jenna a little, but I could see us, I mean me and Ry, make it work. I know we would have. I think he might have wanted to as much as me."

"Oh, Abby, love, don't you see there's something wrong with that? There is no reason that you can't have an even better version of what you imagined a pregnancy would have created. There is nothing stopping either of you from building a future together."

"I know that. I guess I'm just impatient."

"What about him? Why would he take the chance of knowingly getting you pregnant, especially after directly telling me he wasn't 'tryna be a dad yet'?"

"I don't know."

"Well, maybe you should ask him. Listen, love, a baby should not be an excuse to have a relationship or to speed up commitment. A baby does not legitimize anything that can't exist on its own. If either you or Ryan feels like you need to justify your feelings for each other or the commitment you might want to make to each other by bringing a baby into the relationship, you are going about this the wrong way." I spoke gently, but deliberately.

"We aren't or weren't trying, Mom."

"I know, love. But you weren't exactly preventing either. It just seems like something deeper is at work to me."

"What do you mean?" I tried to explain. "Y'all seem to want something to push you forward. I'm not sure. Just remember, the only justification you need is your feelings. Start by being honest about them. It just seems like some strange thinking may be at work here, for you and him. Don't rush. Be a little more intentional about it, and responsible. We don't need to create pandemonium in our lives. I promise, that happens on its own."

"Mom, I know—"

"I know you know. And I know your life is your life, no matter what I say or do. But, please remember that I do know a few things. I've lived just a little. I love you, sweetie, and I want to save you from the bad decisions I see you make, but I know I can't. Only you can do that."

She was crying quiet tears as she hugged me. "Thank you, Mama. I love you so much."

I know she meant it, as she always does, even when her actions don't, but I wondered if the tears were over her disappointing me or over losing something she never had with Ryan.

Chapter 6

Rules, not Wishes

Since she turned twelve years old, I have wanted Abby to value things she still has not learned to value. In the months that elapsed in the aftermath of her first visit to California, I learned and relearned—and will probably learn again—what I have always known: wisdom cannot be forced.

For too long now, Abby has confused freedom with irresponsibility, and although some tough consequences have already come to pass, her behavior hasn't changed much.

Maybe I am confusing wisdom with experience.

The pregnancy episode felt different—as if she really had learned something valuable from it—but then, I couldn't quite tell what. Maybe my inexplicable approval of Ryan made me hope both had emerged from the possible parenthood incident as more responsible. Had they? Both knew that neither was in any position to have a child, yet there they were practicing the very act that creates tiny humans—a fact too easily forgotten—without precaution or hesitation.

Why do I still believe Abby might become a better version of herself with Ryan in her life?

I should have not liked this young man—at all—but there was—and is—a spirit about him that was somehow endearing, a goodness, or at least a lack of negativity, resilience perhaps. I'd call whatever I saw in him integrity, but he lied to me— "yes, ma'am," he said, "I'll follow all the rules."

But, piecemeal integrity isn't enough to sustain people as they rush into the future, brave and new. Or, maybe integrity is mostly a myth. If you look closely at anyone's life, we all fail miserably. Maybe our integrity, like most things, doesn't mean much to us until we lose it. Then we fool ourselves into thinking that we have it when we spend the rest of our lives trying to regain it, like vowing to tell the truth only after discovering the pain of lies. Maybe the wholeness is in the dedication to the process, not in a final product. We are not finished until death, maybe, so until then, the best we can do is learn to be better. I'm still working on it–as Ryan must be, Abby, too. I figure I have at least twenty-five, maybe thirty-five, years left, barring tragedies and cancer. Maybe I'll get it right someday. Maybe I'll see Abby get it right. Since she has met Ryan, I've seen her living more purposefully, more thankfully. I cannot deny his positive influence on her.

I still wanted to speak to Ryan about the situation, but my energy was so spent that I took the easy route and resorted to a text:

> Phew! Well, 25 days and at least 5 new grey hairs later, I'm relieved not to be becoming a grandma yet. I'm sure Abby has filled you in on the goings-on, but I wanted to say just two quick things. First, and this is sort of serious: try not to create a crisis that leaves few options in your future. A baby isn't necessary to legitimize a relationship. Don't force the future you think you want. Leave time for decisions. You're a smart guy. You know that already. And second, repeat after me: Rules, not wishes; rules, not wishes, rules.

The message wasn't completely genuine in conveying all the concerns I had over the situation, but even with its light touch, I hoped to make him think a bit. The response did not come back immediately, but later that day I read what I imagine is the best apology he could muster at the time: "Yes, ma'am. I do know that, and really had not planned on a family until 26 or so, when I am out a few years and financially stable, but no matter what would have happened, Abby would definitely have a good future."

I let it go at that, sending a simple, "Thanks, Ryan," in reply.

Ryan was hard, not so much to figure out, but to affect. He projected the illusion of being in control, having it all together, so-to-speak. But I doubted it. He knew how to say what people wanted to hear, how to read people well while guarding himself in a way I didn't understand then, a way that made him appear open when he really wasn't. In some ways, he seemed to be a person who refused to learn—not about things—after all, he was very receptive to grammar—but about himself, maybe? He projected a personality of controlled spontaneity, if such a thing can exist, but the control didn't always apply, or at least didn't apply equally in all areas, and the spontaneity, I suspected, was more like lawlessness within him. I had seen the evidence strewn in the background of photos and heard it in the polite responses as they contrasted the wild realities. He was a charming renegade who had been essentially on his own since he was fifteen, pretty successfully, all things considered. I wondered, though, what he may have missed as a young man without a mother's guidance.

When I was young, I'd walk into our kitchen, wallpapered with yellow teapots and daisies, to see my brother sitting on the Formica counter, long legs allowing his toes to graze the floor despite the height, and talking to my mom about who-knows-what. The conversation would often shift when I entered the room, and Zeke would flick my ear or try to put his giant, usually smelly feet on my shoulders if I got close enough. I suppose being five years younger made me both an easy target and an ottoman. If I stayed, he would offer my mom some conciliatory parting words, telling her where he would be going or not to worry, and she would always say, "Alright, sweetheart, I love you," but she did worry, and rightly so considering Zeke's eventual death.

I have that wrong—maybe not rightly. Worry did nothing to prevent tragedy, except allow her to cope with it. No, that's wrong, too. Love did that. Zeke knew she loved him, and she knew that—which may be the best anyone can do. Watching my parents struggle through their grief and feeling my own taught me that grief and love are really the same emotion. Grief is simply love which has lost the object eliciting its expression. Grief, like love, wells up within a person, but instead of escaping through laughter, conversation, or the millions of other manifestations of wordless love, it lies trapped inside despite spilling over at the eyes. Hopefully, we learn to live with it, to inhabit the grief, to carry it and continue. I had seen what it looks like when a mother loses a son, and words cannot begin to describe the pain.

I did not know what a son's loss of a mother held, but seeing the living relationship between my brother and mother, I imagined similarly ineffable devastation. Ryan lost his mom suddenly and unnaturally, violently. He found her. The pain he carried must have been unspeakable. I did not think he had learned to cope with it, yet I knew it was not my place to heal him or to call him to task about any inconsistencies in his life.

Ryan was, however, dating my daughter.

Regardless of whether there was a label on the relationship, recent events proved it serious, so the man he was becoming concerned me. I wanted Ryan to be a man of substance, not dissonance.

Sometimes I talk like I have it all figured out. I don't. I've lived a small life dotted with failures and sorrows. But I have paid attention. Still, what I don't know fills the universe and what I do fills my head, an infinitesimal speck in the vastness of what is. In fact, I know that I don't even know all of what's there, in my own mind. I'm occasionally struck by an epiphany over something that seemed resolved. There is always more, and with every new life I encounter closely, I find relevance in something I thought I had figured out.

Ryan sharpened my perception of Abby, of life, of the past. Some memories bury themselves in the deepest recesses, the bottoms of our brains, waiting to be acknowledged when something calls them forth, sometimes unexpectedly. I try not to have them sink so far, to cope with life well enough so that my dreams are not haunted by the unknown, but who knows what's hidden from me. Somehow, I have a balanced perspective of myself, little over or under played, little unprocessed. Facing the events of my life as they occur has kept me constant. I manage, but mostly by vacillating, swinging too confidently toward some judgment then immediately chastising myself, realizing I could be convicted of every crime mankind has ever seen, at least metaphorically. I am no arbiter of truth. I am well-aware that I am among the condemned, not a strong or consistent or honest or unbroken chain of self, but a steady rhythm of its sway, a perpetual pursuit. Maybe the quiet motion of my life is meant to help others find a pace. The way a hypnotist's dangled pocket watch can send a mind into memories long forgotten must count for something.

Chapter 7

Feral Boys

The summer months, July to August and most of September, were quiet. Until September 17, that is. Abby was going back to California at the end of the month. Such are the dangers of a daughter with her own income and long-saved birthday money. Honestly, my biggest problem with her four-day plan was that she would be missing class on Monday. She assured me that college students a-plenty skip their Monday mornings with no more an excuse than Sunday night.

I wasn't one of those.

At least she would be on a flight home as Dr. Castro meandered through Maslow's hierarchy of needs, which she assured me she could catch up on either by reading the chapter or listening to me drone about the importance of self-actualization, a topic familiar to her. When I asked her why she was spending upwards of $700.00 on a trip when he was planning to take leave in October to come home, she responded like any eighteen-year-old in love would: She couldn't wait that long to be with him.

Silly me.

"Should I even bother saying it this time?" I asked.

"Saying what, Mom?" I could tell by her tone that she already knew.

"The bit about tiny humans, you know, how they're created and all."

"Oh, I think I've heard that one before," she said, as if I were setting up a tired joke.

"Well, you can remind Ryan, then. That might be a good idea. Tiny humans are a huge responsibility. They sometimes grow up and fly to California swearing that everything is fine only to find they've come home with unexpected souvenirs."

"Ok, Mom. Are you talking about STDs or babies because I can't tell?"

"Both. I hope he's been checked."

"Oh my gosh, Mama, you make him sound like a dog that needs to go to the vet."

"I said nothing like that! All you on that one, love. But hey, it's worth asking about. Dog tags are a thing."

"Wow, I'm done here," Abby said laughing.

I do love our relationship. Even when I disapprove of ninety percent of her choices, Abby knows I always love her. That's another trick I learned from my mother. I watched her worry about me, Ella, and Zeke all of my childhood. Daddy was more about control, but no matter how much he tried, he couldn't tame Zeke. After a certain age, I suppose imposing limits becomes pointless, especially since adolescents are designed to test them well into young adulthood. As I've said, all you get is a sneaky kid at some point. My mom, however, was less in the business of control than of unconditional love. Guidance, yes, that was always available from her, and is, even today, but she realized that in the scope of life's meaning, having her son know that she loved him was far more important than having him submit to her control. The former allows for relationships while the latter often ends them in regrettable ultimatums, ones that cannot be enforced or are enforced to the point of estrangement. I try to guide Abby, though she exists in a whirlwind, which makes it difficult. That and her love of feral boys make caging her in any way nearly impossible.

Scott and I look at one another and shake our heads over Abby's decisions more often than parents should, and any onlookers probably assume it to be a gesture of frustration and confusion. It isn't, not always. It's acknowledgement. I'm not sure of how we got away with Jenna. The odds of our having a child who in twenty-six years has never given us a reason to distrust her are slender ones, but there they stand, a svelte five-foot-nine with a degree built by summa cum laude self-discipline, a slew of accomplishments and accolades, and a first job that pays more at its starting salary than my twenty-five years as a teacher. When I really consider the facts, Jenna is the child who should leave us shaking our heads, impossible to believe. She has known from a young age what I only concluded after no less than eighteen years: Smart people learn from experience, but smarter people learn from the experience of others.

Jenna listened and watched life with an artist's careful attention. She also asked for advice and trusted our words, and somehow, with them to guide her, she has crafted a life both disciplined and beautiful. It is common to hear the story of hardship and admire the person who overcomes it, but no less admirable—perhaps more—are those who are wise enough to make the right choices from the start. Scott and I only pretend not to know where Abby comes from; she is the one who is truly "flesh of our flesh." As for Jenna, who knows what happens in the metaphysics of inheritance. The two of us together were bound to yield unlikely results, I suppose.

The night I met Scott, I was out for revenge. My boyfriend of about sixteen months had unexpectedly announced that we should see other people, that if we wanted to be sure of each other, we should explore life a little more. Well, clearly, he already had an invitation into uncharted territory. Rather than grow weepy over his proposal, I agreed in a be-careful-what-you-wish-for sort of way, but why not? The moment he suggested seeing others, I had already decided that it was over, but I entertained the fiction of possibility for him. On the Thursday night of his first date with Jennifer, a curvaceous and flirtatious platinum blonde—the antithesis of me—I set out with one of my girlfriends for ladies' night at Lakeview Tavern, a semi-popular dive just off campus. It was early summer, but I already had a dark tan from hours of running and horseback riding and wore a white top to up the St. Tropez factor to a level of exoticism I hoped would attract some attention. It did. The bartender, a young man in his mid-twenties, served up Sex on the Beach, saying that seeing me made him think of it—and to think such things were ok to say, perversely flattering even, in the eighties. Three or so shots into the night, I saw him walk in.

In movies, the angle narrows slowly to a close-up, the background music starts playing as all other sound quiets, and you see his eyes. They're green. You see them scan the room and know that he's looking. You see that he stands out, tall and muscular, that people get out his way, not just because of his size, but because he radiates some rare combination of confidence and amity, but amity that should not lull you into thinking he's harmless. He's not. You see him move closer to where you are. You see him look at you, and suddenly, you see yourself differently.

That's what happened in my revenge-and-alcohol-fueled quest to "meet someone new," as I had announced to Celeste before we set out for the evening. That is exactly how I met Scott, who at twenty-five was unlikely to be in a college bar, but he and his friend Dave frequented Thursday nights because their old college teammate, Nate, was my Sex on the Beach buddy behind the bar. He was a wealth of information about Scott—from the moment he saw that I saw the six-one dirty-blonde walk in.

When the slow-motion of my mind ended and the music became the noise of the night again, I realized that Nate was waving the very focus of my attention over to the bar. He must have noted the completely rapt expression on my face because he said, "Don't worry. I'll introduce you." A thousand thoughts registered, but foremost among them was do not be the girl whose boyfriend eventually loses interest in her ever again. Do not be too agreeable, accommodating, compliant. With my ex-boyfriend, Rich, who was also my first boyfriend, I was all of that—and resented myself for it. I had a small voice, if any at all, in the relationship. Before meeting him, I had been the only one among my high school friends who was not dating someone, and that was problematic because of the proms and parties of senior year. I was never the girl boys would approach. I assumed it was because I was so thin and plain: at seventeen, I stood five-foot-seven and weighed all of one-hundred-and-eight pounds. My brown eyes and hair did nothing to make me noticeable. I was a dateless wonder, the type of girl whom other girls would console with "I just don't understand why..." and compliment with words such as "different" or, occasionally, "exotic," but I knew that in a Christie Brinkley world, all of the consolation just meant "not pretty."

Looking back, I cannot believe I was so foolish. My ex-boyfriend was what is technically known as "a catch" by most standards. He was attractive in a tall, dark, and handsome Latin way. He was also quite an intellect and proud of his private school education. I don't know why he agreed to Celeste's suggestion of a genuine blind date—those were the days before social media—with me to a public-school homecoming dance, other than that he was free. The night started well, with my thinking he genuinely liked me, but it revealed horrid moments. Rich knew everyone, it seemed—people from my own school whom I did not know. At one point, I excused myself to the restroom and left him talking with a mutual acquaintance of his and Celeste's, while she came with me to complete the requisite bathroom pair. Upon our return—he had his back to us—I heard Rich's conversation with Celeste's friend.

"So how did you end up here with Colleen?"

"You know, I'm not sure. Celeste asked me to. Seemed like a chance to meet some new faces. As far as Colleen," and here he smirked and gave his head a small shake, "I'm just doing a favor for a friend."

Celeste turned and looked at me, slightly panicked. "I'm so sorry," she mouthed.

I didn't respond to her, but walked up to Rich and said, "I'd like you to take me home now." He responded as if he couldn't understand why I'd ask such a thing and said, no, not yet, it was still so early. Only when I could not stop my eyes from filling did he realize I heard him. The profuse excuses began: I misunderstood. What he meant was.... he was glad to be there with me. He hoped he could see me again. I was beautiful.

I was stupid, too full of forgiveness.

The rest of our relationship, like the rest of that night, felt too long and wrong from the start. Although we had some fun finishing high school together, he pushed the relationship faster than I wanted it to go sometimes. We began college—I at the state university, and he at a nearby private one—and I felt like the default option. When nothing better was going on, there was me. I was foolish, but had I not been, I would not have been at the bar on the night when time slowed down and life turned into a movie scene.

Things have a way of working out, I suppose.

Scott and I have done better than work out. I feel like his first choice, and I know he is mine. After a bold beginning with him, I mellowed into my authentic self, the one who is more full of quiet mercy than mischief. I've had my moments, though. The night we met is missing some time for me—blank spots in my mind filled with vodka and peach schnapps where memory should be—but I remember most of it, though. Scott's version differs slightly. When the angels stopped singing, Nate introduced us. I learned the three of them had recently gone on a canoe trip together, and that's when the photos emerged. In the dim light of the room, Celeste and I scanned the pictures—a group of about seven young men, three in our present company, carrying on the recently ended glory of their own college days. There was a cabin strewn with beer cans, a friend pulling a contorted face uncomfortably close up to the camera, a creek with six bare asses lined up on its shore—swimsuits puddling around the twelve ankles. I moved on quickly, blushing in the darkness. When I got to the last picture, Nate announced that, oh, he had forgotten one. He handed it to me. It was Scott launching himself into the river from a rope swing, sans swimsuit. Upon seeing that I saw it—I can't even imagine my face—Scott laughed hard, clearly pleased that his full-frontal glory was on display. To this day, he teases me that "there's one big reason" I was interested in him.

After recovering from the embarrassment, I talked with Scott over Billy Idol's rebel yelling for a while, and then we decided to go outside where we could hear one another. We stood near the already-taken patio tables just out of earshot. The noise of the night became a white hum that paled in contrast to Scott's deep voice.

Scott told me he was a football coach and teacher at a local Catholic high school. I told him I was a secondary education English major, and I hated football. I rode horses. He hated horses–fell from one as a child. I told him he needed stronger legs, that holding a horse between your thighs required you to do more than just sit there. That drew a smirk. The conversation meandered in and out of innuendo until it tangled us together against the high garden wall of Lakeview's patio. There, pressed between a jazz mural and the man I did not know could exist in such close proximity to me, I began the life I love.

When the phone in my room rang the next day, I immediately thought it was Celeste. Reaching across the length of my twin bed, I answered with my usual "Hello." Hearing a man's voice say, "Colleen?" I was surprised.

Although Scott had asked for my number, I certainly didn't expect to hear from him so soon, if at all. As I sat wrapped cozy in my equestrian-themed quilt with the phone cord wound around my arm, I smiled, thinking of the mischief in his eyes. His resonant voice evoked feelings (if not clear recollections) from the night before. My mind may not have remembered the words, but my body didn't forget, despite noise and alcohol. I playfully accused him of not even knowing what I looked like. Honestly, his hands, calloused from years of weightlifting, probably recollected more than his eyes. He was accurate, if not flattering. He said I was really small but not short, really dark, really firm—the hands talking—and had "cute little freckles or moles" on my face, and wavy brown hair.

He knew.

He also remembered that I loved horses and literature, which he did not, yet he went on to ask me lots of questions about both. By the fourth, rather than answer, I called him on his game.

"Listen, I know what you're doing," I said lightly.

"What, Colleen? I'm just trying to get to know you better, just asking about things you love."

"Well, Scott," I replied with emphasis on his name, "it seems to me that you are, first, using my name, because people tend to like hearing their names, therefore, like the people who use them, and second, you're trying to get me to talk about myself because when people do that, they perceive the listener as an excellent conversationalist even if the person has said very little."

"Damn. How old are you again?" he asked with feigned disbelief.

"Old enough to have had Psych 101."

"Fair enough," he laughed. "Seriously, you might find this hard to believe, but I've talked to a few women before. You're the first one to catch on to that. Most, especially younger girls, just talk and talk about God-knows-what, probably thinking that I'm hanging on every word."

I said, "So, what you're saying is that you actually aren't listening at all— or more likely, listening for keywords that let you know when to snap your attention back to the conversation instead of whatever game you're watching while you talk?"

He laughed again, congratulated me on figuring out his ploy, and asked more questions, but this time about important things—my family, what I wanted from life—a real conversation. And he listened. We talked about the night before, too, and I explained the events that led me to be there, explained Rich, and explained that my behavior was out of character for me, which, at worst, he might not have believed, but at best, didn't seem to matter. He had an ex whose name was Lindsey, and at one point, a ring was involved in that relationship, but it was recently over. He asked when he would see me again.

Our relationship moved quickly. The summer became fall. It's funny to think that I attended more high school football games during my college years than I did in high school. No one could have predicted Scott—this not-completely domesticated, highly pursued, down-and-dirty football star—in my quiet life. Ella and Zeke were his age, and people they knew, knew him, but they did not, not personally. Everyone apparently knew of him. Once, after we were engaged, I was in the checkout line at the grocery store, and two girls behind me, who were several years older than I, were gossiping—about me. One asked the other, with some shock in her voice, if she had heard that oh, my God, Scott Hildebrand was engaged. "To who!" came the grammatically incorrect response. They went on to say that I was "some young girl nobody ever heard of." I was "probably pregnant." I wasn't. I admit that my injunction against promiscuity—with all the complications sex introduces to unready lives—was not quite as strong as it is today, but I knew about the tiny humans and the STD's and how to prevent them. Mom made sure of it.

Anyway, Ella and Zeke were skeptical of what a man with Scott's social resume could see in their little sister. They didn't trust his intentions or his history during the first few months, which were actually all we had with Zeke. My parents, though, liked him very much, seeing him as an All-American football hero, which he was, even if at a smaller university. The getting-to-know-each-other phase was filled with dates, family dinners, and some light talk of the future, but that changed quickly. The tragedy of October, Zeke's drowning, made the future seem more urgent. By December, we were talking seriously about marriage. My mom asked what our hurry was and suggested we wait until I finished college, saying I was only nineteen years old.

I told her that we just couldn't wait that long to be together.

Chapter 8

Southern Comfort

Though Abby's September trip to California was short, she couldn't wait to tell me about the "so much" that happened. She texted often while she was there—updates of her whereabouts and plans, selfies in front of panoramic views and bathroom mirrors, and several videos. Ryan was quite a guitarist, as proven by his taking impromptu requests from Scott when Abby FaceTimed us. His rendition of "Sweet Child O' Mine," Scott's and my unofficial song, was a bit rough, but he nailed "Patience" down to the whistle.

Waiting for Abby at the Southwest concourse, I scrolled through the messages she had sent over her long weekend—mostly spent at the barracks, it seemed. Although she and Ryan looked as happy as happy can look, I noticed the background, as I always do. The creamy white cinder block walls; the neatly made bed with its geometrically patterned comforter in muted shades of blue, green, gray, and white; the headboard shelf lined with supplements promising fully pumped workouts and gains; the neck of a guitar against wall; and almost out of the shot, a small blue ice chest topped with bottles of Jack Daniels, Fireball, and Crown Royal lined up like ready soldiers awaiting an unseen enemy. In the foreground was Abby wrapped in Ryan's illustrated arms, like southern comfort from two thousand miles away. *What was she doing in this world?* I thought.

At the airport, I expected Abby to be all smiles, and she was when she saw me, but I saw her first. She walked among the crowd from the gate with an expression of loss on her face, something pained, sorrowed. I watched for a moment before calling to her, wondering what might have happened in the time between her last texts and now. They read, "At LAX now. Ry says ;)!" and "Just boarded. Love you!" I assumed that a winky face, in its playfulness, meant all was well, but her downcast eyes made me wonder. When Abby heard me call her name, she looked up, smiled big enough, and walked more briskly over to me. She greeted me with, "Hey, Mama. I already miss him so much." There was my explanation.

On the ride home, Abby explained that she and Ryan grew closer over her short trip. They talked about some difficult topics she couldn't quite share with me out of respect for his privacy, but she said the honesty and intentions they brought to their conversation were both brutal and beautiful, and she loved him more for it. Though no labels were put on their relationship, she felt committed to him. I asked if he felt the same. She thought so, but no one can ever know anyone else's heart completely, she reminded me. She said I had raised her with the grace to allow others to become who they should be, so she would wait and could forgive any flaw she saw in Ryan, especially those she knew he was consciously working on. Besides, she added, she was far from perfect.

This child, my child, was and is a conflation of oppositional defiance and utter proof of attentiveness to every word I had ever said. She has an uncanny ability to use my own advice against me.

Then, I asked one of the hardest questions: Was Ryan's drinking one of those flaws? At first she said no, that he didn't behave "too dangerously" and he was not an angry drunk—he drank responsibly, never alone, only "to have a good time." I reminded her that, once upon a time, I had a brother. He fit that description, too. Sometimes, we understand the definition of "dangerously" only after the outcome. She didn't like hearing that and countered with "he knows how much is too much." But, I heard doubt in her voice.

Maybe the doubt was my own. With the frequency of these summer visits, Ryan was no longer a distant idea. He was as real as gravity no matter what Scott and I thought of the weight of the relationship. He was often the last voice Abby heard at night, sometimes the first in the morning, and constant in her mind. After the concern of pregnancy, I was uncertain he would be a lasting presence in her life. In fact, I thought the whole pregnancy ordeal, once it was over, might have run him off, but here he was nine months later with no reason other than choice. He was a text, a phone call, a flight away.

Abby's visits in June and September and Ryan's frequent phone calls made him more present in our lives, but Scott and I had difficulty believing some of what Abby believed of him. I doubted that Ryan had a grasp of what "too much" meant, and Scott doubted that he had resigned himself to "wingman" when he and his Marine buddies went out. Even the average person's appeal increases when he wears a uniform. For guys like Ryan, the increase would be exponential. Scott told Abby as much, but her response was that she talked to him just about every morning and night. Did we think he was calling her between women? "Maybe," is all Scott said to Abby. To me, he said, "Absolutely." Ryan was attractive, charismatic, and kind, so there is no doubt he drew lots of attention. He was a combination of potentials, a high-risk experiment, so much combustible energy beneath the warm glow.

October provided another opportunity to know Ryan better. He was coming home again, this time with a friend, Chris, just for fun—to visit over the long weekend of the St. John Parish fair, an impressive ordeal of local music, carnival rides, vendors, and livestock. St. John's was just over an hour from our home, and we had taken Abby and Jenna once when they were children. They had fallen in love with the baby goats, fancy chickens, and sugar-coated funnel cakes, which—if you ever go—you should eat only after riding the Tilt-A-Whirl. As the afternoon sank into evening, I recall the goats and chickens growing quiet, the beer out-funneling the cakes, and the music growing louder as the passers-by became livelier. We packed up our girls and left before nightfall. That must have been at least twelve or thirteen years ago, before I could even begin to predict the dangerous curiosities my youngest would explore.

Now, Abby was going to the fair's opening Thursday night hand-in-hand with Mr. How 'Bout an Adventure, Darlin? Certainly, she would be aligned more with the beer and passersby than with the baby goats. How time changes. On Friday, Ryan would be going only with his old friends, showing his new friend some Southern hospitality from ground level. He and Abby would play the weekend by ear, have dinner with us on Monday, and then he and Chris would fly back to California on Tuesday. The visit would be short, but Abby couldn't wait for us to see him again. It would be his first time in Louisiana since March. He and Chris would be staying at his house, not with us, this time.

In the weeks before the fair weekend, Abby spent more time at Ryan's house than our own. Ryan's brother had continued living in the once-flooded home, but little had been done to restore it after Ryan initially cleaned it up in March. For two weeks, Abby went straight to Twin Pines, the area where Ryan's family lived, when she got out of class. Twin Pines was about fifteen minutes north of and more rural than our neighborhood. It was dotted with small lakes resulting from the river's changing course over who-knows-how-many years. At one time, there had been a thriving campground there, complete with horseback riding, bass fishing, and water skiing by day and campfires, stories, and s'mores by night. As suburban roots spread wide, Twin Pines folded into itself, closing the campground and leaving only the few families who had been there before the pop-ups and RV's. Ryan's was one of them.

The house, to Abby, was a project through which she would prove her devotion. She mopped and vacuumed and scoured what was scourable and would return home with bundles of who-knows-what needing to be laundered. Halfway through the second week, she was no longer cleaning but decorating. A few throw rugs and comforters disappeared from the upstairs linen closet, which was fine. She wanted the house to feel like a home again. She wanted to surprise him. She wanted to prove her domesticity, to prove herself highly "wifeable" in the most traditional of ways.

Unfortunately, most of the evidence of her hard work was destroyed with an impromptu homecoming party on the Wednesday night he arrived.

Abby told me about Wednesday when she spent the Friday of boy's night out at home with me. Ryan and his friends were a wild bunch, not that she wasn't perfectly fine with that, but some of them were just, as she put it, "not good people." She had foolishly left her car unlocked in front of the house with an envelope containing her week's pay in the glove compartment. Ninety of the $120 dollars was gone in the morning. She said he apologized for it, explaining that some of these "friends" were people he was "not very close to," friends of friends who had come just because they heard the word "party." There were girls, too, whose behavior she did not like and who did not seem to realize that she "was still a thing to Ryan." Just the wording of that made me bristle. The relationship I had been watching and worrying about for nearly a year was simply "a thing." No, more accurately, she herself was "a thing" in Ryan's full social life.

I am too old-fashioned for such dismissive language. I, maybe more than she, wanted clarity. I did not want her or the relationship to be only a "thing." But, the relationship wasn't mine to define, and that's what I told Abby— that she and Ryan had talked enough to know what they meant to one another, and she could either trust their conversations or doubt them, but if she doubted, she should make sure the evidence came from his behavior, not that of others toward him. He couldn't control his acquaintances any better than she could control hers. After all, didn't guys still text her? She conceded that they did, and though she might be kind enough to carry on a conversation with them, she had no romantic interest in them. She decided to trust her and Ryan's potential together. In hindsight, I wondered if my advice was worth the breath.

I've been holding it ever since.

Although the physical toll of the party lingered in the form of a broken table, several new and unidentifiable carpet stains, and a borrowed comforter sporting a constellation of cigarette burns, the emotional damage of Wednesday night was gone by the time the band closed Thursday night with, according to Abby, a sweet rendition of the Cowboy Junkies' "Misguided

Angel." She said that when Ry held her and danced so slow and close and kissed her right there in the middle of everybody, well, anybody with eyes could see what they meant to each other. I could see what it meant to her. In fact, it all mattered so much to her that I restrained myself from asking how much he had been drinking. I wanted to believe her, to believe what she believed. I guess I did, at least halfway.

Being a parent never gets easier. When children are tiny and demand so much time and attention, their need is a kind of difficulty that most parents expect, but as they grow and become more independent, they usually tell you less, so their need, the difficulty of their lives, appears less pressing. When they are eighteen years old, however, and still confide so much in you, you may find yourself in a different kind of difficulty, the variety that is not solved by a dry diaper and warm bottle or by a Band-Aid and a kiss or even a long conversation in which you listen more than talk. Your best advice cannot override the emotional tyranny of a reckless, young heart insistent on learning every lesson the only way she has ever known—by being broken against the very thing she believes will save her.

Over that weekend, Abby spent time with Ryan at his family's property amid guitars and gumbo. Although he had only two siblings, he had what seemed a network of neighbors, cousins, aunts, and grandparents who were always available to celebrate his being home. Abby called Scott and me on Sunday afternoon because Ryan wanted to invite us over, too. As sweet as it was to offer, we declined, probably less the fault of the stack of essays needing to be read before school the next day than of my own apprehension over feeling out of place. I wonder if going would have changed anything. I don't see how it could have.

When Abby came home later that night, she said how wonderful it was, how everyone in his family can sing so well, and how there is just something better about eating outdoors—the gumbo richer, the sweet-tea sweeter, the stories funnier—and his family, even his cousins, didn't rely on their phones to entertain them. They played bluegrass instead. Hands strummed mandolins, banjos, steel guitar, and bass, and voices sang the afternoon into sunset as she and Chris watched them play, occasionally singing along. It was so simple and easy, Abby said. As she was telling everyone goodbye, Ryan's grandmother called her aside. She told Abby she was so glad to see her again—the last time was his father's funeral—and that Abby was "such a lady." His grandma said she liked Abby so much more than "all those little hussies who chase after Ryan." This, of course, elated Abby. I hoped Ryan shared his grandmother's opinion.

I had the opportunity to assess what his opinion might be the next day, when he and Chris had dinner at our house, which almost didn't happen, according to Abby, because Ryan had received multiple invitations offering far more exciting ways to spend his final night at home. In fact, I'm sure Chris would have preferred Bourbon Street to Kismet Circle, but dinner with the Hildebrand's turned out well.

Abby went straight from her afternoon class to Twin Pines to pick them up, calling me to make sure it would be okay if they showered at our house before dinner. Evidently, Ryan's house had working plumbing, but only cold water. I told her yes, that was fine, and I wondered where they had showered for the last four days. Our Octobers are not exactly cool, but a hot shower after a long day feels good even in August—in an air-conditioned home. Did the air and heat work at Ryan's? I decided not to ask. Although Ryan seemed incredibly open about his life and family when we talked during his last visit, he also appeared slightly embarrassed that the "normal" he grew up with, learned to live with, especially after his mother's passing, was not even close to most people's definition of the word.

Abby arrived at home with the two young men, and after introductions and hellos, she showed Chris to the guest bath, and Ryan went upstairs to her shower. When the water was safely running, she came into the kitchen, purse still on her shoulder.

"Are you going somewhere?" I asked.

"Mom, no," came the reply with the requisite rolling of the eyes. "Look." She took out her wallet and from it pulled four crisp twenty-dollar bills and a ten.

I looked at her quizzically. "You found your money?"

"No. Ry asked if we could stop at the gas station on the way here. He said he needed to just run in for a minute, so me and Chris waited in the car, and when he came out, he gave this to me."

"Wait, had he—"

"No! He went to the ATM because he said since my money was stolen at his house, it was his job to make it right. I told him no at first and wouldn't take it because, like, yeah, I need it, but so does he, even more, but he said he'd be insulted if I didn't, so I did."

"Well, I guess that says a lot about him."

Ryan and Chris emerged from their respective showers at nearly the same time. As we waited for Scott and Jenna to arrive, we talked about the fair as they sat around the island and I seasoned the pasta. Chris said he liked the first band they heard on Friday night, a "swamp pop" group who played a little of anything they wanted from Buckwheat Zydeco to Led Zeppelin. Ryan liked the living history village, something about having to take the time to do things with your hands, not just for fun, but for survival. He thought things were too easy now—nobody appreciated artisanship anymore now that laser cutting was possible. Abby still loved the baby goats best.

Jenna arrived before Scott, and with her usual social grace, joined the conversation, asking both Ryan and Chris questions about their military service, life in California, and plans after their discharges. She was their age and knew some of the same people as Ryan, though she had not been more than acquaintances with most students who went to Park. They discovered that they had been a part of the same district art competitions throughout junior high, when Ryan was still in the talented art program, in which both Jenna and Abby had participated, too. It had served Jenna well in preparing her for her career in graphic design, but as Ryan teasingly pointed out, in seventh grade, he must have had the edge since he won the district-wide Keep Our Community Clean! Poster competition.

Once Scott came home and cleaned himself up from football practice, we sat down to eat, with the conversation turning inevitably to sports. Chris was a black belt, but didn't play any team sports, saying that his smaller stature always made him feel awkward around dudes that towered over him, which is why he began karate—well actually Jeet Kune Do. Upon hearing that, Scott lit up (there is no bigger fan of Bruce Lee). In immediate response to Chris's revelation, Scott promptly quoted, "Mistakes are always forgivable, if one has the courage to admit them," to which Ryan said, "Amen," and Abby and Jenna, in sisterly unison, said, "What?" I suppose it was a weird little moment, but Scott laughed and Chris explained that Bruce Lee said it because "the dude was more than just an actor and martial artist; he was, like, a philosopher, man." After the bonding over Bruce Lee ran its course, the conversation came back to regular sports, namely football and baseball, which Ryan played until his mom died. He said he quit when it got too hard with looking after Marissa, his sister, and taking care of Travis, his little brother. Ryan quickly shifted back to ball games, in particular, Monday Night Football, which was about to begin. At that point, I asked if anyone would like dessert.

Ryan took that as a cue to clear the dinner plates, which he rinsed and stacked neatly in the sink, saying he wasn't much for sweets, while everyone else indulged in brownies just out of the oven and topped with pecan praline ice cream, which was completely decadent, especially for a Monday night. I walked over to the sink and thanked Ryan, not only for the dishes, but also for replacing Abby's money, which I know must have put quite a dent in his own budget. His response began with his usual preface to anything he said to me.

"Oh, yes, ma'am. I couldn't let that go. She was so upset."

"She should have locked her car."

"Well, true, but she didn't expect that I'd have such asshole people at the house. I'm sorry. Excuse my language."

Smiling, I said, "No problem. Anyway, I genuinely appreciate your replacing it. It shows an uncommon sense of responsibility and integrity."

Ryan looked down and smiled rather than smirk, revealing that still-missing tooth and saying, "Oh no, you're making me blush! But thank you. That's a real nice thing to hear."

Abby brought the boys back home to Ryan's not too long after that since they had to be at the airport for a 6:00 flight in the morning, and while she was gone, Scott, Jenna, and I talked about how well dinner had gone, how Ryan—though a little rough around the edges—was such a diversely talented young man, about how his efforts to improve his place in life were so admirable considering his disadvantaged past. We genuinely liked him and were beginning to believe in the future Abby saw with him, which, one month to the day after that dinner, made receiving the news of his arrest so devastating.

Chapter 9

Strays

Trying to parse life out into understandable increments within the long stretch of time is a daunting task, each moment bringing a set of possibilities unimaginable just a moment before. I will never understand the seeming coincidences, the synchronicities, that leave me certain that every detail's timing is full of meaning—if only I could see it clearly.

On the morning of Friday, November eighteenth, I woke and went to school, as usual. At lunch, I received a call from Abby, who had spent the night before with a friend, Sophie. Abby had known her for several months, and they quickly grew close through their emerging interest in religious faith, especially as they tried to reconcile it with less holy practices lingering in the recent past. She called me that day because she and Sophie went to a small get together where a girl not much older than herself discussed her journey of faith, and it moved Abby to tears. She wanted to tell me she was sorry, that she realized she had not been living the way anyone needed her to live— not as a daughter to us or as a girlfriend to Ryan. She said she understood how contrarily she had behaved over the years despite having absolutely no reason to defy the values we tried to instill in her. She said she understood she should be helping to cultivate those very values in Ryan's life, too—instead of embracing the constant party. After all, she said, she wanted what her father and I had for herself "and Ry" someday.

Years ago, Scott and I had been involved in church, but by the time Abby was old enough to remember, we had mellowed in our faith a bit, and I embraced a spirituality less rigid than the scheduled stand-sit-kneel variety prescribed by the religion of my childhood. I sweat my psalms on Sunday morning runs to choirs of mourning doves cooing as the sun rises over the trees. The cadence of my breath and stride brings a balance to me that I never found in church. Nonetheless, I was happy that Abby had begun her own spiritual journey. As she spoke, I recalled our days in church, when Scott and I would counsel so many young people and hear similar outpourings, all generated by a rush of emotion, by a moment of repentance fueled by guilt or gratitude. Either way, many transformations were short-lived. Something so suddenly sprung seldom has the roots to sustain lofty aspirations. I hoped Abby could see the need for slow growth, but her endeavors often became a frenzy of emotion when she had epiphanies. The problems developed when the newness evaporated like lovely bubbles, leaving only a residue of intention.

Abby's intentions are always good. It is her actions about which I am skeptical. Yet, despite her history of unfulfilled promises, I believe "this time" will be different every time. The most recent "this time" had begun just less than a month prior, when Abby returned from bringing Ryan and Chris home the night they had dinner with us. She was elated for two reasons. The first was in her arms when she walked through the door. No bigger than a loaf of bread and mottled with black, white, and hints of tan throughout her mostly gray coat was our soon-to-be-named rescue, Opal, a little stray wandering the back roads near Ryan's house. I immediately said we could not keep a puppy, that we simply did not have time for one right now with work and school and Jenna having moved into her own place. Who would be here to take care of her? The timing was wrong. Abby, true to form, had a compelling reason to keep her.

She pleaded, "Please, I need her. I feel like God sent her to me. He wants me to be responsible for her, and you want me to have a better sense of accountability, don't you? I promise I will. I know I will need your help, but I swear, I will pay for her to go to the vet, and I'll take care of her. Please, we haven't had a dog since Sage died and that was when I was sixteen."

She paused, holding the puppy, then continued, "But Mama, Daddy, look at her. She is so small. I couldn't just leave her on the street. I don't have class until 1:00 on Tuesdays and Thursdays, so she would only be alone for a little while before you get home. And Monday/Wednesday classes are over by noon. Weekends, y'all will be here and if you don't want to bother with her, I can take her with me. I'll take her everywhere. Well, except to class. And work."

Abby was beginning to see Opal would be more responsibility than she first imagined.

Scott also said no, but I was moved, as I always am. I said I'd see what I could do. I am too soft-hearted. Abby and Jenna both inherited their love for animals from me, and this certainly wasn't the first stray Abby brought home. I suppose the three of us were unofficially in the rescue business, though Abby was the only one who volunteered at the local no-kill shelter. In fact, that was always her back up: If caring for the newest project became too hard, she would bring the little orphan to the shelter. But that never happened. The routine was that she would pour her heart into the new pet for several weeks—until life became busy and interesting—then I would assume responsibility. Abby was always bringing "projects" home which would become too much for her, and I would be the one to sustain them.

Little Opal proved no different. Today, that loaf-sized pup is my sixty-five-pound tank of a running partner, though she did help Abby cope with the barrage of slings and arrows November brought. Abby saw that dog as the beginning of the spiritual growth she needed to face the coming months.

The second reason Abby was so happy that night was, of course, Ryan. She explained excitedly, as she bathed the flea-ridden puppy, that on their way back to his house after dinner, Ryan asked Abby if she'd like to come out to California again in December. She said of course she would but didn't know if she could afford it by then; she had planned to visit over Mardi Gras or Spring Break, depending on when he would be deployed. Abby said that Ryan just smiled at her and said, "Merry Christmas, Sugar, it's already paid for." To Abby, it was as good as a proposal.

November eighteenth was the Friday before the Thanksgiving holidays, and with Abby's call at lunch, I looked forward to getting home to hear the details and to talking with her more deeply over the break from school. Although I was unsure of what to make of it all, Abby's life seemed to be taking on direction, even if the course were not what I would have planned for her. I had become more comfortable with the idea of Ryan and began to believe that maybe his interest in her went beyond her wild side, and although Abby was a vastly different eighteen-year-old than I had been, I also began to give her the benefit of my doubts, believing her actions and intentions were beginning to align rather than be so wildly disparate. My memories of Abby's childhood and adolescence spread themselves across the lawn of our past in patterns meandering beautifully but, too often, where they should not go, like picnics in mine fields. Maybe that would end with nineteen and the possibilities it brought, I thought.

It did not.

When trouble arrives with its alarms and chaos, we pretend to think it has come suddenly, but really, we know it has been softly approaching all along. After speaking to Abby at lunch, I checked my phone again before leaving work, even looking at her Instagram. I noticed a new comment on the last picture she posted of her and Ryan, one Chris had taken of them saying goodbye at the airport. She—her glasses above a wide smile and her shirt so huge she seemed pantsless—looked so young and small next to him, a classic James Dean in a white tee and jeans, showing only the slightest hint of a smile. The comment was from a friend of his whom Abby had not yet met. It said, "Abby, need you to contact me ASAP." I knew whatever it was about could not be good.

When I arrived at home, the house was empty, except for the sound of crying—wailing—the sound of bottomless heartbreak. Everything is a bit fuzzy now, but I know Abby was supposed to be at work or school, yet there, sitting on the back porch steps holding her knees to her chest and unconsoled by puppy kisses, was Abby, tears streaming and words incomprehensible. I rushed to her.

"Sweetie, what are you doing at home? What's wrong?" I asked, sitting beside her.

"I got fired. Or quit. I'm not even sure, but I had to leave. Mom, it's Ry, Mom!"

"Is he hurt? What happened, sweetie? I saw your Instagram," I said. She could not answer. Her breathing grew short and shallow. She turned to me and threw her arms around my neck, burying her face in my hair. No mother wants to hear such pain in her child, an absolute wreckage, no words, only the utterances of loss between irregular breaths. She was hyperventilating, drowning in air. I took her hands and cupped them over her mouth as I attempted to calm her down.

"Breathe, baby, just breathe with me. Shhh, try to control it. I'm here. Another breath."

Slowly, she gained greater composure, but the tears still soaked her cheeks in a steady stream. Finally, she spoke. "Mom. It's so bad. I can't, I can't, I..."

Another jag of panicked breath began the first several times she tried to talk. I told her not to say anything but to nod when I asked, "Is he alive?" Yes, he was. "Is he hurt?" Yes, no—confusion and heavy sobs answered me. "Did he hurt someone?" Yes, yes, and a cry of something—of grief, of anguish—exploded into the small space between us. "Oh, Abby what happened? An accident?" She shook her head, still crying. "Shhh, try to calm down, Sweetie. It will be alright. Breathe. Slow, deep breaths. I'm sure it will be alright." I held her tightly, her head against my chest as I tried to model the cadence of breath. We sat in silence for several minutes, little Opal curled in her lap, and she, in mine.

Her next words shocked me. "Mama. He'll never...he won't be alright again. He's in jail."

Every imaginable horror went through my mind: He had been driving drunk and killed someone. He was in a fight and killed someone. He had been caught with drugs. He was accused of—I stopped myself from thinking anything worse. I said nothing but stared at Abby, collapsed in my arms. I couldn't understand how a young man who had sat in my home and seemed so likable—seemed to have a plan for a better life—could be so derailed by behavior worthy of arrest. Finally, I spoke.

"For what?"

"Assault. Assault with a deadly weapon," she said.

"What! A gun?"

"No, no Mom. His hands, just his hands!" She sobbed. "He hit a cop."

"Oh my God, Abby, why? Why? What was going on? Where was he? Was it a bar fight? Since when are hands 'deadly weapons?'" I had too many questions, and she didn't have any answers.

"I don't know, Mom," she shot back in frustration. "Derrick commented on a picture for me to get in touch with him. You saw that. But I was at work this morning. So, he DM'd Sophie, and she called him, and then she came to the restaurant and told me, and Mom—" she began sobbing again as she continued, "I ran to the bathroom crying and I couldn't stop. I haven't been able to stop! My manager told me to go home. So, I'm here, and I don't know what to do! Mama, what am I supposed to do!"

"Shhh, try to calm down, love, shhh," I held her tightly for a few minutes and let her cry.

When she caught her breath, she tried to tell me more. "Sophie told me that she talked to Derrick, and he said that last night, well really, early this morning, Ry went out with some of the guys on base to some club, and there's something about a girl, but Derrick said that cops came, and Ry punched one in the face and broke his jaw. They beat him up really bad, Mom."

"Oh, Abby," she began to sob again. "Sweetie, I'm sure there is more to it. Maybe it isn't as bad as you think—"

"No, it's worse, Mom. I know it is. I talked to Ry before all this last night, and he said he wasn't going anywhere. He was playing guitar with Chris and David. And what's worse is that I told him I was glad he wasn't because I told him, I said for the first time ever, that I was worried about how much he was drinking. And Mom, he got a little upset over it. So, now I wonder if that's what made him go. But he said he was staying home. That was a lie, I guess. He was out drunk, out of his mind probably trying to pick up some ho and now he's in jail!"

The sadness showed its underlying anger. "So, where does this leave you?" I asked with hesitation and a hint of annoyance.

Not looking up, she took a fractured breath and said, "I don't know. I need to talk to him. I don't know anything. Maybe I never have." Her voice was small, as if her body were struggling to find the force to push the words past her lips.

My own tone regained its composure and compassion. "When will you talk to someone again? Will you be able to talk to him?"

"Chris is supposed to call me this evening. Or Derrick. I need to talk to him! I'm so, so confused and sad and angry, Mom. How could he do this? How could he ruin us like this?" she asked, still through tears.

"I don't know, love. You know Ryan much better than I do. Maybe there's an explanation."

"There has to be," she said more to herself than to me. Then looking at me, "Something just isn't right about it all. David said that when they questioned him at the hospital after everything, they asked him if he knew where he was, and he said New Orleans. And when they asked if he was military, he said, no, not yet, but he was going to boot soon." Pausing for a minute, she repeated, "Something is very wrong, Mom."

"I'm sure you'll get the whole story eventually, love. If you still want it."

"What do you mean by that?"

"Well, Sweetie, from what you've told me, I'm guessing this relationship—whatever it is—is pretty much over."

"I don't know. I don't know. I need to talk to him, Mama. I need to."

"When will you be able to?"

"I don't know."

"Does his family know about it all? His brother or sister? Grandmother?"

"I don't know. Derrick told Sophie Chris said he would call me. The police or hospital or his CO might have called them, but I haven't heard from them yet. Maybe I'll call Travis later. Mama?" She looked at me as I cupped my hand under her quivering chin. "What if I love him anyway?" The sobs began heavy again.

I closed my eyes to hold back my own tears, but sending them inward, the pain of her words sank into me, commingling with my fears. Was he really so unhinged? Or, was it simply an unfortunate night, a bar room brawl that could be cleared up? Maybe the officer's jaw wasn't broken, really. Maybe Ryan would be out by Monday, once things were explained, but even if that were the case, what did all this say about him? He was clearly not in control of himself. He told her he was staying in. He told her he loved her. He was flying her out in less than a month. I wondered what all this would mean.

Abby did talk to Chris later that night. She knew more and told me most of it, leaving out some details that I'd learn in increments in the months that followed. Chris had said the officer's jaw was not broken. It was his orbital bone, which would require facial reconstruction, and his vision was impaired. There was also a girl. From what Chis could find out, Ryan was leaving with her when she realized she did not have her phone. She believed Ryan did, and somehow she accused him of stealing it from her and began hitting him. He pushed her off and pinned her at arm's length–by the throat. Her friends came running and called the cops. Ryan was walking away when an officer told him to stop. He didn't. The cop caught up to him, grabbed him from behind, and with a flashlight in his eyes, Ryan turned around and swung hard. The cop went down, and chaos followed. Back-up, ambulances, five felony charges, and a few misdemeanors later, Ryan was in the county jail without any hope of bonding out.

He was lucky they didn't just shoot him.

Chapter 10

Behavioral Evolution

I did not love Ryan Freeman then.

Then, I believed the best Abby could do was distance herself from him and the difficult future his lack of self-control guaranteed. How could a beautiful and bright young woman from a supportive, loving family want to be associated with a man so broken that he had destroyed his one path to a better life? All indications suggested a dishonorable discharge in Ryan's near future—along with an inescapable felony conviction. His would be a difficult life, one I did not want Abby to share, but my wishes seldom factored significantly into her choices. She made a habit of making choices without my consent for at least five years. At the age of eighteen, Abby did not need to complicate her life with Ryan's bad decisions; she had made her own.

He was one of them.

Abby and I discussed the tentative December visit in the aftermath of Ryan's arrest. At first, I told her she should not go; there was no reason for it, nothing she could do for him. I had even suggested that she forget him, focus on ending the semester well, move on. Scott told her more pointedly that she did not want a life with a convicted felon. Did she understand what a felony would do to his future—how hard finding work would be, how limited he would be? That what had been rough for him before this would seem like a cakewalk? Even as we spoke, the words all felt wrong to me, so harsh, like we were playing the roles of concerned, upstanding, suburban parents saying what concerned, upstanding suburban parents should say—and losing their souls in the process.

Before this? Before this, he lost both parents. What were we saying, feeling? I was unsure. Abby knew—she could tell my words had a hollowness to them that I somehow could not fill with conviction—and she cried in endless confusion. I did not know there could be so many tears, like oceans from thimbles. We waded through sorrows for days, uncertain of whether Abby would find her way up. Scott and I held the course, though. I certainly didn't want her flying to California in less than a month to see him, much less through thick glass, like a museum exhibit—a testament to The Failure of Behavioral Evolution.

But things change.

It may have been the recognition of my own harsh judgment of Ryan, of the idea that his failure of behavior was completely within his control, that changed me—convicted me of my own failed humanity. People are most critical when they forget their own pasts, which, even if lived with the lightest touch upon the earth, offer evidence of missteps, misfortunes, and mistakes they'd rather forget. Most may not want to acknowledge past imperfections in the present, but every error paves the way to where we are. There's wisdom in knowing that, but it is hard won, painful to hold, and difficult to apply.

No sooner had I thought so callously about Ryan than my conscience ignited the memories within me of my every moral failing, and not only of my own, but also of anyone I had ever loved enough to forgive (often more easily than I forgave myself). I was no one's judge, especially not Ryan's. I had lived nothing close to his life, had no excuse of financial hardship or a lack of guidance or even of insurmountable sorrow. Still, I could accuse myself of crimes so selfish one would think I had no regard for those I loved. Yet, their hearts held space for me, even through my worst moments. Though I struggled to find true north in navigating that November, I eventually found it and have stayed faithful to it since.

The day after the arrest, Saturday, Abby received a call from Chris, who explained what he knew of the situation. He told her that because Ryan was active military, he would be transferred to the brig after his arraignment until his preliminary hearing, and from there, back to county jail while being processed out of the service. The nature of his discharge was still a matter of question. His service itself did not warrant a dishonorable discharge. In fact, it had been quite commendable, but there were stipulations about "discreditable involvement with civil authorities." Once would be enough for a dishonorable discharge.

It was during that transfer, on Tuesday, that Ryan's CO allowed him to call Abby. She was outside with little Opal when her phone rang, showing a

San Diego number that she did not recognize. She said his first words were, "Abby, I am so, so sorry. I love you," which was the gist of the whole conversation. A certain disbelief hung in their words, she said, but not about their truth. Both could not believe what was happening, but here it was, and it was too painfully real.

Ryan said he had talked to his grandmother and that she was looking for a lawyer, although he had a military lawyer and public defender. Evidently, the DA wanted to pursue the maximum sentence of thirteen years, an accumulation of time for each charge, and the public defender's suggestion was to take a plea of seven years. He needed a private attorney, a good one.

Abby began searching.

I also began my own search and learned more about California and military law than I ever imagined I'd know. Ryan had mentioned something about a "mayhem" charge hanging over him, and that was terrifying. It seemed like something more suited to a terrorist attack with a machete in a public place than a street fight, but with the victim being an officer and with the recent ambushes on police in retaliation for various shootings of unarmed men, the time called for a severe penalty for attacking a cop. I wondered for a moment what would have happened had Ryan not been a blue-eyed blonde with a regulation military cut. He was indeed privileged to be alive. Nonetheless, a mayhem charge would increase his sentence by years. Legally defined, mayhem indicated maliciously depriving another human being of his or her body—loss of a limb, permanent disfigurement, loss of sight. Ryan had broken the man's eye socket. The officer needed reconstructive surgery. This charge seemed possible.

But then it didn't. "Maliciously" indicated intent. Ryan didn't even know where he was that night. Can one have malicious intent but not be conscious of himself? Abby was right. There was more to all of this. I changed the direction of my research.

Abby had been busy, too. She had read countless reviews, combed through website after website, and made several calls to lawyers' offices before finally speaking to Ryan's grandmother and passing on the names of several attorneys in San Diego. They settled on Peter Blair, who seemed to specialize in seemingly hopeless criminal cases, and just as importantly, accepted a flat fee rather than charge an hourly rate. Abby planned to speak with Mr. Blair in December. The trip, about which I still had reservations, would happen, against my better judgment.

Ryan had arranged for his friend Derrick to register as Abby's host at the hotel on base, even though he would be out of the brig and back at the county jail by the time she arrived. Derrick would also pick her up from the airport and bring her to see him. Abby had never met this friend in person, but he had been with Ryan several times when he and Abby FaceTimed. I had worries that she tried to assuage by assuring me that Ryan trusted Derrick with his life, and after all, she said, Derrick had been the one to contact her when "everything happened."

I still didn't like it.

Knowing I was in the room while he spoke to Abby, Derrick offered a description of himself as a "dark-haired Ryan who happen[ed] not to be in jail" as proof of his trustworthiness. Given the situation, I wasn't very reassured, but seeing Abby's desperation to do something, anything she could for Ryan, I reluctantly agreed to the arrangement.

Even today, I second guess myself about Abby. I do not know what I am doing as a parent, even after almost twenty-six years—but those are Jenna's years. Maybe the first four make all the difference between them. I just don't know, but the last twenty-two have been so uncertain with Abby. I never know what is best for her, and if I think I do, I look at my solution to her problem from a different perspective and see how it is no solution at all. In my fifty-odd years of life, I can conclude that I've learned extraordinarily little of what there is to learn in the world, only how to control myself and find meaning in my own mistakes. When dealing with others, I am powerless to make a difference. Differences must be chosen, not imposed. I've learned that, too, but knowing it doesn't negate my frustration.

That November initiated new lessons for me along with some reviews of previous ones: the refresher on forgiveness, for one; the exposure to California and military law was another. Most meaningful, though, was my self-assigned task of learning to love a stranger's son like my own. Granted, I felt unsuccessful in rearing my own children—at least half-unsuccessful—and now here I was initiating myself into the role of pseudo-parent to a young man who lost both of his own and seemed lost himself.

In researching the California Department of Corrections and Rehabilitation, I discovered the county jail had email. Who knew? According to the website, inmates would receive the email within twenty-four hours of being sent. It would, of course, spend time in the mail room first, where it would be read for content that might compromise the security of the inmates or community. The website cautioned that "there should be no expectation of privacy" in the missive. I wondered, for a moment, who these people were, those who read incoming inmate mail, electronic and otherwise. Did they ever wonder who the inmates were before arriving? Who the writers were? Did they ever get caught up in exchanges, recognizing an out-going letter as a response to an incoming letter they had previously read? Were they ever saddened or humored or shocked or moved in any way by what they held in their hands? What they held in their hands, it seemed to me, could be the difference in the quality of someone's life, the difference between the will to withstand hardship and the weakness to succumb to it.

On the morning before Abby left for California, I arrived at school earlier than usual and found myself clumsily thumbing the tiny keypad of my phone, typing a jail email to Ryan. I had decided that no matter what became of him and Abby, he should not feel cast away. I was honest, but hoped he would find some comfort in my words:

December 10, 2016

Good morning, Ryan. Did you know that you could receive email? I discovered it as I googled everything under the Web that I could to find out what was going on with you and what Abby would be walking into. By the time you receive this—btw, hello, person who reads Ryan's mail—you may have already seen her. I just wanted you to know two things: first, letting her take this trip was difficult. I did not want her to go. There is too much I don't understand about your situation and about the one she will be in while she's there, but she's determined. And second, I've done lots of thinking—about you, about how you've ended up where you are, about forgiveness. I'm willing to hear you. I'm willing to reserve judgment until I know more. I'm willing to let my daughter draw her own conclusions. I hope you are holding up okay: regardless of fault, I'm sure this is painful for you. You are in my prayers. –Ms. Colleen

I wanted him to receive it well, and I meant it. Whether Abby would return telling me her contact with Ryan was over or that she was more committed to him, I had no way of knowing. I had imagined a variety of outcomes. The one that did materialize, however, was not among those I had anticipated.

Chapter 11

All In

Within a week or so of her return from California, Abby began toying with the idea of cutting her hair. Her hair is beautiful—lustrous sable falling, at the time, nearly to her waist, fit for a shampoo advertisement.

I should have known then, but I didn't.

Throughout history, women have had complex relationships with their hair, and though that may sound superficial, it is painfully true. The Bible says it is a woman's glory, as do several folk and fairy tales, Rapunzel, for instance. Hair holds some mysterious power, I suppose, even for men. Ask Samson or Delilah—or the makers of Rogaine.

Most women in my family have long hair, at least shoulder length. I cut mine drastically only once, shortly after Jenna was born. Doing so did not make me more secure in my new role as a mother, though. When they were young, I let Jenna's and Abby's hair grow long, furnishing them with unflattering bangs for the first few years, then allowing them to take control of their styles, which, I suppose, unsurprisingly, mimicked my own: long and natural. As I eased into my fifties, I was again tempted to give into societal expectations and cut my mid-back length, but as grey strands began to emerge I opted instead for the unconventional: a silver mane. I might be eighty before it turns completely, but I will someday be Grandmother Willow with braided locks of white, skin like bark, and wisdom enough—should I live an eternity.

Cutting one's hair drastically is a statement, be it of power or punishment or grief. When Emily Dickinson lost the love of Susan Gilbert to her brother Austin, she gathered her long auburn hair and cut it short. Susan and Austin were married that autumn. Even as recently as World War II, women have been publicly shamed by having their hair shorn: French women who slept with German soldiers—the evidence swaddled in their arms— were the main attraction in the "ugly carnivals" after the country's liberation in 1944. Self-chosen, taking up shears suggests an assertion of power, a rebellion against the feminine stereotypes so long in place. Ask St. Rose of Lima, Joan of Arc, or Sinead O'Connor. Self-inflicted, cutting off such a symbol of allure and identity could also be a cry for help at a breaking point, a desperate need to redefine oneself. Ask Britney. I suppose Abby's motive was a combination of all of it.

When Abby came home in December, she talked about how hard seeing Ryan "like that" was—about how he was so sorry, confused, and scared of whatever might happen next; about how he didn't know how what had happened—what they said he did—could be a part of who he was. He guessed it was true, or mostly true, but it made no sense. He had never been violent, not unprovoked, and never to that degree, he said. He had certainly never lifted a hand to a woman before, no matter the punches thrown at him, the cigarettes put out on his back. Before this, he had never been so abandoned by his memory. Recovering it, finding the reasons would be a monumental task. He, much less myself, had no idea of how long it would take, how far back it would reach, nor how penetrating it would be.

Upon Abby's first phone call home when she was in San Diego, she told me that she had arrived safely, that Derrick picked her up at LAX and checked her in on base, and that she would see Ryan Saturday and Sunday, and then not again until his court appearance Tuesday. I asked how Derrick was, and received a simple "fine" in response, which did not seem odd since the trip certainly wasn't about meeting Ryan's friends. I asked about the lawyer, Peter Blair, and she said she would get to speak with him in person after court—he had already called her at Ryan's request to tell her Ryan had given his consent for him to discuss the case with her and to request letters, if she could gather them, attesting to Ryan's character. Of course, she asked me to write one, and of course, I agreed. She also said he told her that he would be requesting a continuation on Tuesday to buy more time, gather more information, and attempt to negotiate the proposed plea down. It all sounded like too much for her to handle, but she assured me, she could.

When she called again after visiting Ryan on Saturday, she said he really appreciated the emails I had sent. There had been two by then. The first very sober and the second much lighter. They started a series of correspondence that touched every emotion within human experience.

In my investigation of the California Department of Corrections, I discovered all the programs offered to inmates—Reading Legacies, numerous veterans' programs, and, of course, AA and several counseling opportunities. My second email told him about these and Jail Guitars, a program started by a member of The Clash back in the eighties. It allowed inmates who could play to teach others, which sounded like something that might make Ryan's time there more bearable. I also suggested several books, all of which dealt with a search for self and peace and answers to the ultimate Why's. Suggested Reading Selections for Ryan Freeman included Jon Krakauer's *Into the Wild*, Viktor Frankl's *Man's Search for Meaning*, and Tim O'Brien's *The Things They Carried*, along with Donna Tart's *The Goldfinch*.

He told Abby he had read them all already.

Whether Ryan saw himself in any of those books or whether he read them simply for entertainment, I still don't know. How others read, how they process—if they process—fascinates me. I overthink everything, yet somehow still miss the obvious and important, so maybe being a contemplative person has less benefit than I would like to admit. But, I have tried to raise Jenna and Abby to be thinkers, people who assess and reassess, reflect. That's what I was hoping to cultivate in Ryan, too, not knowing it was already there to a degree. Ryan had problems with controlling his impulses, and so did Abby—despite her own ruminations—and I thought my writing to him and his reading of lives that struggled in ways like his would bring him some clarity. Without reflection, we are only driven by the basest of desires, with thoughts only of our last great satisfaction and hope toward the next, no better than beasts, who remember nothing except pleasure and pain.

Contemplative people seem less likely to give themselves over to their worst tendencies, I think. Seeking instant gratification almost always results in a loss of self. I had been preaching that to Abby all her life, but I have since learned it isn't the only way to surrender sovereignty of oneself. Sometimes, we give it up willingly in the name of goodness, compassion, love—or what we mistake for it.

Sometimes it's taken from us.

Abby called or texted every day of her visit and saw Ryan as often as visiting hours would allow. On Sunday evening, she called me, sounding a bit happier than I expected, so I wondered, foolishly, if charges had been reduced—or dismissed. Of course, they were not, but something new had materialized, something that did not seem right to me. After nearly a year of talking long distance, seeing one another occasionally, and facing the certainty of a felony conviction, Ryan asked Abby to be his girlfriend, officially.

Nothing could be a worse idea.

I did not share her enthusiasm. Although I liked Ryan and wanted to help him, I did not want to see Abby manipulated. Her emotions were high—they were always high—but with all this, her thinking could not be clear, not rational. I tried to explain to her that although he was searching for stability, it was unfair of him to ask it of her, especially now that he had no other options. For her to commit to an exclusive relationship with him at this point would be extremely difficult—requiring too much sacrifice and maybe more self-discipline than she could muster, I told her. She wholeheartedly disagreed. What began as a pleasant phone call became contentious.

"But Mom. With or without a label on it, you know I'm committed to him. I have been since I met him. I'm not interested in anyone else, ever. I know that more than ever now. Besides, he was planning to ask me on this trip anyway, not just because he's 'out of options' like you said. Remember, he paid for me to be here!" she argued.

"I know he paid for it, love. But this just doesn't seem—it's wrong! He has no idea of how long he'll be in there. You have no idea of how this will affect his future. Neither does he! I just think that if he really cared about you, he wouldn't pull you further into this mess he's created."

"I want to be in it, Mom! You know he has no one! I know more and have done more for him at this point than anyone! He needs me!"

"Abby, he's not in a good state of mind. And his family is helping him. His grandmother is paying for his lawyer, so don't give me that!"

"Mama, you don't understand!"

"I understand that he's scared right now. What happens when he's not, when he's out? Does he still need you? How will you feel if you spend the next year waiting, and when he's released, he decides he doesn't feel like staying home to play guitar again?"

"It's not going to be like that—"

"That's how it was," I cut her off with the ugly reminder. Silence sat between us for a moment, and then without her previous fire, sounding wounded, she quietly spoke:

"We've learned to be honest. I want to be there for him. He needs me. I just want to love him, Mama, and I believe him when he says he loves me."

That's where it began, or, rather, where the relationship became something new, something other than what it had been, though its history was unchanged.

On the Monday morning of her visit, I woke up to a texted picture, which I'm sure she was not supposed to take, of Ryan—behind glass, holding a short-corded phone, tan jumpsuit and all. He wasn't looking at the camera, but down at his other hand, with an expression I couldn't quite place, something between resignation and despondence. With it, she said, "Ry asked if you could please keep sending him emails. They make him happy." The request was manageable and heart-rending, so Ryan became a part of my weekly routine. Each Tuesday and Saturday, I would tap out a message of no more than 4000 characters, with no expectation of privacy. Usually, emails were on the lighter side, though occasionally, I'd have something more substantial to say. Tuesday afternoon, just after dismissal and the day Abby would come home, I found myself full of thoughts and sent Ryan the maximum word count in email number three:

December 20, 2016

> Hi Ryan, I'm about to leave school for the airport to pick up Abby. I know the last week was nowhere near the visit either of you had planned, but I hope there was still something to enjoy about it, maybe even some productive thinking that came from it. I'm anxious to see Abby and hear what she has to say, and for the record, I did ask her after being there—visiting you, going to court, seeing the reality of all this—if she was still "all in." She said yes, of course. This is a tough place for me and her dad. It's strange; we want to be supportive and understanding, but we are looking at ourselves thinking we must be crazy to allow our daughter to be involved with all this. I have to say, however, Scott is managing it remarkably well, though some of the details may be missing for him. I think I have reached a weird mental place where I want what is best for you, yet realize I don't know what that is, but if it includes Abby, I pray that it is also what is best for her. Anyway, I suppose I am trying to say that all this scares me. I don't know if you've noticed the few times you've been to our house, but I am a tame person who likes things in their proper places. And this is a messy situation. But, I trust it will work out as it should. I just want you to learn something valuable through it all. On another note, Derrick described himself as a brown haired you who happens not to be in jail. Does that make him a good guy? Abby hasn't said much about him. I hope you are well, and I am happy to hear that you finally got your tooth! I look forward to seeing that fully-toothed smile in person.

I suppose the first benefit of Ryan's incarceration was that the United States Marine Corps made good on his dentistry needs.

Despite the seriousness of the situation and my growing concern for Ryan, Scott and I tried to regard Abby's relationship with him as something that would pass in time, something she felt necessary right now but would tire of when the frustration of timed phone calls, no physical contact—not even every few months—and a limited future became glaringly real. In the meantime, we accepted her wishes, even supported her through them, as we too easily, too often have. Again, she would have to experience life on her terms, feeling the impact of consequences imposed by reality rather than by protective parents. Punishment hurts most when it is self-imposed. But sometimes it starts so subtly, it's hard to recognize.

After Abby's return home, just before Christmas break, she sent me a selfie captioned "look what I did." There she was, missing about nine inches of long hair, smiling, but not in the eyes. Her bob grazed her jawline. I did not stop to think about why she might be redefining herself so drastically. I suppose I assumed it was her new role as Ryan's official girlfriend, her attempt to prove her domestication—either that or just a whim.

Honestly, I was thinking more about Ryan's life, about what could have pushed him to where he was, and why I should be concerned with it. The answer to the second part was obvious: Abby. The first part, though—there was so much. In frustration, confusion, and compassion, I watched and thought until I had to write. Not another email or even the character witness letter, but five-plus pages of handwritten emotion poured out of me. I am not sure whether I was writing to Ryan (the salutation addressed him) or Abby or myself, but I discovered that I had lots on my mind. I eventually gave it to Abby, telling her to do what she thought was best with it.

Chapter 12

Spilling Ink

December 12, 2016

Dear Ryan,

I woke up to a texted picture of you this morning that broke my heart. You look so sad in it, and I'm sure you are. I wonder what you were thinking, what you've been thinking lately, and how your thoughts about anything may have already changed because of this. I have put so much thought into you recently, and into why I can't stop thinking, and while part of the answer is obvious— Abby— another part is terribly confusing. You are so important to Abby; consequently, you are important to me, and while I'm fairly sure you'd drop in priority if Abby were no longer a part of your life, especially if things were to end badly, I'm also fairly sure your well-being would cross my mind for years to come. Having taught for over twenty-five years, I've become a quick study of people, especially young ones, and I equate anyone I meet under the age of thirty-five to a could-have-been-student. I know if you would have been mine, I'd have loved you, as Donna Reynolds does. I've had students a bit like you over the years: the ones who are smarter than they allow most to see, who understand their own potential yet channel all that energy into things less than beneficial, who have everything, every quality, they need to get what they want from life but somehow get lost along the way or are persuaded to want what they should not. You remind me of another young man, named Brian, close right? He was a brilliant disaster in high school; so smart but distracted, musical, too worried about girls, too willing to try whatever anyone put in front of him, and too unapologetic for his misguided behavior for too long a time. He also became a Marine. I still hear from him occasionally and am happy to say he and his wife have settled into a quiet life and are expecting their first child. He will be an excellent father. Maybe I've imposed the idea of him onto you, and that's simply wrong. You have your own story.

I am at fault for creating ideas around people, and I have undoubtedly done that to you. Letting people be who they are is tough. I always want the idealized versions. I suppose I should stop worrying so much about who everyone else is and take a good look in the mirror sometimes. Sometimes we learn forgiveness best through the blame we encounter within ourselves, and I, like everyone, am not innocent. I've been thinking that recent events have caused you to take a serious fall on my Mom Rating Scale, but sometimes I'd rank myself low. I've been riding around on a high horse for a while, I guess, thinking I can fix people even though I'm far from perfect. I have made progress though. I wish I could help everyone do the same. My class recently asked me what my superpower would be if I could choose one. I go back and forth between wanting the ability to say exactly the right thing to help people heal from whatever sorrows and wrongs they feel and wanting to set people on fire with my eyes. Okay, not really, but being able to deliver a good shock, like a dog's shock collar, that would be great. But anger always cools, and I'm left with all my emotion bottled up, not knowing what to say until it comes pouring out in ink. Like this. I wish, in the thousands of words I've said to you, I knew what to say. I wish I could mend the past, protect you from every bad decision you have yet to make. I know how futile that is, though. I've been unable to protect my own child from herself—unable to protect myself sometimes. I do pray, though.

I've learned by proxy for a good bit of life. Seeing others, such as my brother, suffer the consequences of his drinking and disregard has taught me to respect limits. Maybe that has also made me boring, but I believe it has kept me safe and made me wiser. Not everyone—like Abby—learns this way. Experience teaches most; reflection, only some. How do you learn, Ryan? What have you learned? I don't need to know those answers, but you do.

Living deliberately is an art and doing so does not mean living without spontaneity. It means living with purposes that do not oppose one another. It means living with an understanding of what you value and why. At least that's what it means to me. My definitions aren't the only ones. The ideas of purpose and value send me into reassessment daily, and although I do not always like what I find in myself, I know I need to see it to move past it. I've done lots of that lately and am still in progress, trying to move past ideas that have resided within me, quietly waiting for me to realize how wrong they were. There is a short story one of my students brought in after finding it on Tumblr. She liked it but didn't quite understand it. She thought I could explain it to her. I think it says what I'm trying to learn—and trying to teach. It's called "The Egg." I'll send it to you. Hang on...I just printed it, for what it's worth. Enjoy.

To be honest, Ryan, the more I think, the more I'm convinced I know very little. I'm full of a desire to understand life and of the awareness of the impossibility of doing so. I'm a huge fan of paradox and ambiguity, which is good since the more I try to grasp, the higher the bar is set: the more unanswerable the questions become. In my mostly safe little life, Abby's choices throughout high school presented me with challenges I hated—I know you know what pain there is in loving someone and being powerless to help them. That's how she's made me feel. Seeing her grow enamored with so much that could destroy her was—and is—my biggest struggle. Learning that loving someone is more important than controlling them is a lesson my mom taught me and one that, if she had not, life certainly would have. Seeing my youngest daughter grow deceitful and secretive as a young teen and wild and reckless as she grew older felt like a rebellion against everything I hoped to instill within her, rebellion against me. Although I said some regrettable things to her during that time, I determined that loving her took priority over controlling her at the cost of resentment and alienation of family. It led to a more honest relationship if not better choices. It also led to you. I'm quite sure you would have had little interest in her if she had been the rule-follower I wanted. And that's okay.

I think she shares with me a few principles that I believe are absolutely true. One, I've mentioned to you before, Romans 8:28, regardless of the particulars of faith, God, however you define God, does work all things for the good of those who love him. (I won't get caught up in the pronouns...the limits of language). My second fundamental truth is that everything is connected, which stems into this: there is a reason for everything. Sometimes we are lucky enough to discover the reasons; most of the time we're not. One day, I'll tell you a story about that. Right now, though, I can trace the path in my memory that brought you into Abby's life, and I can make sense of it. I can even see one version of the future; of course, it isn't the only version. I also know that my job isn't to control any of it. It's yours and Abby's, together or apart, your choices, reactions, assessments, reassessments, and reflections will determine your futures. You've probably heard before that the best predictor of future behavior is past behavior, and I believe that's true, as far as pop psychology goes, unless there is some marked change, a shift in perception that breaks a pattern. People of faith might call it repentance, but that sounds so judgmental. I prefer to think of it as simply learning, which is what we were created to do—to learn in order to create. I hope you both learn from this and that because you do, you can create better lives for yourselves. Ryan, I don't really know you, not well enough to understand how you have put yourself where you are or what is best for you in the future, but I want to offer some comfort along the way, and guidance, if you need it— if you'll accept it. Whatever comes of this, I want you and Abby, together or not, to grow wiser from it, to live more deliberately, more aware, with lives not marred by avoidance and escapism, but filled with purpose. I know the pain of failing oneself, and I know the peace of redemption. I hope to celebrate your knowing that success, too, one day—the success of the will to overcome, to prove possible the idea that all that is happening is part of a divine confluence of events meant to make life more beautiful and bearable for those we love.

You know, I am unsure of why I wrote this. It seems more of a journal than a letter, but for some reason, you were my imagined audience. I apologize if it assumes too much. Maybe I've said something that makes sense to you, I hope. Or, you might just think, "What a weird old broad!" (Do men even say that anymore, "broad"? It seems very military to me...I think my grandpa, who was an Army man, said it all the time...I'm rambling now...okay, done.) Anyway, my mind is a bit more settled, after all these words. Thank you for reading this long-winded rant.

As ever,
Ms. Colleen

Chapter 13

Interior Landscapes

Somewhere in the days between Abby's cutting her hair and Christmas, a letter came in the mail for me along with one for Abby. She seemed more excited about mine than hers, but she had the grace to let me read it first. I guess I should not have been surprised to receive it, but I was. Somehow, I imagined my emailing and writing to Ryan as a one-sided endeavor, but I was pleased to see that he understood reciprocity. I noticed the handwriting: small, but not too; even; neat, respectful of margins; familiar in that I've read work resembling it from certain students—a positive association. Even with an occasional "ain't" in there, his grammar was better than most of my freshman comp students in August. Ryan sounded like himself on paper:

Dear Ms. Colleen, Well dear Lord! Haha, this has been one hell of a month. I just wanted to start out by saying thank you for caring so much about me even though you've only met me a few times. I haven't really had that good feeling in a while. I mean, my family is perfect for me and everything, but they get busy with their own lives, so they show me love mostly only when I'm around them. So, this is nice. I can't wait to be able to come back and have another conversation with you. There are so many things I need to fix in my life right now that it ain't even funny. I'm even losing hair right now as I'm writing this. Seriously, like 7 just fell on the paper. Considering everything that is going on right now though, I'm glad this happened. God was giving me pretty straight forward signs that I ignored. And I can't use my screwed up past as an excuse. I'm considering this a blessing because I was going to die pretty soon if I didn't get this reality check. I've learned 3 things with all this so far. I've got one hell of a right hand, God's going to get me through another obstacle in my life, and I absolutely love your daughter. I swear, I think she was sent to save my life or something. Even though I've got more issues than Time *magazine, she hasn't given up on me, and I want to thank you for that. She obviously got that from you and picked up a lot of your other good character traits, too. I know I'm not doing so hot right now on your mom rating scale, but I'm also a person who never gives up. When I'm finally able to get out, I know there's still a lot of work to do. And depending on my charges, it very well could be more difficult than I can imagine right now. But, and it's a big but in my eyes, God has trained me to deal with the worst. I can walk through Hell's fire because I know they'll eventually burn out. Life is going to be difficult for me, and Abby knows that. And as much as it sucks to say, I won't be able to get her a big house, nice cars, beautiful jewelry, and brand-new clothes for a while. However, I will be able to give her the love she deserves. I will protect her against literally anybody or anything. She'll always be beautiful to me no matter what she's wearing. And honestly, a small home is better than a big house anyway. Homes have stronger foundations than houses do, that's why they survive life's storms. Anyway, thank you for everything you've done so far. Love, to me, means many different things, so with that said, I love you and your family. Love, Ryan Freeman P.S. I drew a picture with a lot of symbolism in it. I figured you'd like it. It's weird, but it says a lot.*

Obviously, Abby had decided to send the handwritten letter I wrote to Ryan, which meant she had also read it. I was glad. I wondered though, what Ryan assumed about us, about me, with his references seeming to place importance on houses, clothes, cars. I suppose my saying that I liked things in their proper places, or even just our family's outward appearance could have caused the assumption, but his comments about that were not what I studied within his letter. It was his drawing. It amazed me. It suggested a young man who knew himself, saw exactly where he was, and had a mind that reached deep into the unfathomable to pull out images explaining what words cannot convey. I took in its details, which emerged in my mind as a poem:

A barren landscape
dotted with destruction
along a checkered path paralleling death,
a toppled rook, a crooked king,
an unseen thirst quenched in toxic measures
to the last drop,
a wild western hemisphere beside a void
of possibility,
of ease unknown–
questions unanswered lie beneath the mischief
and the sadness of consequence,
of pushing the limit,
of being the illustration of what can happen
under the watchful eye
—amid the signs—
that allows what is.

He titled his drawing "The Signs Are There," but for the poem it inspired, it didn't feel right. Titles always trouble me. Calling things by their right names, an idea posed by Pasternak in *Dr. Zhivago* and borrowed by Krakauer—well, really McCandless—in *Into the Wild*, resonated with me. To know something or someone well enough to see what or who they truly are matters, and I was looking at a self-portrait, not of appearance, but of thoughts, of reflection, of self-awareness. In the mystic, Dali-esque landscape, I saw the acknowledgement of so many poor choices. Ryan—a guy who, as Scott once said, "shits charisma," and seemed unbreakable no matter what he threw himself against—brought his past to the page, ghosts within him populating the vista with hushed violence. Both whimsical and unsettling, the drawing captured Ryan's attitude and experience, and his accountability. He put himself where he was, and he knew it. It captured his riotous past.

Shortly after his arrest, when Abby felt that strange combination of anger, betrayal, and compassion, wondering why he would have gone out that night after speaking to her, wondering even more why he would be leaving a bar with a woman—she wrote, too, a short poem, and read it to me. I don't recall exactly how she began, but she ended it with, "You're a riot in California," and she was right. Whatever chaos was within Ryan, he had done a good job of containing for a long time.

Although I knew his home life had been a rough one and his mother's death would have been enough to send most people irrecoverably into anguish, Ryan seemed strong enough to carry his childhood without too obvious a struggle, at least outwardly. He seemed to dance with the ghosts of his past more than close his eyes against them or rage opposed to them, but I guess *seemed* is all. I couldn't help thinking that aside from the alcohol, something more provoked Ryan's reaction the night he was arrested, maybe something even he could not yet identify. I wondered where the situation— of a young woman threatening him, accusing him—sent him in his memories, conscious or not. What combination of factors had come together in a way he had not experienced before—the way things seemingly mundane suddenly explode, like a roadside IED everyone mistakes for trash?

The young man I had come to know over the last year did not seem so volatile, so dangerous. How could a person who had withstood, who had appeared worthy through so much misfortune in his life, suddenly lose his value in a span of unfortunate hours? Ryan's hours that night were filled with a series of decisions, poor enough in isolation but compounded, devastating. How could a life of setback and surmounting lead here? How could all the respect won from the small victories vanish in a haze of unremembered events? It can't.

A person is either good but going through hardship or confusion, or he is a fraud—is there anything else? Unless I had completely misread Ryan, he wasn't a fraud. He was struggling, which was obvious now, but had it always been? I didn't know him well enough to know yet.

Although life had already dealt so harshly with him, Ryan seemed able to look at it and not hold existence itself suspect. Even in this situation, he owned his actions although he didn't understand them—didn't even remember them—completely. He knew there was no disputing that while his mind went wherever some detail of the moment sent him—deep into a wordless remembrance of who-knows-how-long-ago—his body fought. The bruised and broken skin and blood dried black across the knuckles of his right fist told a story he did not doubt. And because he knew, he willingly accepted whatever fate awaited. It would not be an easy one.

Inside the darkest places within us, those we are most afraid of, is often the salvation we desperately need. Ryan said he was glad this happened, that he was ignoring signs, that he probably would have died soon without this "reality check." I was glad to hear him acknowledge so much, but I disagreed with something he said, too. He said he could not use his past as an excuse, but I wondered what had really happened in it and how much, if any, he had resolved, how much he really faced—and overcame. He was skilled in distraction and escapism. Now, already a month gone by, he had no escape other than books and inmate programs, no solace at the bottom of a bottle, only emails and letters, and those from very few, often only us. People say the past cannot change the present, but it can, especially if we run from it. Memories surface and rearrange life in ways we had not previously imagined. Ryan, like all of us, had work, challenging work, to do in finding the patterns of his life, but he willingly began, and willingness makes all the difference.

Thankfully, Ryan was admitted into the Veterans Moving Forward program, which has its own red, white, and blue module at Vista Detention

Center, and there, he was far better off than with the institutional gray of the general inmate population. The program made good on its intentions to help inmates who served their country. Ryan had access to various classes, training, and most importantly, counseling. He took advantage of it all. Although he had not mentioned it to me in his letter, he told Abby he had been evaluated for several possible psychiatric disorders. Aside from the obvious depression and alcoholism with which he was coming to terms, the most significant diagnosis was PTSD.

Having returned from deployment to the Middle East less than a year before his arrest, Ryan had recently witnessed atrocities, lost brothers in arms, and experienced the stress of uncertainty in the way only the military can, and though all of that exacerbated his condition, I immediately knew it was not the cause. Hearing the gunshot, smelling the iron hanging in the air, and seeing the blood pool around her body—that was Ryan's trauma. I lost my father to a sudden heart attack, and although I was married with two children of my own, I felt like the foundation had fallen from beneath me. I cannot imagine how a fifteen-year-old boy facing a parent's violent death would feel. Ryan's PTSD reached back far, and I believed the events of that November night triggered something deep within him, but what, I can never really know. What I knew at this point was that my daughter loved a young man full of complexities that terrified me, and part of me considered what it would mean for her future, should their relationship last.

The other part was discovering a rare person. In some ways, Ryan had been only an idea for over a year, an outline drawn with select details and brutal truths, but that frame began to fill with my best imaginings for who he could have been and could still become. Over the long correspondence of his incarceration, I grew to love Ryan, even when Abby couldn't. But, I'm getting ahead of things again.

Chapter 14

Christmas Parties and Greek Mythology

The days leading to Christmas were thankfully quieter than those before Thanksgiving. The most tension—or maybe second most—occurred when Abby pleaded her cause to Scott about supporting Ryan as his girlfriend. Although he shared my opinion of Ryan's timing and motive in inviting her commitment, whether it was conscious or not, Scott told Abby in terms gruffer than my own that she was an insurance policy.

But he also said he wanted her to follow her heart.

Scott had grown up in a home that prioritized logic over love, security over the singing of angels. Hearing this philosophy throughout his childhood left him hoping for something more in his own life. He told Abby he wanted her to listen to herself, to the small voice within her we knew was there but that she had grown skilled in silencing. He wanted her to make wise decisions and to be wise enough to know when to ask for help with hard choices. She promised she would. I think that's a promise she continues to break, and in doing so, continues to suffer without awareness and ownership over the absurdities that arise in her life.

Jenna, who had moved into her own apartment after graduating, came home for the holidays, but she offered her sister no advice. Having orchestrated her life so differently and being in a content relationship for two years, she could not relate. Jenna absorbed every bit of guidance we ever provided her, and she, too, tried to encourage her sister toward good choices, but in her own, unobtrusive way. She offered that odd filial support best communicated through facial expressions, cartoonish sounds, and that odd, wordless language of siblings, although the late-night voices told me they did talk more deeply when they were alone. Jenna brought Ryan up by name on Christmas morning. After opening gifts in front of the fireplace, Abby sat cross-legged on the floor among crumpled gift wrap holding Opal in her lap, not quite expressionless, but definitely distracted by her thoughts.

"Hey," Jenna said in her sister voice as she reached over and poked Abby's foot.

"Hey," came the squeak of a response, the spell of sadness only half broken.

"Ryan?" Jenna questioned.

"Yeah, everything's just so hard," her voice trailed off and the tears began. Opal began licking her cheeks.

"I emailed him the other day, wishing him a Merry Christmas Eve's Eve." I said.

"Wait, what?" Jenna asked her most frequent question. "He can get email?"

Abby nodded, looked up, and said, "Yeah," which came out as more of a chirp. "I did, too, last night."

"Well, it's Christmas morning, with, you know, good cheer and all that. We should email him and wish him a Merry Christmas," Scott chimed in, surprising me.

So, with each of us on our phones, we gathered around the coffee table, gift wrap still strewn around us. Abby and I walked Jenna and Scott through the how-to-email-an-inmate process. Having just sent him one of some substance two days before, I lightened this one up by telling him about the awesome elf socks I was wearing for the occasion and warning him, should he ever spend the holiday with us, to avoid Uncle Tim, who had a somewhat creepy propensity to kiss female relatives hello a bit too enthusiastically and would corner anyone he could to lecture them about the evils of Big Data (about which he's probably right). I'm not sure of what Jenna said to Ryan, and Abby—she told me she told him about how happy she was that her dad, of all of us, suggested this little email party. Scott offered encouragement, the kind of coach-y advice I've heard him give to his players, but with a difference. He read it to us, and there was a note, a deep one, of sincerity and understanding in his words. Although he never addressed it aloud, I believe Scott saw a bit of whatever it was that Abby and I noted in Ryan that was reminiscent of him. The difficult childhood, the natural charm, that ability to walk into a room and own it—or at least think he did, as I would tease Scott. Some aspects of Ryan were very familiar. The likeness made me wonder what might have become of Ryan if he had had just a little more stability in his life, even the kind a series of stepdads can provide.

Abby felt so much better after we all hit send. Seeing her smile, genuinely smile, was good. She brings so much of the adversity she encounters on herself, but that doesn't make her up-hill battles less painful to witness. I still worry about her constantly: about her habits, her burdens, her goals, her future, her present—how what we are living at this very moment will affect her, where it will lead, what it will teach.

I was and am learning, as always, to let go.

As I talked with her, wrote to Ryan, tried to offer advice when asked, and navigate everyone's emotions, I knew I had no control over any of it. What would happen simply would. The complicated machinery of life can keep a mind too concerned with where future becomes present, which too quickly recedes into past. Tracing that path busies me too often. I vacillate between believing an understanding of the process creates meaning and purpose and believing it's futile to attempt to sort out. Meaning and purpose usually win. Sometimes, though, I wonder if that's just the lie I tell myself to cope.

The ordeal with Ryan caused me to wake everyday wondering what newness would develop—whether a letter with some revelation would arrive or whether Abby would dissolve herself into a puddle of tears over something she had or had not done, whether any of this would suddenly make sense. If we are really honest, the draw to the future is just to see what happens, to test our theories about how far up the mountain we can push our boulders, our burdens, before they roll back over us, and we begin again.

The absurdity of life overwhelms us all sometimes. We parse the world into so many pieces that we can no longer place them, figure out how they fit together. We somehow believe that some parts should have nothing to do with others, but that isn't right. We cannot live through disconnected experiences and feel purposeful. We cannot take our hands from the boulder and step to the side to pick up something shiny. If we do, what we have worked toward will roll at crushing speed past us, where it will surely destroy someone.

We must meet our responsibility, make sense of it, and find the continuity in it, even in the horrible parts. In fact, broken as we may be—flattened too many times—we have to address the task before us simply because it is ours. I have never understood why people complain so much about conducting what is necessary to maintain their own lives. We are accountable for what we create. To ignore or avoid the work is to succumb to fate; to face it is to create the opportunity to reflect on it, and find the absurdity of it all, which is what allows us to live outside the suffering—to laugh, to replenish ourselves, to begin again. Meeting that responsibility, we keep those around us safe, shouldering the burden, being ready for the weight—not if, but when—it rolls back. Life is just life. The goal is not reaching the top. It is the observation and embrace of the toil, the struggle. It is showing up ready. It is, as Camus said, imagining Sisyphus happy.

Abby wasn't ready.

Chapter 15

Risk Assessment

The holidays were harder than I knew for her. Alternately hopeful and lost, she distracted herself with shiny new friends, friends of Ryan's she had gotten to know. In fact, to my disappointment, she chose to spend New Year's Eve with them, with a girl named Lisa, who seemed like a terrible idea to me. Although I liked Ryan very much, I did not like what or who surrounded him. His friends from home, most of whom forgot he existed unless he were hosting some excuse to behave badly, weren't the reliable sort. Lisa was, at least, dependable. I know Abby was seeking vicarious approval from them and trying to grow closer to Ryan through them, but her behavior reminded me of her high school secrecy, her missteps. Nonetheless, she was her own person, as always, and swore that no one was a negative influence on her. She, in fact, claimed to be the instigator in most untoward situations—just what every mother wants to hear. At least she took responsibility for herself.

The day after New Year's Day, a letter addressed to "Everybody Hildebrand" arrived. Four carefully folded sheets of loose-leaf paper, each with our names in large, neat print on the outer fold, bore Ryan's appreciation for our Christmas messages. Scott's letter began, "I'm not sure if you've ever been to jail before, but I recommend not going." Ryan went on to tell him about the workout routine he had devised, the dietary challenges of jail food, and the thanks he felt for our help and encouragement when he knew how much easier forgetting him would be. To Jenna, he also expressed thanks and added he could cross "spend a holiday in jail" off his bucket list, and to me, he spoke of looking forward to spending some future Christmas with us, asking how the house training was going for Oatmeal—what he had taken to calling Opal—and being completely willing to entertain Uncle Tim's conspiracy theories, but maybe not kissing him. Abby read her letter—hers covered the front and back of a page—quietly on the sofa with a sad smile, something between reassurance and longing.

Life was settling back into a routine for all of us with the start of school on January 4, 2017. Scott and I resumed our usual days filled with coaching track (for him) and the grading of essays (for me). Of course, I still spent a few minutes on Tuesdays and Saturdays emailing Ryan. One of the first post-holiday emails dealt with the continuing enigma of Abby. At lunch, I sat at my desk phone in hand and tapped away.

January 5, 2017

Hi Ry,(I'm feeling rhymey today.) Here's one for you: What do you get when you cross a wanna-be badass with someone so sensitive that kittens make her cry? Abby. You get Abby. Oh my, let me tell you—the child is an absolute empath. Every little thing—prayers, a stranger saying, "have a nice day," a Facebook What's Your Secret Power quiz—you name it, it makes her cry lately. She has way too many emotions. I think it is precious. I love her. There isn't a part of her that's afraid to express her feelings. I just got off the phone with her, and she was all-out sobbing over anything and everything—joy for the growth she's feeling in herself, sadness that you are not here to share it with her. I told her she should write it, which would not only include you, but help her figure herself out, make sense of life as the pen moves across the page. That's what I do, anyway. Writing is so cathartic. I know this whole jail thing is awful, but the time it forces on both of you to reflect and the way it creates the need to write just to stay in touch is almost a gift. Ok, maybe that's too optimistic, but it's sort of true. If she writes to you and you to her, consider how in years to come, you'll have these pages from the past that will allow you (both, maybe) to see how your perceptions changed, how circumstances did not dictate your identity, how your relationship not only withstood this but strengthened through letters. That's a love story to rival *The Notebook*. No pressure, though :) Enough of that. I know you have a court date coming up soon, so that has been heavily on my mind and in my prayers. Well, the vet just called and said Oatmeal can come home (she was spayed today), so I'm headed there to pick her up right after school. Am I terrible to have scheduled her appointment today so that she'd be sluggish our first week back so I wouldn't have to walk her? Oh well. Love, Ms. Colleen P.S. What did 0 say to 8? Nice belt.

Before a letter from Ryan would arrive, he would often respond through Abby. To that one, he said he needed a minute to "think of a good G-rated joke." I guess too much time around Marines and criminals can tilt one's sense of humor toward tawdry. He called her every other night, which did get a bit expensive, but as she said, she was working again, and considered the cost an investment in her future. The idea troubled me, a little, but then it didn't. My daughter dating a convicted felon sounded outrageous and unacceptable, but Abby dating Ryan was fine, especially as I knew and understood him more. How the felon and Ryan were the same person was paradoxical, and it was something few people knew. With Ryan's having been stationed in California, simply saying he was still there became an easy way to avoid questions if I were asked about my girls' lives, but some people knew, and none of them understood, much less approved. Ella, especially, objected.

My sister put the question directly to Abby: What if he has a flashback and hurts you one day? It was a question I had talked with Abby about myself, early in the events. It was the first hesitation I had. Abby told her what she told me, which was that Ryan has never hurt a woman—the police report proved it. The most serious physical mark on the cell phone girl was the impression of a single tooth on *her* fist. Nonetheless, it was a chance she was willing to take. Still, Ella's disapproval was palpable, and it landed squarely on me, especially after she found out that I wrote to Ryan regularly. Before school had begun again, Ella, my mom, and I had lunch together at a little outdoor cafe. The day was crisp but sunny, and the scent of coffee lingered in the early afternoon air. I stared at the menu deciding whether to have pancakes or a cheeseburger, both choices I'd later regret. It was then that she asked me—her voice full of disapproval—why I still wrote to Ryan.

I told her, "Have you ever seen news stories or documentaries, like ESPN's, about people who are full of potential but have had such rough lives that they end up going down a bad road?"

"Yeah," she waited for something more. My mom, who I knew liked Ryan, at least before all this, sat pretending to be more interested in the menu than in the conversation.

"Well, right now, this boy is important to Abby, and even without her, he's a person with a whole history, and he's actually very smart and talented—full of potential. I just think about those stories, and when they end well, people feel good, like their faith in humanity is renewed or something, but when they end badly, everyone looks at each other and says, 'What a shame. Someone should have done something.' I guess because I've gotten to know Ryan, I've decided to be the someone."

"I just don't think it's smart. She should forget him. You should stay out of it. I mean, what kind of life would she have? She's only eighteen. She's too young to be making decisions like this."

"I agree; she is too young. And who says the decisions are final? She might get tired of waiting depending on his sentence, or he might move on from her once he's out. It's just life right now, but he's a person. He's alone for the most part, other than us."

"He shouldn't be her problem. Or yours."

"Jeez, Ella, it's called compassion." My mom shot me a surprised look.

"Colleen, don't you know I've learned that having compassion for someone isn't worth hurting yourself or your family in the long run?"

"I'm sorry. I know, but I guess I'll have to learn that one for myself," I said.

The conversation about Ryan ended there, Ella punctuating the discussion with a stern yet silent "You'll see." We learned not to talk about Abby and Ryan, at least not out loud, but whenever, if ever, Abby brought him up around her, I was the one who received the disapproval, communicated all too clearly in that wordless language of siblings. Ella has lived a different life than I have, so I justified our difference of opinion with our contrary experiences—mine, years in the classroom learning to care about other people's children; hers, years in the corporate world, learning to protect her interests.

I knew that Ella did know something about compassion, though. Years ago, right after Hurricane Katrina, she took in my niece's boyfriend. They had been dating for about a year and were both seventeen. He lost everything except his parents, who were not very present in his life from the start. After the storm, he was part of the rescue efforts and pulled bodies from the flood waters in lower St. Bernard, where a nursing home, among other residences, was lost. He had seen too much and harbored his own issues with nowhere to take them. Ella, after her family relocated and settled, opened her home to him. He lived with them for several months. Then, my niece broke up with him when he got another girl pregnant. He had been cheating on her the whole time. I guess Ella learned the vulnerability of compassion then.

Knowing when the pain is worth the risk may be impossible. Only in retrospect can such assessments be made, but in that reverse view, vision is skewed, especially when we see someone we love hurt. Would I regret allowing myself to care about Ryan? Maybe I would, but my regret would not make his life any less valuable than mine or Abby's. We tend to think the people closest to us are the most valuable—our family, our friends, our communities. Proximity becomes the primary condition for love in that way, and there is no closer proximity than that of mother and child.

I completely understand the defensiveness of protecting one's own from all the Others. Yet, the Others are someone's children, too, so how do we value our own most? Do we really believe that "we're all God's children" or that "all men are created equal?" We certainly say it when it's convenient, but I don't see many people living it. Instead, they live and love according to proximity. Accidents of location create value, and if someone is from the wrong side of the tracks, well, you know the story. Getting caught up with people "like that" is dangerous, according to conventional wisdom, but when "like that" simply means someone you have not allowed yourself to know, how unwise is it, really, or how rational? I do understand protecting one's own, but I also understand that every soul has innate value. I don't really understand how we should know whose lives we should bring into our own. I don't know how to know who is worth the risk. All I know, I guess, is that life puts tasks before us—from caring for a litter of barn kittens to grieving the loss of a brother, a mother, a father—and they will roll back, so we may begin again, wiser.

Chapter 16

Bound in a Nutshell

In mid-January, Abby began college courses again, still commuting from home. She received her grades from the previous semester, which ended so tumultuously. Honestly, I was expecting the worst, given that studying for finals was not exactly her priority in early December, but she fared pretty well. She would have to work hard this semester to keep her scholarship. Skimming by with a 3.0 left little room for future lapses. She only scheduled twelve hours, arguing that arranging her classes so that she attended only two days a week would allow more time to work and would cost less in gas. She had a point, so with no room for error, the semester began, and shortly after, she began a new job as a server at a local restaurant.

Falling into a routine after the holidays with Jenna's living forty-five minutes away and Abby finding her footing in school and getting a job, I assumed responsibility for most of Opal's care. Before work each morning, I'd take her outside, make sure she had food and water in her pen, and promise her a walk when I got home. Her mystery DNA revealed itself more clearly every day. She was definitely not a retriever, but thankfully, she was also not a digger or chewer or barker. Had she been left to her own devices on the street, she would have been a cat-killer, but she keeps her instincts in check around Snowflake and Pepper, our cats who come and go as they please, having deftly avoided coyotes for the last five years. Abby's patterns were beginning to resemble theirs—coming and going as she pleased. I was not fond of it and voiced my disapproval more than once. Something was not right with her, but she denied any difficulties other than the obvious depression over Ryan. As always, she assured me that "everything's fine." I doubted that. For years, Abby's interaction with me ebbed and flowed predictably. She would cling to me when she was scared or needy and avoid me when she knew I'd be disappointed in her, when she was disappointed in herself. I had seen little of her over the early weeks in January.

Balancing concern and disapproval requires the skill of an equilibrist in the wind. Walking the tightrope of emotion that runs through Abby and Ryan's situation demands, at once, intense concentration and casual disregard. I only navigated one of them well enough to avoid plummeting— the one who was not my biological child. With my research into the prison system and PTSD, I focused more on imparting what I could to Ryan in a manner that showed my concern without seeming intrusive. I suppose with Abby, I was just presumptuous. I was concerned for her, but I too often expressed my worry as anger. In the few conversations Abby and I had during those weeks, I said things that wounded her, not knowing she was already huddled around more pain than she could bear. Weeks more would pass before I knew.

With enough distance between us to keep my touch light, I began my latest email to Ryan with an Opalism, what I began to call the anecdotes about her.

January 10, 2017

Ryan, so, first, this is going to be one of two emails because I have so many things to say, which I know you are super excited about :) and second, I did a thing. Well, I've done lots of things lately, but this one is just silly. Sort of. I created an Instagram for Opal. Turns out, she's pretty funny, and kind of deep. Who knew, right? She comes up with the greatest hashtags. The account is Opal_ism, because Opalology was taken. And sounds like a study of gemstones. She said she expects, "that tattooed, blond guy who was here when [she] was a puppy to follow [her] eventually." I tried to explain, first, that she's still a puppy no matter how bad-ass she thinks she is and that if she's going to use social media, she needs to use it responsibly, which means maybe not accepting every follow request that comes along, but I guess you'd be fine. The hardest part for her is the necessity of opposable thumbs. Ok, I've kept that fiction up long enough. Did you realize I was so lame? I crack myself up. Really, there's a party in my head every day. (But I'm kind of awkward at real-life parties.) But seriously, I made her an account, and manage it in first-person-Opal-point-of-view. Ridiculous. It's mostly an excuse for me to follow Abby. She finally got a new phone, and changed her passwords to everything, so now I'm locked out of her Instagram. I think she had forgotten that she used my phone to log in once, which had given me secret access to her life for the last year. I'm a bad snooper, though, because I didn't even know direct messages were a thing until Opal got one from Jenna. That's probably good. Lord knows what horrors I may have encountered in Abby's DMs (scary, right?!). Anyway, I am super annoyed at The Child (what I affectionately call her when I am peeved at her). Seriously, I texted her last night and told her how glad she ought to be that she was not born a hamster because I'd have eaten her by now. Is that mean? And gross? I can't always tell because I have a sort of dark, twisted sense of humor sometimes. It surprises people because they usually think I'm all rainbows and halos, which I guess is nice. Not related-as far as space for these emails #nospaces=morespace.So hopefully,it isn't too squished up.I'm creeping up to the maximum word count pretty fast,so I am going to wrap this up here and save the rant about The Child for the next email.But before that,I wanted to say an unrelated thing.It's a line from *Hamlet*,which I love to teach:"I could be bound in a nutshell and count myself the king of infinite space." I hope you understand what he means.I think you will bc I think you are pretty swift<3

Part II(which you have to read despite my over-caffeinated rambling bc:captive audience...too soon?)Anyway(prepare for rant:)The Child went to get coffee with a friend around 5:30yesterday,and I didn't hear from her until I texted her at 9:30,when she was with Sophie.Which was fine.I woke up at 1:00.Not home.It's 3am in the morning(put my key in the door and-oh,wait,sorry#partyinmyhead) still not home.I get up at 4:00and call.She forgot to tell me she was staying at Sophie's.I'm sure you've gleaned thus far that I'm not a controlling parent(little interest in exercises in futility)But I would like The Child,for whom I have made many concessions,to show some consideration and respect.I keep thinking,"One day…"I am too full of the softer side of human nature,all mercy and compassion not enough justice and consequence.If and when you become a parent, good luck finding a better balance.Ok.Rant over. So,how've you been?What is there to occupy you during the day?Do the programs I read about actually exist or are they just for the benefit of public perception?I hope you are reading.And writing.Not letters, necessarily, but for yourself, journaling, telling your story.Do you have the things you need?By the way, I'll be happy to write a character witness letter for you.How does the commissary work?Do you need socks-you said yours had a hole?I bet you didn't realize what you were getting into when you asked that I keep emailing you.Be careful what you wish for!Anyway,I hope you are managing as best you can and keeping your spirits up.Here's another joke to help:Why wouldn't the shrimp share his sandwich?He was just a little shellfish.That ought to make your day!And believe me, I know you are so excited right now because,well,lots more where that came from!Speaking of superior entertainment,is there anything you'd like to read?I would love to send you a book.Also(prepare for more serious tone/aka caffeine come-down)I told Abby that I'm a little afraid I'm imposing an image on you that might be inaccurate,which worries me.I don't want my mind to create you as you are not.She asked who I thought you were.In a nutshell,I said you are someone who is not only intelligent but insightful beyond what and how, who is kind,honest at the cost of discomfort, authentic,and most of all you are someone who understands the beauty of paradox and ambiguity.Ryan,I can't explain why in the space that's left,but I feel a burden for you and believe me,I know enough about enough to have an entirely different reaction.But I don't.I pray for you to have peace of mind,to be strong through this.Ok,wrapping this up bc out of charac<3

My emails to Ryan, frequent as they were, alternated between matters of serious consequence and absolute foolishness. My priority was to keep his spirits up, mostly, to make him smile, since I imagined there were lots of things for him to be unhappy about. I also wanted to give him perspective. He had not listened to a parental voice for nearly seven years, and my impression was that he may have forgotten that people, like Abby, do not exist in isolation, but that their choices touch everyone's lives, spreading like ripples on water—or like tidal waves. His family situation was vastly different from our own, not just in terms of hardship, but in terms of the connections. Like Scott's family more than mine, his was an every-man-for-himself model, not that they didn't love each other. They clearly did, but each member was often left to cope on his or her own. As far as I could tell, Ryan had always held his pain within himself to keep it from seeping past him, from affecting others. If I could ease that pain, I wanted to.

Human nature, full of flaws, puzzles me. How we disperse our sympathies—or not—contradicts common sense, as well as our instincts to love, sometimes. Reason suggests that we should align our understanding and affinity with those whom we know best, having witnessed their lives in the full scope of their messiness, yet we often do not. In fact, we hold the opposite position, finding those closest to us most blame-worthy—we take their messiness personally because we love them.

We know their histories and whether the past provides reasons for current transgressions. We know (or so we think) their weaknesses and whether they were voluntarily chosen or arose from a double helix of dark arts. We know if we share those propensities and whether we, ourselves, have overcome them or succumbed to the fates spelled out in our DNA. From that vantage point, we parcel out compassion or resentment with more intention. Abby grew up with few disadvantages, immense love, and more comfort than most, yet she chose her "curiosities" (her word to validate the behaviors that have caused her such difficulty and consequence). After almost seven years of lessons from her teens still unlearned, my patience with her was short. I was tired of failed teachings—of hearing apologies, acknowledgements, excuses with no altered course before them, and not a single change. I was tired of her seeing her body not as a temple, but as a playground.

Now, things would have to be different. They had been different, as Abby so persuasively compelled me months ago, when she leveraged two thousand miles of distance in her favor to explain how close she and Ryan were, how "emotionally present," in her efforts to win my approval of him. Abby had settled, committed. She was more driven. She loved him. I tried to understand how his arrest and impending sentence shifted her—because while she was still dedicated, something shifted—beyond the sadness beyond the betrayal, beyond the reality of how he landed in jail.

Something seemed bound within her.

She was becoming elusive again, but I could not see what she was avoiding. I assumed it was just the general pain of having to live through what she could not control, which is something I am still learning how to do, always learning. I tried to be patient. I am still trying, though for different reasons.

Chapter 17

Revelation I

Within a week of sending my two-part email, I received a letter from Ryan. I smiled to the point of laughter when I saw that he led with G-rated humor:

January 23, 2017

Dear Ms. Colleen, So, a blind guy walks into a bar...and then a chair...then a table. Haha, as terrible as that joke is, it cracks me up every time. I would just like you to know that I talked to The Child for you. Hopefully, my words of wisdom will remind her to let you know her plans from now on. When I have children, I will try my best to keep my cool constantly, and I'll do how my mother did with me. You asked about my days in here. Well, my average day is as follows: I wake up, make my bed, brush my teeth, read 3 pages of a book, clean the room, make coffee, listen to music, and journal, do whatever classes that we may have that day, get locked up for an hour, read a couple chapters or write letters, call Abby, play the guitar, watch a movie, make burritos, do a private Bible study with a couple guys, read for 2 more hours, pray, and finally go to sleep. That's pretty much every single day. But we do actually do the programs here, so that's pretty nice. And about the socks, I deal with what

I'm dealt but it's fine. When I get out, I'll appreciate every pair of socks I own. I'll appreciate a lot of things that I maybe didn't as much as I should. And I am writing a lot. Mostly journaling my thoughts but writing about some things I thought I forgot about from when I was little, too. Maybe I will write a book one day, but I'd have to use fake names for some people; those are called something specific, huh? Anyway, I don't want some of this stuff to come back and haunt me or hurt anybody else when I'm done with that part of my life. If you really write about raising Abby, I'd love to read that. Will I be in it?! It's great when you know the people or the real story. By the way, when I get out of here, and I have no idea when that will be, but when I do, I might need 2 things from you if you don't mind. Motherly advice sometimes and at least 1 home-cooked meal. I am so tired of bologna sandwiches. Oh yeah, my grandma sent me a book! It by Stephen King and I'm ecstatic about it because it's over 1100 pages. It should keep me busy for at least 2 weeks. And I liked your analysis of my handwriting, by the way. It makes me feel...observed. Anyways, thank you for continuing to write and email me. Time goes by faster because of it, and that helps more than you know. I reckon I'll write again when I get your next rant! Love, Ryan Freeman P.S. I know you're an English teacher, so I'd like to explain something real quick: I only get 1 sheet of paper per letter. That's why I don't indent. Drives me crazy but saves space, like your smash up punctuation emails. Oh, and Hamlet, that dude gets it...there's more between heaven and earth than we can imagine, right?

I could not have imagined the things to come.

Just two days later, she told me. She had been scarce around home all week, so when I pulled into the driveway and she came out to the car to greet me, I was surprised.

"Hey, stranger," I said.

"Mom, I'm so sorry," she began.

I assumed she was talking about avoiding me, and said, "Abby, I worry when I don't hear from you, and—" She cut me off, leaving me completely unprepared for her next words.

"No, Mom. Not just that, everything," she began to cry. I reached out to her putting my hand on her shoulder, but she stepped back, gesturing a resolute "wait" with slightly raised palms. "Mom," she paused and took in a sputtered breath, "I slept with Derrick."

Stunned, I didn't think at all and blurred out, "Abby! What? How could you?" My first reaction was nothing but accusatory, and my own eyes filled with tears. "But—I—I don't understand. This is just so—Abby, I thought you loved him. How? Does Ryan know?" I could not fathom what I heard.

"I told him last night. That's why I didn't come home again. I couldn't. I couldn't face you, too. I can't face anyone. I'm so, so sorry," she sobbed, wiping her eyes again and again.

Shocked as I was, I realized lecturing her about morals right there in the driveway was not what she needed, so I hugged her—she welcomed the embrace—and I said, "Let's go inside."

We sat on the sofa, my purse still on my shoulder. I asked what had happened with Derrick, how the situation became a possibility, but she said she didn't want to talk about it; she was "just very stupid and had way too much to drink with him." I asked, "But isn't he Ryan's best friend?"

"Not anymore," she said angrily.

"And what about you? I guess y'all ended things when you told him?"

"Obviously," her sobs became heavy again. "Mom, what is wrong with me? Why am I such a worthless piece of shit?" She covered her face with both hands.

Reaching for her, I said, "Abby, no. Don't say that. You made a mistake. Do not let this define you. You have to get through it, learn from it, but do not think of it as who you are."

My intuition was completely off as I spoke. I was saying the right things, I hoped, but inside, I wondered the same—what's wrong with her? I had never known Abby to be so focused and selfless as she was with Ryan. I had been telling myself a story about them that moved toward a happy ending, even given his current circumstances. Not once had I considered that she would be the one to jeopardize the relationship, but as I sat so close with my arms around her, all I could think was, *Why does carnality rule her?* I wondered what might change that. I thought her relationship with Ryan was changing it, at least giving her more control over it. She had said almost a year ago that he was thousands of miles away, so all they could do was talk, that just knowing he was there was enough if she could see him every few months. My thoughts raced with possible explanations. Maybe all the restraint and focus required of her between visits was just too much. Maybe the reality of the thick glass and short-corded telephone hit harder than she allowed me to see. Maybe when she encountered a "dark-haired Ryan," she lost control. After all, if he were really so much like Ryan, he would have charm enough to entice most young women, which made me question Ryan's judgment in choosing him to "look after" her.

Some part of this was my fault, I knew, for not being the kind of parent Abby needed. But, I didn't know how to be that mother. I should have trusted my instincts and forbid her to go like a sane parent would have. That would have been unrealistic, though. She would have snuck away—strong willed, defiant Abby. I wanted to ask her so many questions, but I didn't. She was confiding a part of her life most would hide from their parents.

She didn't need my judgment.

It came anyway, through my tone. I was disappointed, angry, and embarrassed, but what was she feeling, this wilted girl in my arms? I imagined her pain. She had said "I'm sorry" to me so many times, but forgiveness wasn't mine to offer, though I did forgive her. Ultimately, that would have to come from herself, from Ryan, but that was unlikely. He was a prideful young man, already haunted by memories. Maybe this was for the best, the breakup I had wanted in the beginning.

Now, I felt the pain of it, too.

Abby did not say much else about the incident, only, again, that she had been drinking with Derrick, and yes, she realized now that doing so was an unbelievably bad idea. She said it "just happened," and she really didn't want to talk anymore about it. She told me the guilt over it was becoming too much for her, which led her to tell Ryan—that, and the fact that Derrick had been texting her, attempting to get her to break up with Ryan. When she rejected him, he threatened to tell Ryan himself. I imagined the weight of the situation was a burden she carried for weeks and said as much to her. She nodded; a strand of short hair caught across her cheek wet with tears. Then I asked where all this left her, to which she simply said "alone."

Her tears were quiet, but continual. She said Ryan hung up on her when she told him, without so much as an angry word. He called back a little over an hour later, saying he needed to "say a few things." I dreaded what they might be, but she said he was not cruel, just hurt. He told her that he really thought she was different, thought she was heaven-sent to get him through this because of everything she had done so far, but he guessed he was wrong. She said she just listened, apologized, and cried. They didn't talk long, and he ended by asking her not to contact him again.

Chapter 18

Truth, Consequences, and Nietzsche

In the aftermath of Abby's confession, I felt the weight of unfinished business. I had promised Ryan a character witness letter and had been emailing him for over six weeks. That our correspondence should end as abruptly as their relationship felt odd, so I did what I always do at my most conflicted.

I wrote.

First, a letter, long and meandering and unsent, and second, the character statement. He would need that for his court date in early February, which was only a bit over two weeks away.

Timing is everything. The day after Abby's revelation, I received his letter. Jail time takes some getting used to. Communicating anything in the moment of its importance is nearly impossible, and the past is always pulled into the present. That seems to be the nature of incarceration, whether behind actual bars or those in which we imprison ourselves. Ryan's letter obviously did not address the most recent event, but it did address Abby's avoidance of me, which, now, didn't need to be addressed. I understood. Always, she has kept her distance from me when she conceals some wrong, whether that be the guilt of some regret she rather not discuss or the obstinacy of willfully choosing some way of life of which she knows I disapprove. I had mistaken her surreptitious behavior over the last month for the latter. I wish I had been right about it. Being familiar to me, it would have been easier to accept.

I had such trouble understanding her, my dark-haired little angel who has grown to be the kind of beauty about whom Instagram asks, "Who is she?" I'd like to know the answer to that myself, as I'm sure she would. How often do people act out, desperately seeking to satisfy some need, and they do, gluttonously, but afterward are left only with the shame of their indulgence? Is that what happened? In some ways, no matter how charming he was or how drunk Abby was, I couldn't imagine her choosing to cheat on Ryan.

A year had already passed since they began talking—in that year, she had shown no interest in anyone else. Only when Ryan reminded her that they were only "talking" and that she was free to see anyone she wanted at home, just as he was free to do there, did she ever indulge anyone else's attention— and it was brief. A boy whose name I can't even remember wanted to "hang out" with her, and she had put him off for months at her previous restaurant job. He came in often, always sat in her area, and tipped generously. She said she knew of him for years but was never interested in him. He was "an entitled private school boy who would live off Daddy's money his whole life," she said. Nonetheless, he persisted.

When Abby came home from California last June, she thought she and Ryan had become more than "talking." In the weeks after, she was hurt every time she posted a picture of herself or of her trip, and Ryan didn't like it, but when I asked her if that was significant, as I had wondered while she was there, she reminded me about the deployment and terrorist rules. I couldn't figure out what was true and what wasn't, but I knew it wasn't my business, so I left them to sort out whatever it was they were doing. Anyway, Ryan assured her that their commitment to each other was not exclusive, and the restaurant boy persisted, so Abby went out with him. Once. Her final assessment was a metaphor:

"How was it?" I asked.

Abby explained, "You know how, back in high school, when we went prom dress shopping and I tried on the gorgeous white one I eventually bought, but Sophie made me go to three other shops and try on way too many other dresses that were okay but didn't fit right or were too floofy or plain or just not me, and all it did was irritate me?"

"Yes."

"Well," she continued, "it was like that. I've already found what I want. Why keep looking?"

So, was Derrick, through Crown Royal lenses, that good of a knock-off? Was Ryan that poor of a judge of his friend's character? Was Abby so dissociated from herself that she couldn't corral her inhibitions? I didn't understand what had happened, couldn't see how it was possible given what I knew. Then I realized: Maybe I didn't know anything. I knew what I saw, though: her. And whether it was her fault or not, I hated what was happening. The waves of remorse that I knew washed through her had to be destroying her, but Abby would not talk about it.

I've learned that it is important not to avert your eyes when what you see frightens you, which might be one reason I have kept close watch over Abby through this ordeal. But, not looking away is especially important when what you see is in yourself. I wanted Abby to understand that, and Ryan, too. Nietzsche said that the strength of a person's character can be measured by how much truth he or she can tolerate, by how much it must be watered down, falsified essentially. Trying to understand them individually was an undertaking in itself but attempting to make sense of them together was impossible. Maybe because they weren't "together," never had been, not as a couple really. They had a relationship but having spent no more than a handful of days in one another's presence—well, they had never been a couple. What were they? I suppose all of life is that way—too nuanced to grasp without the most focused intent. Reducing it down, fixing it into a formulated phrase denies the complexity—and the beauty.

Still, somehow, something beautiful will come from all of this.

Chapter 19

Character Witness

All along, I didn't want to like Ryan as much as I did. Before his arrest, he was charming and kind, if on the wild side. After his arrest, he was honest and vulnerable, and willing to look within himself. So, even then, before I knew the depth of him, I liked him. How foolish of me to stay in contact with the worst-case scenario Abby had ever concocted for her future plan, but I did.

Those who thought I was unwise to write to him while he and Abby were together would think I'm beyond foolish now. He has even read most of this so far, this excessively long rant about raising her, and he loves it. Maybe I'm foolish for sharing it with him. Hopefully, I'll have a life long enough to let me figure out the foolishness within me, but I say that facetiously. Writing to Ryan doesn't feel foolish. It feels like the right thing to do. I know it is, still.

That Saturday, I did not write to Ryan. Instead, I wrote about him.

January 27, 2017

To Whom It May Concern:

One year ago, my daughter told me that she met someone for whom she wanted to change, someone who motivated her to be a better person. Naturally, she piqued my curiosity, so I probed for details. Upon receiving them, caution stirred within me, for while she gushed positivity, I bristled at the idea of my eighteen-year-old's being so rapt with a young man—a Marine home on leave, nonetheless—nearly five years older and from one of the most horrific backgrounds I have ever heard. While his story engaged my compassion, it also signaled the possibility of complications. Having lost my brother to a tragic accident when I was eighteen and my father in my late twenties and still feeling the pain of those losses decades later, I could not fathom how a young man who, at age fifteen, lost his mother to a violent death could be well-adjusted. Moreover, he had subsequently endured the loss of his home, first, to a natural disaster and then, later, to fire, all while caring for a younger brother and a sister slightly older than he and while attempting to navigate life amid the addicted behavior of his disabled father. In my mind, such back-stories were the stuff of fiction. But, then I met Ryan Freeman, who is, indeed, quite an unbelievable yet very real young man.

As the months progressed, my daughter's attention to this Marine proved to be more than a brief phase, so I entertained her interest, which was easy to do since Ryan was two-thousand miles away and posed no immediate concern. After all, the relationship seemed like a parent's dream: my daughter's feeling of commitment to this young man negated her interest in any local boys and made her more purposeful in her studies and work. All seemed no more than a harmless long-distance romance, but in March of 2016, she came to me with a hefty request. After receiving news of yet another misfortune in Ryan's life, the death of his father, she learned that he would be coming in on leave to oversee the funeral arrangements, and he needed a place to stay. You see, the already-compromised home in which his brother was still living (while his father was in a nursing home)had been flooded by the recent severe rains and river crests in northern St. Tammany. "Could he stay with us?" was a question I was not expecting. After some deliberation and investigation, we did allow Ryan to stay in our guest room and have no regrets about doing so.

Over the few days Ryan spent with us, I grew to understand what I heard from an acquaintance who taught him in high school—that I will never find another person who has remained so optimistic through such adversity. Ryan impressed me. As we talked, he shared some of his past, and while I marveled that so much tragedy could occur in a life so young, I was awed by his clear attempt to comfort me through the discomfort of listening to his story. Ryan does not want sympathy. He is an incredibly self-reliant young man who does not want to burden others—in fact, he did spend several nights of his leave in March on a damp mattress in a flooded-out house because he did not want to "wear out his welcome" in our home.

As a high school and university teacher with over twenty-five-years of experience, I consider myself adept in "reading" young people, and in Ryan I see a rarity. As part of the millennial generation so famously consumed with self, Ryan possesses an altruism that is admirable but that does not always work to his benefit. In his lightening our conversation with self-deprecating humor or stories of good times after disclosing some of the challenges of his young life, I saw not only the attempt to ease his audience's distress, but also the suppression of deep-seated emotions. In not wanting to burden others— and perhaps in not wanting to appear weak or needy—Ryan has done a disservice to himself. Anyone who has lived through the catastrophes he has experienced cannot successfully cope alone. Ryan has tried, however, and in many ways has made excellent decisions for himself.

Graduating from high school may not seem to be a monumental task to most people, but to "Kids in Transition"—our district's name for homeless, often parentless students—it is. Ryan graduated. Having the foresight to create a future apart from the challenging past of one's childhood home, family, and friends is often a difficult decision, and many lack the courage to remove themselves from their familiar yet unfortunate circumstances. Ryan displayed that courage in choosing the military as a means to a more productive life. Loving fiercely and wholeheartedly is something many people struggle to do within themselves, for some equate love to vulnerability, to possible disappointment and pain. Ryan, however, knows that the pain of lost opportunity, of loss itself is far worse, so he comes home when he can, and I have been amazed over the last year to see that when he does, others flock to him with their needs rather than ask what he might need himself. Yet, he does not complain. He helps.

I believe I am a well-educated, logical person, so I realize that a single year of sporadic visits, conversations, and texts is far too little time to garner a complete and accurate assessment of anyone's character—a single anything cannot define a person. But, as I've said, I've taught for twenty-five years and have known thousands of teenagers and young adults only for a single year or semester. Occasionally, I will have a student who is so uncommon, such a rarity, that I feel privileged to have had the honor to teach her, to have known him. Such people are not perfect; indeed, they are subject to every flaw humanity has to offer, but their authenticity, their effort, their concern, and their courage make them exceptional. Ryan is one such person. In him, there is resilience, the only word in the English language which simultaneously conveys misfortune, determination, and hope. Ryan has strived to overcome the impossible odds life has placed before him more admirably than anyone I have met outside the covers of a book.

With sincere regard,
Colleen Hildebrand

I thought composing the character witness letter would help me compose myself around Abby and Ryan's situation. It didn't. It pulled me in deeper, broke my heart more. I don't know if I should have, but I asked Abby to read it. She did, and she cried. "It's perfect," she said, hushed through tears. I downloaded the letter as a PDF complete with a signature and sent it where it had to be sent. I hoped it would matter just a little. It probably didn't.

Even after sending the letter off, I felt an emptiness, an emotional weight I have seldom encountered. I knew the reasons for it, and among them was the reality that Abby and Ryan's story would end here, but there was more. So much felt unfinished. I ached for Abby because I understood the immense pain of failing oneself, and I thought of the irony in my writing to Ryan of that pain upon his arrest. Could they see the parallel? Was there a parallel? Why was I constantly seeing patterns of meaning that I could not trace to a conclusion? I carried—still carry—the synchronicities with me, wondering what they might mean. The weight of Ryan's and Abby's respective wrongs, while seeming a balance to me, seemed to drag them under. Abby would need me, the little I could offer. Who would Ryan have? I typed an email and read it, then read it again, hesitating before finally hitting send in a thoughtless burst.

February 2, 2017

"There are no events but thoughts and the heart's hard turning,the heart's slow learning where to love and whom.The rest is merely gossip..." Annie Dillard wrote that.It resonates with me.I've been so sad.Join the club,right?I can't recall a time of deeper,more personal pain than when I disappointed myself so gravely,caused massive heartbreak for others.I wouldn't wish such monumental hurt on anyone.I once found myself doing the very thing I swore was not within my constitution ever to do.Young and dumb,I walked into a failure so great I wanted to quietly end my life over it, over losing the trust of those I love,over the humiliation of wrong choices,and over the betrayal of my values,my upbringing, my failth.But time,God,and forgiveness I did not deserve moved me past the ruin, teaching me not to allow regret to define me.Nearly 30years later,I continue to learn from that mistake,becoming more measured and aware of how I carry myself,more compassionate, certain of myself,and forgiving of others.Hopefully, more wise.I do not believe someone truly repentant should be nailed to the single error of his life.I hope you've been able to see this in me since I've been writing over these weeks.My mom and sister don't understand my support of you-it's been a source of tension;not knowing you,they think any charge against you should elicit fear,not forgiveness,yet knowing the darker aspects of my family,I see pardon as the only option.Some people forget or fail to learn,but the truth of the human condition is as ugly as it can be beautiful,and it applies to everyone.We can hurt and heal.When you emerge from your circumstances a wiser man,I hope you find a wonderful someone to love who will never define you by your mistakes,and I hope you are wise enough not to wed others to their past wrongs forever. Ryan,I've tried to save Abby from her impulsivity for years, and I've failed.She must save herself,and she knows it,feels it now,at the cost of you. Losing you has taught her more than I could teach her in almost 19yearsThank you for that,for meaning so much to her that she finally understands. In the time to come,I hope you find some redemption for her even as she tries to live it for herself.I'm uncertain of whether you'll still want to hear from me, so please know that I will continue to pray,notice the odd coincidences,and want a beautiful life for you<3

I thought that email was the only closure I would have on the lightning strike of Ryan Freeman in Abby's life. I hoped he would see in it that people are just people, all flawed, and while forgiveness seemed too much to ask, I hoped he would not hate her. Not even ten days after I sent the email, a letter came. It was short, apologetic and filled with sorrow. It began with, "I'm writing this with more pain in my heart than I have felt in a long time. I loved your daughter more than I have any other girl, probably more than I ever will again, but…" and it ended with, "I don't expect you to want to write, and seeing your last name would hurt, but I would really like to still get emails or letters from you. Please don't think less of me." It left me hurting for everyone, so I did what I always do.

I wrote.

What any of this year-long saga between Abby and Ryan meant, why it mattered so much to me, what the word matter even meant—all of that both eluded and consumed me. Matter is solid, tangible—reality—but what matters is seldom that. What matters so often circulates in the unseen, eluding our grasp. I was angry at myself for entertaining the thought that somehow this would still all work out. How had I gotten here?

Not so long ago, I wanted Abby to end things with Ryan. Now, I felt so ambivalent—stuck between them, wanting their wrongs to cancel each other out, wanting them to understand what mattered. Abby mattered, and I tried to convince myself that Ella was right, that Ryan's future should not matter so much to me—that I should be able to let this young man—whom I still did not really know well—go, especially so that I could focus on my own daughter's well-being. I knew how badly she was struggling. That isn't what happened, though.

Chapter 20

Calumny as Spectator Sport

Today's ugly carnivals happen online rather than in the streets.

Somewhere along the way, someone, Ryan I guess, maybe Derrick, told someone else, and Abby told me. Within two weeks of that emotionally draining weekend, Abby texted me and said that her name was all over Facebook. Sophie had told her before she saw it herself. Knowing her thin skin, I bristled with worry upon reading her text. I called her from my classroom during my planning time.

"Hey, my love," I said when she answered. "Are you ok? What's going on?"

"It's a comment on Lisa's Facebook under a picture of me and Ry from October when he was here. At the fair. There were a lot of comments. I only read a few. Mom, I'm ruined," her voice shook. I could not tell whether it was with anger or shame.

"No, love. You aren't. Don't look at all of that again, and remember, people's attention spans on social media are short. They'll find something new to gossip about by tomorrow. And besides, who are these people anyway? Not your friends, right?"

"No, I only know a few of the names. They're his friends."

"Well, sweetie, be strong. This is none of their concern. And how good of friends can they be to him? He told both of us he hasn't heard from anyone since his arrest, and that's almost two months ago. These people are not anyone to you. They're spectators, gawkers. So…" I trailed off, staring at the waves of wood grain on my desk.

Abby began in a slightly more composed tone, "What confuses me though is how they even know. Ry asked me not to tell anyone. He didn't want people to know, so I don't know why he told Lisa or anybody."

"You know, love, it seems that Ryan would have a hard time explaining his motives for a few things lately so don't waste time thinking about it."

"I guess, to hurt me, huh? To make sure people know I'm a worthless piece of shit, which I suppose I am." Abby said it so soberly that it concerned me much more than it would have if she had been sobbing, like last time.

"Abby Glynne Hildebrand, do not say that about yourself ever again. You are not a worthless anything. You are human, which means that you are just as vulnerable as anyone, and just as forgivable. And believe me, anyone pointing a finger at you probably has hands way dirtier. Can we please remember the reason Derrick picked you up at LAX to begin with— because your boyfriend-not-boyfriend-ex-whatever is in JAIL," I spoke slowly, sarcastically, "for hitting a cop when the WOMAN HE LEFT A BAR WITH called them. Yes, your judgment was bad, your actions, wrong, but you are no worse than him, or me, or anyone. It was a mistake." I picked up a pencil as I concluded, as if to wield authority more effectively, I guess.

"Mama, thank you. I know." She was crying now. "There's just so much wrong everywhere around me and inside of me. I feel like… like a graveyard, love turned to rot. I want it to just go away, but it feels like it never will."

"Oh sweetie, what do you mean?"

"I don't even know." She took a shaky breath. "I let people use me. I don't know. I wrote that today at school, a poem. I feel like a graveyard. Will you read it when you come home?"

"Of course, I will, love."

"Mama, I just don't want to feel like this. I want it to go away. But now it's worse. Now everybody knows. They'll always remind me. They'll always hate me."

"It will go away," I said, tapping the pencil, eraser-end down. "Most of those people don't even know you. Don't let their opinions matter. You will get past this. I'll read your poem, and we can talk when I come home. For now, stay off social media. I'll be home right after school. I love you very much, and listen to me: you will never do anything wrong enough to change that. I know you are a good person, one of the best. No matter what. I love you."

She spoke softly as she hung up, "I love you, too, Mama."

I was livid. I pulled up Abby's Facebook on my phone, and there it was. Scrolling back not too far, I saw it, the picture of Abby and Ryan sitting on a bale of hay laughing with each other, the picture that became an invitation to comment on their relationship and my daughter's moral failing. Only one comment showed. It was from a name I'd never heard before, but Eddie simply said, "2 sides to every story." At least Eddie had some sense, but the other twenty or so of the fifty-two comments that I read were not so accepting of alternatives. After reading that "only a slut of fucking outrageous proportions would cheat on her Marine while he's deployed," I had enough. "Deployed?" These people didn't even know where Ryan was. I reported the comments as cyberbullying. I never told Abby.

When I got home that evening, Abby wasn't crying. She was nestled into the sofa pillows with Opal, her phone on the coffee table. "It's all gone," she said emotionlessly. At first, I was unsure of what she meant, but then she said Sophie reported the comments. I was relieved. I sat down next to Abby. She looked so small. She was my height, but she looked so small. She said nothing else. She only sat staring off into some memory I was not invited to see, and that was fine. After a few minutes, I turned towards her. She did not look at me, but I spoke to her.

"Love, what do you need right now? Do you want me to read your poem?" She pointed to her journal beside her phone on the table. I read silently:

I feel like a graveyard
Filled with the remains of what was
I sit idle, stagnant, harboring the losses
Of others
Allowing whoever pays for a plot
To dig into me
Burying their pain
Leaving memories like wilted beauty behind to rot
In their rightful place—
With the rest of the dead.

"It's a sad, beautiful, poem. It's hard to hear, love. I don't want you to feel that way, but I'm trying to understand that you do. What can I do?"

"Nothing. Just be here."

I didn't know how to just be, not then. I desperately wanted to say whatever could make her right. I didn't know how else to react other than to tell her it sounded like she was holding in a lot of pain that she was trying not to feel, and I said that to no reaction. Then I asked, "What do you want?" I realize now that was the wrong question.

Still staring, she said, "Him. I just want him."

That wasn't what I was hoping to hear. I asked, "Have you written or emailed him?"

"Not yet. At least not put it in the mail yet. Will you still write to him?"

"Sweetie, I did email him, just to say I knew. You can read it."

"No, I don't want—I can't. Not now. I mean, write to him, though. A letter. And keep writing."

"Love, what should I say? I don't want to be intrusive. This is between the two of you."

For some reason, perhaps because of my own conflicted feelings, I couldn't tell her I had hand-written, too, already, or that he had written to me. His letter and my rambling journal-in-response were tucked neatly into my book bag, waiting for something.

"I know," she still spoke dispassionately, numb, "but he'll need somebody."

"Well, from the looks of Facebook, he has more than enough people willing to rush to his defense. I'm sure he has friends who are there for him."

"No, Mom, he doesn't." This was the first thing she said with any emotion. She continued, "Like you said, he has spectators. He's entertainment to them. They don't know the difference between caring and gossiping. It's like people just want to seem important and feel like they have a little piece of him. I hate that. He'll get a few letters from girls who want to fuck him, but that won't help anything. He needs someone real." Her voice broke just a little as she finished, "Mama, please don't abandon him. He'll need you."

I finally told her a bit guiltily, "I did write to him, haven't sent it though." Permission, the letter was waiting for her permission, I realized.

"Good. You should. Keep doing that," she said with some energy.

"But, Sweetie, I have to know, has he said anything to you that would change my opinion of him?"

"Nope," was all I got.

"He hasn't berated you or called you awful things?"

"No."

"Are you sure? I remember the idiot incident. I know he can be harsh."

Before his arrest, back in September, Ryan hurt his knee, dislocated it dancing or cutting up in some way, and shortly after the first injury, reinjured it proving to someone he could do a backflip. Abby told him that he would end up killing himself if he didn't stop acting like an idiot, which set him off. I think it was the only time he posted something on Instagram with her in mind. Ryan tolerated Abby's posting and tagging him, on Facebook, too, but he never reciprocated, even after he bought her the ticket to California, there was no public acknowledgement of her place in his life. He just explained the social silence away with "because of Isis."

This posting of his, though, was unmistakable, though the audience who understood might be small. It was a collage of risks he had taken and injuries he had sustained throughout recent years: jumping from a high cliff, neck brace, snowboarding flips, crutches, bloody leg, and so on. The caption began, "I am not an idiot." It went on to detail how he was someone who tested his limits, who wasn't average, who "was damn sure not you." Abby was "you." It struck me as unkind and small-minded to target so vehemently someone who, at the heart of the matter, was expressing concern. I wondered if that version of Ryan had said anything to Abby yet.

"No, mom. He hasn't called me a 'fucking, cheating slut,' or a bitch, or a whore, or anything. He just told me to leave him alone forever."

Her even tone was terrible again. I would have preferred screaming or tears, defensiveness. "Ok," I said, and asked nothing else. I did suggest, though: "Listen, sweetie, I know that you are dealing with a lot, too much, so I want you to think about seeing someone, professionally, to help sort through all of it."

For the first time, she really looked at me and spoke with a feeling that came from her self-interest rather than her interest in his well-being. I think the feeling was indignation. "Mama, I don't want to talk about this with anyone, no one! Besides, if I do, I have you." Her voice held some combination of certainty and desperation I could not make sense of. Something in it told me our conversation was over. She couldn't cope with any more pressing right now, no matter what my intentions. She hugged Opal to herself more tightly, and I looked at her for a long moment.

She broke my heart. I have such trouble understanding her—this beautiful, complicated combination of genes that is half mine. I know how much she loves me, but that is hard to reconcile with how much she defies me. Yet, she still needs me. Eighteen —nearly nineteen—years of direct experience, trial and error, and I still don't know how to do what's best for her. My eyes filled. She saw them. "Ok, but if you change your mind…" I got up and kissed her head, her hair, that short hair, barely grazing her shoulders. She didn't move. She looked so small. How her tiny stature could hold so vast a sadness surely defied some laws of physics.

Chapter 21

Batshit Crazy

The mysteries that circulate unseen in the ether must intersect like a million spider webs—etheric cords connecting past to present, soul to soul, self to something greater. That, or our brains gravitate toward batshit crazy when we're under emotional stress. I favor the first but recognize the likelihood of the second explanation.

Inexplicable events have occasionally touched my life. I've mentioned the dream of my brother and conversation with my father, but also, Scott and I have experienced at least one oddity together. One night, we had just turned the lights off and got into bed when Scott jumped up yelling, "Oh, shit!" Naturally, I shot up, too, turning the lamp on and asking what was wrong. He told me he felt something tickling his head, like fingers or a bug crawling through his hair. I imagined a roach, and roaches in hair are a definite no. We turned every light on, shook out the cotton sheets, looked up and down the soft white walls, under the bed, in the pillowcases, and found nothing. The ten to fifteen-minute search satisfied us, and we went back to bed, where Scott talked a bit more about how weird it felt and placed his fingertips lightly in my hair, dancing them across my scalp like a parent might to reassure a child of her presence. I told him that it didn't feel like a roach at all.

It felt like his mom.

He looked at me as my statement hung in the air. I was never sure that Scott really grieved properly for her. She passed away in 2005, just after Katrina. The hurricane didn't kill her, but it exacerbated her stress as she was undergoing treatment for pancreatic cancer. Scott has said little about it over the years, but I know he carries it like lead in his soul. Anyway, after I said that, he looked at me like a deer in headlights and said, "Alrighty then, back to sleep. Goodnight, love you!" I chuckled at his good-natured avoidance, turned out the lights, settled my head on the pillow.

Then, I felt fingers dancing through my hair.

There are, indeed, more things in heaven and earth, and I can't explain any of them. I certainly do not claim to be clairvoyant, clairsentient—clair-anything—but I do wonder if it's possible.

Strange things happen. I feel things unfold before they do sometimes. Really, I guess I'm just intuitive or subconsciously perceptive (or imaginative enough to make my own reality a little more magical), but on rare occasions I have physically felt something I could not explain. I say all this to preface what I know sounds implausible.

Even with Abby's approval—rather, encouragement, which is more odd—I had not yet put the letter in the mail. I felt ambivalent about it. Even now, I feel a twinge of embarrassment for having my personal version of crazy committed to paper—though it would not be the only time that occurred—but I shared with Ryan an experience I had had one Saturday morning driving to school to monitor Saturday detention: in the car, I had a song stuck in my head in that annoying way that songs get stuck, even the ones you don't like all that much. The song was "Champagne Supernova," with its nonsensical lyrics. The line on repeat was, "Someday you will find me caught beneath the landslide…." Just driving along, singing silently, my eyes filled with tears. I supposed it was just the worry and stress over Abby, I wrote to him, but as I turned into the school parking lot, the drive lined with coral-colored crape myrtles lit like flames in the morning sun, my brain shut the song off to say a prayer for Abby, Jenna, Scott, everyone I love—as I always do before starting my workday—and for Ryan. Afterward, from nowhere, from somewhere in my mind that did not feel like my own, came a voice saying, "be a mother to him."

I wrote that in the letter I was still toting around, and I felt crazy for it, but I told him. I said other things, too, mostly about how hard seeing the pain of the situation was, about how uncertain anything in life is. I just rambled with worry about both of them, about forgiveness and pride, and balance—about too much—but it was what Abby asked me to do. I sent the letter after an unexpected phone call.

Evenings around the house had fallen into a familiar routine. I would arrive home first and change out of my work clothes, which were apparently more appropriate for a law office than a classroom (according to students) before tidying up the house and taking Opal for a walk. She was getting big, almost forty pounds at five months old, but was still too young for a two-mile run, so we walked the neighborhood or mostly the trails just over the little bridge behind the house for nearly an hour every day, with breaks to smell every deer track, lost feather, or remnants of previous travelers undetectable to me. Sometimes, traces of skunk would waft past us, or the scent of sweet olive in the spring, and I'd wonder if that's how she smells everything, with that intensity. How could she not be overwhelmed with newness? I wonder when and why people, many of them, turn off or become numb to the little miracles of nature, to the little miracles of their own natures, to their capacity for wonder. By the time students enter my class at sixteen or seventeen, many of them have not noticed a wildflower or a ladybug, dragon fly, or mourning dove in years. Some have never seen a four-leaf clover.

We have busied ourselves right out of the beauty of nature. That's a problem.

The number of kids with Individual Education Plans specifying generalized anxiety disorder would probably go down if they could remember the childhood joy of dirt. Maybe my walks and runs have kept me calm, or better able to pretend to be, and Opal has been a great reason to get outside every day. When Abby brought her home, she argued that she needed Opal. Really, I did. I always feel a comfort in getting away from the paved roads and street signs, preferring to notice what nature might have to say in her signs.

When I returned home from Opal's walk that late January afternoon with the setting sun already touching the tops of the tallest pines lining the small lake behind the house, I saw that both Scott and Abby were already home. The smell of garlic and chicken I had put in the crock-pot before leaving overtook the memory of sweet olive when I walked in the kitchen, where Abby was sitting at the island.

"Hey, love," I said as I kissed her on the top of her head when she bent down to scoop up a not very scoopable Opal.

"Hey, Mama."

"How was today?"

"Decent. I got a B on my biology quiz."

"That's good! I'm really proud of you for pulling your grades up, you know, despite everything."

"Um, thanks Mama. I, um, have to ask you something. It might be kind of weird for you, but you can decide."

"Oh, lord. What, Abby?"

"I got a phone call last night. From Ry. Not really to talk to me. He hates me, I think. He wanted to know if I would ask you if he could call you."

"Oh, Abby. How do you feel about that? I mean, I've written to him these two months, but you know…" My voice trailed off because I didn't know what I expected her to know—that speaking was harder than writing? That by default, I was on her side if there were sides in this?

"He's having a really hard time, Mom. He was having a hard time before this. And he just said that he doesn't have anyone to talk to about it all since he can't really talk to me and doesn't want to. He respects you. Anyway, he wanted to know if you would talk to him."

"Sweetie, I have no idea of what I should say to him. I mean, I hardly understand the situation myself. What I do know is how you feel and how I can't help but see it all as brought about by a series of bad decisions dating back to November, not by a single decision made in a vulnerable moment. And I don't think that's what he wants to hear."

"Probably not." She paused, looking down at Opal, who was sitting surprisingly still in her lap. Abby, eyes big and soft and deeply brown, looked up through wisps of her fallen hair, and quietly said, "But will you? You're the closest thing to a mom he has right now, and he really needs one. Please?"

The words fell like an anvil—a cartoonish crushing of my soul. How were those words–like echoes from my recent Saturday drive–possible? What was happening here? A rush of something—significance, confusion, wonder, a few unnamable emotions—washed across my face with mild heat, like embarrassment, but with greater weight. The change within me must have been visible because Abby asked if I was angry, which I was not. Finally, or what felt like finally, I answered, "Yes, love. I'll talk to him. I'll email him to tell him."

"You don't have to. He's calling tonight, around 8:00."

"But—"

"I gave him your number last night." I looked at her questioningly, and she gave me the closest thing I had seen to a smile in over a week, saying, "I knew you would say yes."

My phone rang at precisely 8:00 p.m. Abby, her pixie hair still dripping from her shower, was sitting next to me on the sofa, and Scott was across from us on the other couch. "Is that Ryan?" he asked. I tried to keep Scott informed to the comfort level he could manage. He certainly didn't want to know everything, but I wasn't letting him off too easy; after all, Abby didn't inherit her adventurous spirit from boring me. He was the other half of those beautiful genes. I had told him of her trouble, and he had listened, pained and embarrassed over her behavior as I was—at least according to what we knew then. When I told him about the incident with Derrick, Scott just shook his head and said, "I just don't get it, seemed like she really loved the dude. This whole situation is just so fucked up." I agreed.

Upon seeing the otherwise unidentified San Diego number, I got up and went to my bedroom with Scott's advising, "Listen more than you talk," and Abby's saying nothing but following me out of the room with her eyes.

"Hello," I said, sitting on the edge of the bed.

The other end began, "You have a collect call from [pause] Ryan Freeman [pause], an inmate at Vista Detention Facility. This call will be monitored or recorded. To accept the charges, press or say 'five.'" I pressed five.

"Um, hello, Ms. Colleen?"

"Hi, Ryan." I felt foolish, not knowing what to say. "How are you?" certainly didn't seem like an appropriate question, so I left my greeting at that, a greeting, until the honesty broke silence. "I have to tell you: I feel a little uncertain here. Despite the thousands of words I've written to you, I'm not sure of what to say."

"Yes, ma'am. I understand. Thank you for talking to me. Not just tonight, but in all the emails and letters, too. I can't tell you how hard this has been, and I don't hear from anybody much."

"You're welcome. I'm sure my rants aren't always useful, but I try to keep them entertaining."

"Yes ma'am, they are. Well, um, I guess you know all about what's goin' on with me and Abby?"

"I'm sure I don't know everything, but yes. It hasn't been easy here, either."

"I know. I just don't—" he cut himself off and began again. "I just thought she was so different. I can't understand it. I don't know what to do."

"We, I mean Scott and I, we don't understand either, but as far as what to do, isn't it done? I mean haven't y'all ended things?"

"Yes, ma'am, I reckon we have. But it just don't feel right. I'm really losing my mind. I just don't know anything right now. I'm accused of doing things I'd never do, that I must've done because evidence says so, and now this." His voice was not strong and assertive, not sure at all. It was shaking, emotional.

"Ryan, I don't want to pretend to understand anything, especially about your life, not better than you, anyway, and I agree that the young man I met in March did not seem like someone who would be where you are now, but listen to what you just said: you must have done something you did not think yourself capable of doing. That seems familiar. There was an entire night before the event, and she forgives you for that."

"Yes, ma'am, I understand what you're saying. It's just hard. But I do forgive her. Well, I'm working on it. I want to," he said.

"Abby has told me that you don't think everyone's telling the truth about what really took place the night of your arrest. I know you don't remember it. I don't know. Sometimes truth is more subjective than we think. Abby won't talk about the Derrick thing with me, but I have the same feeling about that as you have about your arrest. It just doesn't feel right. There is more to it than she is saying. All she ever wanted was to love you. It makes no sense." I had rambled too much. I stopped myself and said, "I wish I knew what to say in person. I'm better on paper. You'll see. I'm afraid all I can offer is an ear."

"What would you do if you were me? What would Mr. Scott do?"

I paused, slightly caught off guard by so direct a question. As I responded, I tried to say the words exactly right, as if I could impart some magic that would sweep clean a past littered with more debris than I could fathom: "I...I think I told you in my email. I, well, both of us, would forgive. There is malice and there are mistakes. I don't think either you or Abby ever meant to deceive or hurt each other. Being able to tell the difference between the two takes time, but more importantly, it requires that people swallow their pride a little. Pride, more than so many other things, keeps people from being happy. That probably sounds crazy, but—"

An automated voice broke in, "You have sixty seconds left on this call."

"Oh," I said, surprised by the interruption. "Well, I don't know much, but..." I let my voice trail off. With so little time left, the pause felt very wrong, but I really didn't know what else to say. I wanted to say they could get past it all, but I couldn't suggest that. It was too much.

Ryan finally said, "Thank you, Ms. Colleen. I'm trying, and really, it means a lot that you talked to me. And please keep writin'. It's about all I have to look forward to in here."

"I will, Ry—."

The call disconnected. I dropped the letter in the mail the next morning.

Chapter 22

Nice Jugs

As the semester continued, Abby continued to sink deeper into reticence, absence, and confusion. Her need for me turned out to be brief, and in my constant reaching for her, I believe that I unintentionally pushed her away. I know she needed time to find and redefine herself, but most of that just looked like rebellion or avoidance to me at the time. I had convinced her to see one of the counselors available at the university, and she did once, but she missed her second appointment, and her third, and then confessed that she just didn't want to go. Going ruined her day because all she could do afterward was cry, and she couldn't go to class crying all the time. On that first day, she had one class prior to the appointment, went to it, then skipped everything afterward, including a biology quiz. So, she stopped going, saying that it wasn't doing any good and that she was better off just writing in her journal. She was also getting thinner.

When she graduated from high school the previous year, she looked so healthy. To her father's delight, she had begun working out, and her body responded quickly. Her quads took on a shape that would make "fitspo" girls envious, and she was physically strong—stronger than me for the first time in her life. We are an odd family, always challenging each other to feats of strength or cleverness or creativity. I recall when the girls were just a little younger, probably twelve and sixteen, and I was running a recreational summer camp they both attended, the competition was especially heated: Who could swing up on Scout, a sixteen-hand chestnut mare, bareback? Who could tread water or hold a plank longest? Who could draw the best dragon or whatever—to be decided by the campers, known for their brutally honest assessments? Who could tell the best campfire story? Of course, the odds were unfair. I was the most experienced with everything; Jenna was tallest, fastest, and most tenacious; but Abby, well, Abby was the coolest. She had that ineffable quality that gave her an appeal Jenna and I could never cultivate, and she was the most artistic. The kids always voted for her dragons.

As she grew older, Abby lost her love of art, though, and I hate to think that it might have been because Jenna began to pursue her own artistic talent seriously by majoring in graphic design, at which she certainly excelled. Abby always made a point of not taking an interest in things her sister was interested in, which has always upset me since they are so similarly gifted. But we've never compared them at home. In school, though, I knew Abby faced "your sister" comments from every teacher they had in common. I try not to saddle siblings I've taught with that weight, largely because of Abby's resentment of it. Each of my daughters is most definitely her own, and free to be that. I believe both of my girls would say that they've had the freedom to define themselves, although once, again at camp, sixteen-year-old Abby, trusted counselor, in a fit of self-assertion claimed it was my fault she never played with the other campers as a child—that I didn't force her to submit to my authority.

We took care of the submission then and there.

She apologized through tears of laughter from a very unnatural position pinned between the floor and me, saying she knew she was a willful, sneaky kid. She was right, though. I've never forced her to do anything she felt strongly disinclined toward, and being a loner as a child myself, I understood that the kittens were better company anyway.

But, I should have forced her to continue seeing a therapist. It may have come out sooner, but we'll get to that. Abby, in her then-current state, was wilting, and though I tried to sustain her through what support I could offer, it just wasn't enough. Her patterns reverted to the unpredictable again. Some days she would be home when I arrived from work. Others, she'd be gone without a word. Her friends were changing, too. She didn't see Sophie, who was dealing with her own drama, so much anymore. Abby had become friendly with the group of young people at work, other servers and bartenders, all eighteen or nineteen to early twenties. Scott and I had gone to the restaurant a few times since she began working there, so I had faces to match the names she would sometimes mention. Riley was a seemingly sweet girl who also went to Southeastern University, and she and Abby talked about getting an apartment together for the fall semester. Then there was John, their shift manager. Abby did not like him much.

When Scott and I were there, he came over to our table to introduce himself, which I suppose was a kind gesture, but immediately, I could feel why Abby preferred not to be around him. He was a slight young man, maybe thirty years old, with blue eyes made bluer by their intense pink rims, giving him a sickly look. His manner, for all its aim at cordiality and propriety, was false, stilted, as if his compliment on your pearl necklace would turn into a punchline, a lewd one, as soon as he was off the floor and in the kitchen.

I admit I was already biased against John before meeting him. Abby had come home one Thursday night saying she might quit and look for something new because of what he said to her. She had been carrying a tray with two pitchers of beer to a table when he passed and said, "Nice jugs." Honestly, I was surprised by her reaction. She had heard—had probably said—much worse than that since the anatomy to which he alluded arrived when she was twelve years old. But, in combination with his other notable qualities, Abby decided it was not funny. That was during her first week of work. When she let it be known that she was not amused, he told her to "get over herself" and then informed her that her last table was not cleaned well enough. She swears it was.

Sometime in February, after Mardi Gras, the situation grew worse. Although we have never been a family that could be accused of having Puritanical expectations of our children, we also have not willingly sent them into the world to face the wolves we know are there. One Sunday before an afternoon shift, Abby lolled around the house with more angst than usual. She brought up calling in, even quitting. When I asked what was going on, she simply said "John."

"What did he do?" I pressed, the edge rising in my voice.

"He's just gross. My skin crawls whenever he's within ten feet of me." she answered. "Ugh," she groaned, "my ass is sweating just thinking about it."

"But did something else happen? Has he said something to you again?"

She let out a sharp breath, a puff of sarcastic laughter, "Ha, I wish. No, he didn't say words, just some vulgar grunts as he scooted past me by the register last week. I can't stand him."

"Abby, that's harassment. Seriously, have you told anyone? You need to report that," I demanded.

"Riley was right there. She heard him, saw the whole thing."

"Whole thing? What else was there? What aren't you telling me?"

"Mom, don't worry about it. I'm going to quit. I'll find something else," she said, attempting a dismissive, no-big-deal attitude about it now that I was getting worked up over it.

"Abby Glynne Hildebrand, you will not let some poor excuse for a man intimidate you out of a job you like. Tell me what he did!" At that moment, Scott walked into the kitchen and felt the seriousness.

"What's going on?" he asked.

Abby and I spoke simultaneously, with her "nothing" ending well before my summation of the situation.

"Do I need to go down there?" Scott asked in typical dad fashion.

"Oh my god, no, Dad! I'll handle it. Y'all are making this way bigger than it needs to be!" The sass emerged.

"No, Abby. There is something you aren't saying here because I know you would not wake up and decide first to call in on such short notice and plan to quit when you have a job at which you've made a friend in Riley and earn as much as you do in tips without having to dress like Malibu Barbie. What is going on with this guy?" I demanded.

Abby sat down and put her head down on the table and folded her arms over her head in what seemed an effort to shelter in place, but then she lifted her face. She was visibly sweating. She had tears in her eyes. "I don't want to tell y'all," she said quietly.

"Sweetie, after everything that's happened over the last three months, what could possibly be so bad?" I asked sincerely.

"Nothing. It's not that bad. It's just stupid, and I'd rather not have to do anything about it. I'd rather just quit."

"Tell us," Scott said firmly.

"Well, you know how John is always flirting with me, and I just laugh it off all the time, but I hate it? After he scooted past me and all, later that day he was in the hallway when I came out of the restroom. The hallway is narrow, so when I passed, I turned sideways away from him. He put one hand on the wall in front of me to stop me and the other hand on my shoulder and, um, he got really close, then sort of licked my neck and bit my ear."

"No fucking way. Let's go. This asshole is done," Scott was ready with the righteous anger of a protective father.

"Dad, no. I'll handle it!" Abby cried.

"How? By quitting? By running away so he can do the same thing to the next girl?" Scott retorted.

"You're right. You're right." Abby realized. "What should I do?"

I told her, "You should do it right. Report it as sexual harassment, because it is! Call the manager. What's his name—Greg? And tell him you will be coming in early today because you need to speak to him about a serious situation."

Abby was nodding, with quiet tears rolling down her cheek, nodding and saying, "Okay."

Having calmed down slightly, Scott offered, "I'll come with you, if you want me to."

"Thanks, Daddy. But I can do it. I know I should do this. It's just so hard. What if he says I'm lying? What if he accuses me of starting it?"

I was confused for a moment. Why would those be her first thoughts? Then I asked, "You said Riley was there for the register incident, right?"

"Yes."

"Start with that. And the jugs comment. And the unnecessary criticism about your tables. Let Greg know Riley heard and saw John act that way with you. Then tell him about the hallway, and tell him you want to file an official complaint. I doubt Greg will question your honesty. Anybody with any sense should be able to see the creepiness in John." I tried to give her a plan, an approach step-by-step, and suddenly, compelled by almost nineteen years of habit, I added, "Listen, sweetie. I know this is hard, but I want confronting it to be your decision, not ours. You shouldn't have to feel uncomfortable in your own life." She nodded and pulled in her lower lip before breathing deeply.

"Okay. I'm going to call him now, then." Abby got up and went to her room. Within an hour, she was down, dressed in the requisite all-back attire of servers, and said, "I'm going now. He told me to come straight to his office before clocking in. Please say a prayer for me. I'm so nervous."

"We will, love. Be brave. This is the right thing to do. You can't let guys like him get away with that. Call us when you have a chance, okay?" Scott and I hugged her goodbye and she left.

Drama stalked Abby. I had seen it tracking her through high school—and then all the commotion with Ryan. Abby, as far as I could tell, did not create it, not the arrest part that precipitated the unpleasantness that followed, anyway. When she met him, she told me she just wanted to take care of him, to show him the comfort he never had. She just wanted to love him to safety, to adventure on their own terms. I'm beginning to doubt people get to live, much less love, on their own terms. Fate, God, the Universal sway— whatever it is—dictates so much. I realize that Abby's choices have influenced many of my own, as do those of all the people I love, but I also know she doesn't always look for trouble. It often finds her, rubs its muzzle against her legs, looking up with hopeful eyes. Then, just as she reaches down to pick it up, out come the claws and teeth. You would think the cross-hatching of scars she earned at camp would be memory enough to instill some caution, but no. Abby's wild love has always had too little regard for self.

Chapter 23

Cosmic Jokes

In jail time, "overnight" amounts to two weeks on average, so after the phone call, after my letter, Ryan's response was not slow in coming. It simply had to travel the route of jail mail, which included not only the difficult task of procuring paper, a pencil, stamp, and envelope, but also the waiting-to-be-read in the out-going stack in the mailroom, where it would be scrutinized for "contraband, or censored or rejected based on legitimate facility interests of order and security." Then, it would journey from California to Louisiana. The letter I received was dated February 8, 2017, about ten days after I spoke to Ryan and mailed that dissertation on forgiveness and pride and all the unknowable things that swirl through the ether. It was postmarked February 14. It arrived on February 23, 2017, what would have been my father's seventy-fifth birthday.

Feb. 8, 2017

Dear Ms. Colleen, Well, if it weren't for you sending your letter to me, I don't think Abby would have ever gotten the one that came for her in the mail with this one. I've been working on it on and off for what seems like forever now even though it's been just a month. I had decided not to send it to her. Then I talked to you and got your letter right after that. Thank you for talking to me that night. I just feel so alone sometimes. You know what I was pretty upset about with this break up other than the obvious? I really like you and Mr. Scott. And I kinda worked a little hard to get your approval. I hate that it ended up like this. But on the bright side, I got to meet y'all and I really enjoyed that. Plus, I don't think I'm done with Abby. I have no idea why. It's probably because I'm in jail and haven't really been in contact with anybody else but I really don't feel like that's it. Should I feel like I can get over this? Should I just let her move on from me so she can have an easier life? I still don't know what's going to happen to me and I'm more worried about the life that I want for my family that I don't even have yet than I am about my current situation. It might be because I have no control over this current one. I've given it to God. My future, however, feels like I'm at a fork in the road staring at the drawing I sent you a few weeks back. One thing that I'm tired of though is being a people pleaser to everybody. I wanna do something for myself and not feel selfish about it. The fact that I've slept about four hours this week doesn't make the decision-making process go any better either. Some things I have been taking advantage of while not being able to sleep though have been reading the Bible, writing about horrible experiences in my life (which helps since I can't drink through them now), and writing the letter to Abby. I'm not sure if you saw that thing or not but it looks like something Isaac Newton might have come up with when trying to figure out the laws of gravity. Writing might help, I think. Didn't you say you wrote about your brother? Did that help you cope with and understand things a little better? I can't believe some of the things I'm remembering about my childhood. Like situations that make me understand why I reacted to certain other recent situations the way I did and do. I know Abby's not at all connected to my childhood so it's really weird. It sucks because I thought I'd be able to talk to a therapist about this stuff in here, but they just threw some pills at me so now all I do is write about what I remember and my dreams. No idea what's been up with those by the way. I never get to sleep soundly. When I do sleep I have the most screwed up, terrifying dreams I've ever had. And I think the meds actually make me more nervous around people than I used to be because I avoid people a lot more. Or it could just be that I'm in jail and they're criminals. I guess I am, too. Anyway, I'm talking to the doctor about it ASAP because I don't like how I am right now. Have you ever heard of stuff like that? Maybe it's because I never took medicine much, not even ibuprofen. Being in here is hard. Sometimes I feel grimy, like there's not enough soap and I'm eventually gonna look like these shriveled up old dudes with hairy ears. Sometimes there isn't soap, really though. And Ms. Colleen, thank you for telling me about the song and the voice. It kinda freaked me out. You might freak out a little too when I tell you this. That was my mama's favorite song for a while. Don't feel crazy about hearing a voice either. I think it's her, my mama, doing that. I've definitely seen and heard some crazy stuff in my life that I can't explain, and I'm pretty sure Mama has tried to steer people into and out of my life to help me through tough times ever since she died. I wish she would visit me like that instead of me seeing her in the dreams I usually have though. I don't want to see her that way. I'm trying everything I can to cope. I have so much on me right now. Ms. Colleen, I know you already know the charges on me and everything about why I'm in here, but I swear, I really don't think everybody's telling the truth about that night. It makes me want to cry. I know I've said this already, but it's just so damn hard to accept. I'm accused of something I can't imagine doing and I don't even believe the supposed reasons I allegedly did it. I spent almost five years of my life in the Marines working hard to be someone and I'm about to lose everything. Anyway, I hope I did the right thing by sending Abby that letter. I hope you and Mr. Scott are doing good. And I really appreciate your advice and letters more than you know. Thank you so much for being here for me. Love, Ryan Freeman P.S. My lawyer said he got the character witness letter you wrote for me. Thank you for that, too. My next court date is in two days, but nothin's gonna happen. It's gonna get pushed back again. Probably til May.

Ryan's distress rose from the page like outstretched arms, but his burdens were not mine to carry, not even those born of his relationship with Abby. I could not even help her carry her own, not really. Abby did not share much of her letter with me, but it, indeed, looked like a page from *House of Leaves*, with margin notes filling every available space. Also in the envelope, folded into Abby's letter, was a paper rose, carefully twisted and torn into petals and leaves. It even had thorns on its stem.

With all the romantic drama unfolding in Abby and Ryan's whatever-it-was, forgetting that realities such as lawyers, courts, charges, and sentences existed was easy, but it was all there, mixed in with newly diagnosed concerns, and that was only in Ryan's life. Abby's life had realities, too. School and work demanded her time, but lately, school took second, maybe third priority to more immediately gratifying endeavors. As the semester progressed, her grades slipped into dangerous territory for someone with a scholarship, and C's seemed unavoidable. In biology, a C was her best-case scenario thanks to the missed quiz and a research assignment. She blamed her university therapist, whom she no longer saw, which was definitely not good. Her work situation—that resulted in John being fired—had improved, but her circle of friends had expanded to include a few people I would never have placed in her life, had I much say in it.

The irony is something, isn't it? I never would have hand-chosen Ryan as a part of Abby's life either. Somehow, fourteen—fifteen almost—months had passed since she first said the name "Ryan Freeman" to me, and although I understood him better now, I still did not understand *them*. In all those months, the handful of days they spent in each other's presence seemed too few to believe in the relationship—the relationship that never was. Again, the irony strikes me: my assessing the authenticity of a relationship by measure of physical proximity. They did have something more, or so I had begun to believe. Whatever had held them together, whatever had brought Abby back to herself was seemingly gone. She had heard nothing from him since the letter that arrived with mine. She and Ryan were over it seemed, ending on as amicable a note as anyone could hope given the ugly truths. But I was still there, quietly between them.

I don't know why it was so hard for me to let Ryan go—maybe because Abby asked me not to so sincerely, maybe because of the song (which he had to have mentioned before, lodging it in my subconscious, because…how else…), maybe because he seemed so appreciative. Once upon a time, I had wholeheartedly believed in the necessity of her welfare as separate from his future, but now, when I should be grateful for the divergence, it felt wrong. It felt like neither she nor he was willfully choosing it, as if it—the whole situation from his arrest to her infidelity—were a cosmic joke, a very bad one. And there I was, right where I didn't belong, flailing around in the middle of it. They mattered to each other. I still could not completely understand the balance of wrongs, how hers outweighed his so mightily, but that was not mine to figure out.

Maybe I was just that mom, the one with no life of her own, too busy with her children, misplacing all sorts of emotional energy.

No, that's wrong, too.

I've always adopted people—and maintained my own interests. As a teacher, I am well-practiced in emotional availability. To students, teachers have no past, no lives outside of their own, and a teacher's reality consists of students' current needs, interests, dilemmas. You live only in conjunction with their presence, and in their absence, cease to be. I'm sure many recall the shock of seeing a teacher unexpectedly in the toilet paper aisle in Walmart. Teachers exist because of students. We are there for them, offering some support at lunch or after class, helping them carry the responsibility of demanding parents, needy siblings, or cheating boyfriends and girlfriends simply by listening. Occasionally, greater troubles—pregnancies, abortions, coming out, suicidal ideation, abuse—cause them to linger at my door, and

I'm there, offering direction where I can, reporting issues of serious consequence when mandated. I have always allowed them room to unburden themselves on my shoulders and not let them see me shuffle out from under the weight at the end of the day, when I assume my real identity with its own joys and sorrows to bear. But, Abby is my own, and I share her sorrows. I could not shuffle out from under them.

Ryan reminded me of (and would have been) a student I would have adopted, which I sometimes did without their permission or even their knowing. I'll care a little more for some than others, not fully understanding what makes the difference between this one and that. Maybe it's their degree of need or trust in me. Maybe it has something to do with frequencies and vibrations—all that metaphysical foolishness my dad would talk about. Maybe quantum physics has more to do with connections, consciousness, and behavior than we think. Maybe those unseen waves within us wash outward over others, and those calibrated to feel them are those to whom we are drawn. How else do you just "get" some people? I thought I understood Abby and Ryan, and Ryan, Abby believed, was one of the few people who "got" her. She was the tide under a night sky, the pull between them far more than an ebb and flow. Their absolute torrent made me believe in a purpose to it all, but maybe I was just wrong about everything.

Over the months—years—that followed, my relationships with Abby and Ryan evolved separately, but always with the reality that they were only a question away from each other. For a brief time, they did sink deeply into each other again, when Ryan faced his sentencing, which did not happen that May or that September, when the next date was set, or December, but much later—in February of 2018. There is still so much to tell you, and all of it feels simultaneously like yesterday and an eternity ago.

Chapter 24

Caught in the Spin

Once, when Scott and I were younger, we walked outside in a wind that could nearly lift me. Even between huge gusts, a steady gale caught my hair and clothes, carried leaves like confetti, and occasionally invited the very dirt to rise and dance in small circles around us. Scott said the world was spinning too fast. Sometimes, I think it has been ever since. The idea of "gradual" confounds me—a progress so slow that it feels like stagnation as it unfolds, but later, though "later" differs in measure for everyone, that slow progress strikes as an epiphany: it's over, done, the long past, of which there is so much, reduced to a second whose end just snapped you into a new reality. It's an impossible progression to plot, from "then" to "now," swirling eternities into ephemerality, leaving you to wonder how time vanished.

Time, more than pain, makes us most aware of our mortality. Pain only makes us welcome it. I know that's morbid, but most people have been in places dark enough to want a release from this life at least once. Time and life are paradoxical, though. I have a thought in mind, and I'm struggling to frame it: People couple time and life together, and rightly so, but when you feel most alive, time disappears. People think that death equates to being "out of time," but in life, people lose track of time when they are rapt, caught in a flow that takes them out of their usual awareness into something less bound, less inhibited, something in the realm of the soul. I'm not explaining this right, but passion or purpose offer a different way to be out or outside of time. I feel that flow when I paint, sometimes when I write, when I read, or wander the trails after I run. It's an engagement with creation, I think, and I wonder if that's what heaven, what whatever comes next, after time, is— being caught up in creation itself, a part of its energy.

When I was little, the nuns at school would talk about heaven, describing streets of gold and lots of singing, praising God continuously. The problem was that I preferred grass to gold and didn't have a great voice, so imagining how that would equate to eternal happiness troubled me. Besides, where would the animals be? As I grew older, I began to question, with the encouragement of my dad, everything about existence. He would sit for hours reading Edgar Cayce or *Chariots of the Gods* while my mom would cart us off to church every Sunday. Then Zeke died, and Dad's reading changed, but he saw connections. He would point out biblical passages that the nuns had never mentioned. Chapter one of Ezekiel—of course it would be in Ezekiel—describes the wheel in the sky. That made me wonder. Years later, when I adopted my own eclectic reading habits, Luke 17:21, which says "the kingdom of heaven is within you," resonated with me as I read *The Spirit Molecule*. My father fostered my curiosity, my investigations of existence, imparting to me an openness to possibility I have not seen often in others, possibly because I have seldom been open with my own thoughts in conversations. I masquerade as a traditional Southern Christian while harboring questions and beliefs that could have me burned as a witch, but I'd be in good company.

Please don't get me wrong. I believe in God. Just don't ask me to explain who or what God is. He—for lack of a better word—is definitely not a grandfatherly figure in the sky. I think too many people picture Charlton Heston as Moses on the mountain when they think of God, but God is beyond image, beyond language. We are arrogant to believe we can capture any adequate description of God with words. When I was in high school and read Emerson and Thoreau for the first time, I had a religious conversion of sorts. The idea of the Oversoul made such sense to me. I have adopted it and probably corrupted it in making it my own, but I see God in it, in the creative energy of the universe. That's the only way what the nuns said about praising God for eternity in heaven makes any sense to me. Maybe, dying and going to heaven means becoming a part of that energy, a part of God, if we aren't already.

I don't know what I'm talking about, but as I try to piece this all together, being inside and outside of time seems relevant. This is the crazy in me that I hide fairly well in my everyday life. While I will occasionally drift onto a rambling, pseudo-philosophical tangent in my classes, write an enigmatic poem, or paint something surreal, I'm pretty normal: just a wife, mother, and teacher who tries to do a decent job in each role. I fail often, but also often, I'm the only one who notices, or at least I'm the only one who berates me for it. I worry that I have failed Abby. I recently saw an article on Pinterest titled, "If Your Mother Said Any of These Nine Things to You, You Can Trace Your Anxiety Back to Her," which is such a lovely title. The sayings included "calm down," "don't worry," "hurry," and "let me help you." Has any mother not said these things to her children? I guess Pinterest berates me, too. Anyway, with my failure as a mother confirmed by social media, the world spins on.

Spring of 2017 seemed to arrive overnight, and with it came events of the sort that require gifts and outfits and small talk. A combination of weddings and baby showers dotted the calendar from March to June, birthdays—Jenna's, mine, and Abby's all in March—and Easter in mid-April. Spring has always bustled with responsibilities, especially as school winds down, but this year was especially busy. Jenna's early March birthday, her twenty-third, brought us to dinner at Jade, a Chinese-Vietnamese restaurant that makes spring rolls an art form. There, Scott and I met Jenna and Michael, her boyfriend of almost two years, and Abby, but Abby was late. Jenna met Michael during the spring of her junior year in storybook fashion. Jenna had run cross country in high school, and was quite good, though not quite fast enough for an athletic scholarship offer on top of her academic one. She contented herself with recreational running throughout most of college, as I have done most of my life. I say "most of college" because Michael changed that.

One day she was running on campus and, as she told me, "sort of freaked out when these two guys ran up beside" her. She said the long-haired one did the talking. He told her that their coach had sent them, and that their mission was to recruit her for track and cross country. If they could get her to go talk to him, they would be excused from workouts for the rest of the week. She did talk to him and spent the last three semesters of college running in addition to all else she did. She and Michael graduated together, and Scott christened the couple nickname 8.0 for them since both graduated with perfect 4.0 grade point averages over their four years. Michael was a finance major poised to become an investment banker upon completing his master's degree. They were and are a beautiful couple—brilliant, good, and modelesque—made for each other.

As they sat across the table from us, Jenna, with her effortless beauty, laughed as she recounted the late-night dance session she and her roommate choreographed earlier in the week for a Snapchat audience. Michael attested to their work as high-quality entertainment, vouching for Jenna's impressive twerking skills, one cheek at a time. Cheek isolation twerks, Jenna explained, are quite complex. I did not doubt it. My own cheeks—those on my face—hurt from smiling as Michael, eyes bright blue and shining, bragged that Jenna made him the envy of all the finance teaching assistants at LSU. I had no doubt this brilliant young man would be my son-in-law in the not-too-distant future. That was something to which both Scott and I looked forward.

When Abby arrived at the restaurant, she carried with her a little box which she attempted to hide as she kissed everyone hello, leaving Jenna for last. After she greeted her with their traditional "hey," a little chirp that sounded more animal than human, she placed the box in front of Jenna and said, "I got you a small thing. Be careful when you open it, though."

Jenna looked quizzically at Abby, then pulled the ends of the green silk ribbon, undoing the bow. The little box was not wrapped, but covered in a decorative print of tiny cacti, and that is exactly what Jenna found inside, a very small, very beautiful succulent garden featuring prickly bulbs and buttons of cacti in varying shades of green.

"Abby, I love this! It is the cutest, thank you so much!" Jenna reached out in what would appear to be a high-five toward Abby, but instead of the traditional clap, their hands met in their awkward-turtle hand hug, a sister thing.

"Do you know why I picked cactus?" Abby asked.

"Because I have a history as a plant murderer?" Jenna replied, undoubtedly remembering the orchids I gave them in January. Jenna's was already dead. She thought it was fake.

"No," Abby explained, "because you are a little cactus. You are beautiful when you let someone see you bloom, but you know how to make people keep their distance, too. And you're tough as shit. You'd survive the apocalypse. And thrive. Meanwhile, y'all can put my orchid, which is still blooming," she added with a smirk, "on my grave."

"Abby!" Jenna scolded at the unexpected ending of Abby's monologue, which was mostly lovely. "Don't say that. I mean the grave part. You are way tougher than I am. I would never be brave enough to do the things you've done at your age."

"Like what?" Came the self-deprecation with what seemed a note of genuine perplexity.

"Like going to California and meeting with a lawyer and doing everything you've done for Ryan." Jenna didn't know.

"I guess you haven't heard?" Abby asked, deadpan. Jenna stared at her, confused. "We broke up, or stopped talking, or whatever. We ended whatever it was. Or wasn't? Just too hard."

"What?" The disbelief in Jenna's voice captured the same incredulity I had been struggling with although I knew the story.

"Not right now. Y'all can talk about that later. So Michael, how's the market? You'll be finishing up in May, right?" Scott changed the course of the conversation.

We placed our orders and ate too many spring rolls while we waited for the entrees, and the rest of the evening went along without too much heaviness, a quality, which unfortunately, Abby towed into almost any room she entered lately. Jenna and Michael brought most of their Lomi Lomi—a sinful affair involving bacon-wrapped shrimp—home, and we boxed up a good portion of the Triple Dragon Scott and I shared. Abby had barely touched her Pho, asking us to bring it home for her so she could have it tomorrow. She was meeting Riley and some friends from work after dinner. As we left the restaurant with dinner for the next day, we said our goodbyes in the parking lot, leaning in for hugs and kisses all around. There was a moment, it seemed, between Jenna and Abby, but I didn't hear what they said and didn't ask later. Sometimes sisters need only to be sisters, not daughters. As we all parted ways, a gust of early March wind rushed up and caught the green ribbon of Abby's gift to Jenna resting atop the to-go box and spun it into the night, where I lost sight of it.

Chapter 25

Image Rehearsal Therapy

Easter passed with the customary family dinner at our house and a table full of crawfish and stuffed artichokes and a huge pot of chicken and sausage gumbo on the stove. No one mentioned the previous year when we welcomed Ryan into our home for the holiday. He had impressed everyone in some way, positive or negative. My mom liked him immediately when he helped her carry her usual collection of gift baskets, covered dishes, and store-bought desserts that would remain untouched all day, but my sister and nephew eyed him suspiciously, attempting to discern the tattoo that peeked out from a rolled-up flannel sleeve.

This year, Abby was alone among her sister and cousins, all with their significant others. She sat with Opal, preventing sneak attacks on my niece's little boy, who waved teething biscuits like a priest dispensing holy water— spit consecrating everyone below the knees—as he toddled around the house. Later, we all went outside, playing corn-hole and enjoying conversation in the warmth of the late afternoon sun and the breeze coming across the water. Abby stayed aloof but smiling, inhabiting a post-Ryan persona which, to me, conveyed false aplomb, but to most others read as perfectly fine. When everyone left and the kitchen was clean, the evening settled into just us, Abby and me, while Scott disappeared into the bathroom for a shower that seemed to take at least an hour. Abby curled into me on the sofa like a child much younger, and said, "I miss him."

Unspoken rules had developed between us. I never brought Ryan up to her, and neither of us said his name. "I know you do, love," was all I replied, not wanting to initiate a difficult conversation that would undoubtedly include tears. But, then she asked.

"Have you heard from him?"

I had.

Six weeks had passed since the Valentine's letter, the last communication Abby had with Ryan. I continued to email and write to him through March, through mine and Abby's shared St. Patrick's Day birthday. I had even sent him a hygiene package from the commissary, which had an online store—the wonders never ceased. After reading the letter Ryan sent to me along with Abby's last, with its downplayed descriptions of nightmares and emotional struggles unrelated to Abby, I had researched ways to alleviate the horrible dreams he was having and emailed him what I found, along with the news that he should no longer worry about a soap shortage and that at fifty, his skin will thank him for using moisturizer. The dreams were undoubtedly a manifestation of his PTSD, a subject I had serendipitously learned more about through a novel, *The Hour I First Believed* by Wally Lamb, which I also ordered and sent to Ryan, hoping it might offer insight and encouragement. Having had my fill of Mardi Gras between the ages of two and twenty, I reserved the unique handful of February days off school for reading now. I emailed Ryan to tell him I sent the book and to explain Image Rehearsal Therapy, hoping it might provide some relief.

February 24, 2017

Hi Ryan, I hope you are well and that the gift pack was helpful. Did you receive the book a while back?It's fine if it isn't your taste to read; just pass it on to someone or donate to the library there. I just finished writing a letter I'll drop in the mail soon, and I apologize for its length and its boldness.I don't intend it to come across in a didactic way at all.I worry about intruding on and assuming too much about you,consequently upsetting or offending you,just about every time I send something handwritten.Just know that it comes from a place of concern and love,not judgment.Well,the reason I am writing this in addition to that is to tell you about Image Rehearsal Therapy for nightmares.It is a cognitive behavior therapy that turns out to be really simple, and from what studies say, pretty effective.While lots of therapies involve delving into dreams and nightmares to unpack the symbolism and decipher the subconscious, this simply aims to make them stop. There are three basic steps:1. choose a recent (or recurrent) nightmare2. change the script: let yourself think about the nightmare only for the purpose of changing elements of it.For example,I have this disturbing house-within-a-house, creepy haunted dream now and then. In it, a familiar door (like the one to my room) becomes a portal to some crazy place that is in my house that I have never seen before, and bad things live there. I open it and am usually terrified awake.So, in IRT, I would change it so when I open it,I see no bad things, but a surprise party for me (which is still sort of scary)or change the door to a window that I open and butterflies fly in—or dollar bills, twenty-dollar bills, yes, that's better. Anyway, you alter the scariness out of the nightmare and make it something new, different entirely, but only by beginning with the elements of the nightmare. Then you write the new dream down (mentally unless you want to literally write and rewrite it) to make it more vivid every time.3. Rehearse (read) it and add new positive details.Spend 10 to 20 minutes a day on the dream. Studies say that it can reduce waking stress by about 60%within three months and improve sleep quality in as little as a week. Results lasted in the test group for about 2years(when subjects decided they didn't need therapy anymore).I figured it is worth trying, right?I hope it helps.<3 Ms. Colleen

Not knowing the quality of psychiatric care available to Ryan and having been horrified by the idea of their "just throwing pills" at him, I really wanted to provide him with helpful information. I had even spoken to my school's mental health provider about it, but she said that although she heard of IRT, she had never used it with a patient. I figured it was something, at least.

The handwritten letter I sent him addressed the questions he had written to me in the Valentine's bundle. Should he feel like he can get over Abby? Should he just let her move on because that's what's best for her? Did writing about my brother help me cope? Have I ever heard of having such nightmares about people you loved? I knew the uncertainty of everything overwhelmed him. Being unable to control situations swirling around you is one thing, but being unable to control what swirls within you is another entirely.

I don't think I provided much direction for Ryan in my letter, not on matters of the heart anyway. He and Abby would have to find their way through the ambivalence that kept them within each other's sight but out of touch. They were just two arm's lengths apart, but they never reached for one another at the same time. Each had so much to sort through. People must know themselves and be honest about what they want, who they want to be, and who they have been in order to position themselves for the future, but they must be willing to look into the ugliness they'd rather not see if they want to rid themselves of it, like IRT. In the handwritten letter I sent along with the email, I told Ryan all this.

The response to my letter had arrived several days before the Easter holidays began, but I had not told Abby. Her presence at home had been sporadic at best, evasive at worst. When she wasn't working, which she often did, she stayed with Riley or other friends whose names and connections I could not keep straight anymore. Her life was becoming something entirely separate from my own, which I know is the goal of parenthood, but the way Abby's independence was unfolding felt dangerous. When she was with us at home, she loved us. That was always clear, but when she was gone—well, out of sight, out of mind. Abby existed in isolation. Nineteen-year-old Abby conceived of herself as arriving to life fully formed, like Venus rising from sea foam, forgetting that she would wake in the night wanting to crawl into bed with me and Scott at the age of nine or that our income still insured her health and car. But, she was home now, nestled into me and asking if Ryan had written, so I told her.

"I have heard from him," was all I said.

"How is he?" she asked.

"Struggling," I responded. "He was having nightmares, bad ones, so I emailed him some information, but now they've put him on meds to help him sleep."

"He's always had really vivid dreams, really symbolic ones," she recalled.

"I remember the one you told me about, with his dad talking to him, the one right before his arrest. I've been thinking about that since I got his letter. He's really working hard to put himself back together, to be better," I told her.

"What did he say?"

He said so much, and he said it with such sincerity—a transparency that made me imagine standing at the edge of a fishing hole and looking into a clear depth that revealed coral reefs or some other unexpected beauty. Despite the imagined poetry, I gave Abby the as-written version, straight as Ryan said it.

April 10, 2017

Dear Ms. Colleen, First, I'd like to thank you for the letter and hygiene pack. Both really helped me out a lot, but in different ways, obviously. I also want to compliment you on your handwriting. It actually is a lot like my mom's was. I started writing questions down and answering them honestly. Turns out that you use a different part of your brain when you write instead of talk, and you see things more clearly. Second, the meds they were giving me had a reverse effect on me and heightened everything they were supposed to prevent. Haha, figures. The funny thing is that to fix it, they tried upping the dosage twice, and that really threw me into overdrive, so there actually was something wrong with all of that. It's better now and I'm taking something that keeps me from dreaming mostly so I sleep for a few hours a night now. I do appreciate you not telling me how to make my decisions. I like that you ask a bunch of questions instead. That causes me to find my own way I guess. I was just trying to figure out what other people do when facing hard stuff. As for the old soul, new soul question, I know exactly what you're talking about. Ever since I was young, like really young, people have told me that I have an old soul. It's probably because I understood how things work in life and I can see the feelings on both sides in almost every situation because of things I've already witnessed in my life. As far back as I can remember, people have asked me for advice, and I always somehow came up with it. After mama died, I kinda had to give myself advice on everything since Daddy was either gone or strung out and nobody around me knew what to do about anything. Haha, I obviously made a few mistakes and learned the hard way, but I have learned. Thank you for having confidence in me and putting in your letter that you think I am coping and working hard to improve myself. It was a wakeup call to me on realizing this is the first time I've ever soberly faced my problems. It made me feel sick to my stomach to realize how weak I had let myself become over the years and especially the last few months. People always told me I was strong but that's because I had no feelings anymore. I covered it with alcohol. I wasn't strong, I was numb. Now I need my sister and brother to realize the same thing about themselves. I know I can help them. I love them so much and will do everything I can to help them. Also, please don't worry about intruding or assuming too much of anything about me. Sort of complex but I'm real up-front and open enough to be assumed about. I'm not easily offended so don't worry about sharing your thoughts. I actually enjoy them and like to know how other people, especially people I respect, view me. It causes me to see from their perspective figuring out how and why they got that opinion. Then I can fine tune things I'd like to change about my demeanor or appearance. And thank you for sending me the story about your brother. I like the way you say so much without saying things right out. I appreciate the information on IRT, too. I've been writing the dreams I remember down, but mostly I'm not having nightmares anymore. And I know you didn't ask, and I appreciate it, but as for everything with Abby, I have spent a ridiculous amount of time writing, drawing, making graphs and tables, cross analyzing and studying the Bible trying to figure out what I should do. After finally being able to think sort of clearly, I decided that I never want to feel those feelings again. Once trust is broken that bad and by two people you love not just one, it's hard to earn back anything. I also don't want to hold it over her head and accidently use it to hurt her. I forgive her, but I can't trust her again. I know I'm no better, but I think I'm the only one of us who will make a move. Like I said, I'm not done with her in my life, I'll probably never be, because I do love her so much, and if she ever needs help, I'll be right there, but I got cut deep with this one. I just can't tell who's holding the blade. I don't know. I'm practicing the future I want to see, and I want to keep writing to y'all, so I hope that's ok. I can't tell you enough times how much I appreciate everything, the advice and help, your confidence in me, the information and hygiene stuff, just everything. Until next time, I love y'all. Love, Ryan Freeman

Upon finishing the letter, Abby looked up and asked a one-word question: "Y'all?"

I did not have an answer for her.

Chapter 26

An Agnostic, Insomniac, and Dyslexic
Walk into a Bar

Abby's life grew no less interesting without Ryan so obviously in it, but even when she didn't say it, I believe he lingered in her mind, always on the periphery, if not dead center, like the eye of a storm. After receiving his April letter, I emailed, of course, but my emails had become less frequent (usually once a week) and filled with whatever thoughts fell from my head to my hands upon the keys. Sometimes they were nonsense. Sometimes they were serious. Sometimes I regretted hitting send. Nonetheless, I wrote. Along with the weekly email, a handwritten letter made its way to California about once a month, usually in response to a handwritten letter that made its way to Louisiana. After the letter I shared with Abby, the one that prompted her to question the "y'all" at the end, I had emailed Ryan with some foolishness about my Saturday detention adventures, a short explanation of why *Brave New World* is more relevant than *1984* today, and a few jokes—Why shouldn't you trust advice from an atom? They make up everything. But, I had also written to him, responding more directly to all that he said in his letter. I also rambled, for lack of a better word, about my own memories and observations. After addressing the concerns or needs Ryan would send my way–something that made me feel very purposeful–I allowed myself to write freely, to muse on life—my own and in general—and now, thinking back to some of what I wrote, I wonder if I should regret any of it, my oversharing, as they say. Ryan assured me that every word was well worth reading, but it seemed strange that this young man, this adult something-like-a-son I've adopted–this fairy godson (because I can think of no other title to explain his presence in my life)–should know so much about me. I suppose I attempt to teach un-didactically through stories, which, at the core, is quite didactic.

The rambling in the last letter, now that I think about it, was almost prescient. I wrote it before Abby moved into her own place in June. I didn't receive a reply for a while, which left me wondering if I said something to upset Ryan. Turns out, I had.

April 22, 2017

Dear Ryan,

After a week of spring storms, winter is back this morning with temperatures in the forties. I hate when the weather does this. As if the tornados that skipped across the state were not enough, nature will be gracing us with colds and coughs that linger long after this sudden change, reminding us that we should never get too comfortable. So it goes. That's from Slaughterhouse-Five. *I guess it's what to say when there really isn't anything to say. Life is just life.*

I know you won't be reading this until early May, and who knows what changes life will bring by then, but before continuing, I have to let you know that you were missed over Easter—Abby asked me directly if I had heard from you much. She had been doing a good job of steering clear of the subject of you, at least with me—who knows what she thinks about—but after everyone went home on Easter Sunday, she cuddled up with me on the sofa and asked. I felt like the mom from The Notebook, *not telling her about so much, and I didn't like that. I know you are dealing with a lot, but so is she. Thinking back to January, knowing how things have unfolded for her, I think she was coping with much more than she allowed me to see, and I wonder if she still is. I feel like I have lost her just a little, but maybe that's just what her version of independence looks like. In hindsight, I'm thankful that I've only lost a part. I guess I will never know how close we came to losing all of her. Probably too close. It's been rough, but my intention isn't to get into all of that. It is simply to let you know I shared your last letter with her. I don't know if that is okay with you, but considering that you closed with saying you wanted to continue* writing to "y'all," I thought it was. That part confused her. Me too, I guess. "I love y'all," you said. I didn't know what to tell her. I thought you should know.

Alrighty then...if you are still reading this and have not dropped it like a stick that turned out to be a snake—wait, what am I saying—you wouldn't drop a snake. You'd bring it home and make a pet of it. Or set it free. My brother had snakes. Or tried to. The little ones always escaped. My mom would freak out over it. Usually, we'd find them after a few days wrapped around the outboard motor in the utility room, which made sense since most came from the canal across the street. One, though, a corn snake, super cool looking, ate mice, which I hated. Turns out that Zeke did, too, though he tried not to show it. He was too kindhearted to watch the sweet little mice, who I'd cry over, go down like eight balls in a noodle. He gave the snake away. I guess trying to appear tougher than you are is a pretty tough thing. He wasn't much of a hunter either. There's a squirrel story that ends badly... but fishing—that was my family's forte. Growing up, we had a four-foot above ground pool in our back yard for about nine years, five of which saw people swimming in it. The other four, it was filled with fish. Bass, big ones. My dad, grandfather, and Zeke would fish Bayou Bienvenue or Pearl River and come home with ice chests full, but occasionally, live ones. We actually fed them until they became Friday night dinner during Lent, good old Catholicism. To this day I can't understand how fried fish or boiled crawfish is more of a sacrifice than, say, a turkey sandwich.

Anyway, my brother was quite a fisherman. And a water skier. School wasn't his thing, with his being a touch dyslexic. I wish I had had just one conversation with him about what he believed. That perplexed me for a long while after his death. Sadly, one of my most vivid memories is a moment, a conversation I was not meant to hear but have carried with me for over thirty-five years. He was sitting on the kitchen counter telling my mom some foolishness about hanging out at the state park talking to Bean and Ash—those are friends' names by the way—under a tree when a baby bird fell from it, chirping in a blind, featherless panic, no doubt. He stepped on it and killed it. Intentionally. I hated him in that moment, but as I continued my eavesdropping, I realized he was confessing. He hated himself for it, too. Then I felt bad for him. I wondered what else—if one baby bird weighed so heavily on him—he carried in his conscience. I've never said anything about that to anyone. I've forgiven him for it, though. It's weird. Sometimes I feel like I know him better in death than I did in life. Certainly, that isn't the ideal sibling *relationship. I hope my girls always maintain their weird little connection, but more importantly, I hope they are always present in one another's lives and always care.*

Your concern for your siblings is clear. I hope you can help them, too, but remember that ultimately, people can't really save anyone but themselves. Just being there, available, and offering what support you can is about all there is to do. I'm still learning that, and it's difficult, the inability to save them. You know that already, though. It's the same with children, as I am sure you will someday see. How to support without enabling is tricky, always trial and error and learning again. I suppose on a related but unrelated note, I appreciate the clarity you offered on your feelings for Abby. I understand the lack of trust being too much to overcome and appreciate your knowing yourself well enough to realize that.

You know, I'm sitting here thinking that I told you a snake story earlier, and now I'm thinking about temptations—about the need to let them go rather than cage them and grow fascinated until they escape and destroy us, most likely with self-loathing and self-deception, like metaphorical snakes. Real snakes are just snakes, perfectly fine. But people snakes...nope. Maybe it's the curse of English teachers to make metaphors out of life. I swear I didn't plan it. I feel a short story in there somewhere. I'll get right (or write?) on that after I finish grading the fifty essays I'm collecting Monday. Also, I know you will not get this until after your court date, but please know that I have not forgotten about it; I'm praying that some charge will be dropped or that the D.A.'s offer will improve, or something! I'm also praying that you have the strength to withstand whatever comes your way, which is kind of a pointless prayer. You've already proven your ability to withstand so much. That's a done deal.

So, let me end with a great joke (no need to confine my superior sense of humor to email, after all): What do you get when a dyslexic, an insomniac, and an agnostic walk into a bar? [insert Jeopardy music here] An argument that lasts all night about whether there's a dog! Be well, Ryan.

Love,
Ms. Colleen

Chapter 27

Farsighted

With days growing longer throughout April and into May, time somehow seemed shorter. So much was happening—Abby's impending move, baby or wedding showers every other weekend, and the school year's end in general—that I busied myself into inobservance, collapsing into bed every night with no memory of falling asleep. Certainly, I hardly made it past the first name on my list of prayers, or maybe they are more of meditations. Of course, that first name was always Abby's. Still a bit broken, still unsteady, she came and went without much enthusiasm about anything, especially school, but she managed. Although she lost the academic scholarship, she kept the state-funded tuition assistance, so that would offer some relief for her fall expenses. "Relief" in nonacademic areas of her life was more troublesome to me, as always. She was smoking again, both cigarettes and marijuana, "self-medicating," perhaps. I was certain of this because she did little to conceal it, coming home on occasion smelling like a concert. She knew how I felt about it, but, as usual, that didn't matter, and with legalization so common, my stance on the issue just seemed antiquated to her.

Youth can rarely see past itself, past the day.

Not far down my list of prayerful intentions and amid the red-letter days of May was also Ryan and his court date. He did not expect to be sentenced then because his lawyer was still attempting to negotiate a better plea deal using Ryan's participation in and completion of several inmate programs, including AA and anger management classes, as evidence that he deserved a lesser sentence. But he expected something to happen. It did. On May 9, he appeared before a judge who told him that the young man he was looking at and the young man presented by the D.A. seem like two different people, that he was aware of the PTSD diagnosis, and that he was aware of his military service, and that he was ordering a more complete psychiatric evaluation before proceeding. I suppose that was good news. According to Ryan's lawyer, every day spent in county jail prior to sentencing was good. It kept him from the more volatile environment of any one of the state prisons to which he would eventually be transferred and allowed him to accumulate credits toward a reduced sentence. Besides, having been at Vista in the veterans' program for nearly six months, Ryan had established a reputation, a good one.

Shortly after his May court appearance, Ryan became a trustee. The position, unlikely for someone so young in the system, gave him more responsibility and a bit more freedom. He described his role as a "connection between the counselor, deputies, and inmates who makes sure inmates do what they are told, don't fight, are respectful, and honestly just help make life in jail as easy for them as [he] can." He also said that being able to help people and having some responsibility made time pass a little faster. I had continued my weekly emails, usually filling the available character limit every other week while I held detention but sending something short from home. The last one I sent from school was filled with questions—about his health and sleep, about his progress in counseling, about his impending evaluation, about being a trustee, and about Abby. It was the first time I mentioned her in a long time. I wanted to know if life was better for him without her. I suppose I was trying to figure out if hers had improved without him, and I was having trouble with that.

Sometimes I wish I could be oblivious. Being unaware of others' hope and pain might allow me to live less troubled. Even when I try, I cannot make the choice to ignore what I see and feel around me, though, especially when I see it in and feel it from those I love, that strange proximity. Abby radiated pain and I absorbed it all, though she tried to keep it from me. Without a word, I knew she was carrying far more than she wanted me to know, and while Ryan seemed the bulk of her burden, I knew she was accumulating more through her recent life, much of which was unknown, at least in the details, to me. I knew she had new friends, a job, a lack of discipline in school, and a desire to avoid any conversation with me that required depth. That's what bothered me most. Abby had always been one to dive into hard ideas, even those about herself, and explore whatever meanings she might find. She never covered her eyes at the sight of something upsetting or unexpected when she was young, but now she lived in a haze of obscured vision. Looking inward, looking out—it didn't matter. To me, it seemed my profound thinker had become shallow and distracted by the shiny new things that I knew would rust away. Her instinct for meaning seemed gone, and I could only imagine that it was buried in the last five months. Over that time, she changed in ways I couldn't understand.

One Sunday afternoon, while Scott was at the gym, Abby woke up after getting home in the early morning hours and came downstairs while I was grading papers at the table. Our daily conversations had become those of practicality and logistics—times, people, places. I was surprised when she sat down after we said good morning—although it was 1:30 p.m.

"What are you grading?" she asked.

"Arguments for 102," I responded, looking up at her, hoping to invite her into conversation.

"What about?"

"They could choose their own topics, so anything from the unfairness of dress codes to the inefficacy of border walls. Some are really good. One is about how practicing mindfulness and yoga for thirty minutes at the beginning of a school day can improve the quality of education. There's some compelling evidence. I'd be all for that."

"That would be cool. It would never go over here. Can you see Mr. Therman on the morning announcements doing yoga? That'd be hilarious. Not that he doesn't need it," Abby opined.

In hindsight, I should not have, but I steered the conversation to her, asking, "What about you? How are you coping these days?"

"Mom, really? I'm alive, right?" She intended that to be funny. It wasn't.

I looked at her disapprovingly but not harshly, and said, "Yes. But really. We hardly talk about anything big anymore, and I'm worried about you, especially since you'll be moving soon. Do you think that the responsibility of being on your own will be something you can handle?"

"Only one way to find out," she said, punctuating it with an obviously fake grin.

"Well, you know I worry, and with school this semester—"

"Mom! Can you not! This semester was kind of hard for me! Remember?"

"Abby, I know. I'm not accusing you of anything other than just that—having a hard time. I'm just worried that you haven't really dealt with things. It seems like you are avoiding your feelings. Avoiding me a little." It was more than a little. Too often, the sight of me seemed to remind her of everything she had ever done wrong without my saying a word. Now, here I was saying words.

"It just hurts, Mom! Life hurts!" Her words came out not as a scream, but as a wail, not loud but intense, true. Then the tears came. "This is why I don't talk to you. I'm just so tired of crying all the time. I know you don't mean to make things worse, and really you don't. It's all already there, but I can't talk about it. It's constantly in my head, and I wish I could get it out, but it's there all the time and I don't know what to do. I don't want to be like this."

"Oh, sweetie, I'm so sorry," I said as I reached out to touch her, stroking her hair, as she put her head face-down into crossed arms on the table. As gently as I could, I asked, "Can you tell me how 'this' is? I want to help you."

Turning her face toward me but not lifting it, she said, "Sad, Mom. Feeling worthless—like I invested everything I had and made one mistake and lost everything. Now there's just this. All the time" She wiped her tears away.

"My love," I began softly, believing the "it" she meant was the last sixteen or so months—what they were and what they became—with Ryan. "I won't pretend to understand how you feel, but I know that staying out all night and getting high all the time won't fix it. I know how deeply you are hurting and living at the surface is no way to fix that." She shot me an angry look, but I continued. "You know it's true, love. Investing in yourself, making decisions you're proud of, finding meaning—that's the only way back. It's hard but—"

"Mom, this is not the time. Please! I don't know what anything means! I can't do this right now."

"Abby, what's going on? What is 'right now'?" I asked. She reached for her phone on the table.

"This." She held the screen up to me. There in red letters at the top of the list of her missed calls was "Ry."

"What?" I asked, mostly to myself, a bit stunned. I thought of his last letter, of what he had said about trust. What was he doing? Rather than say any of that, I asked, "You still have money in your GTL account?"

She nodded, "And look at the time. It was 12:30 here, so 10:30. He can't make calls that late." She got up to get a tissue.

"Well, maybe as a trustee?"

"Yeah, probably," was all she said at first. Then, still standing, she said in a different tone, "He's working really hard, huh?"

"I think he is. He's coming to a lot of realizations about his life. Well, you read his last letter."

"Mama, I miss him so much." She stood for a second longer, wiped her nose, and went upstairs.

The explanation for the call arrived eight days later. In fact, there were several explanations. Both Abby and I received letters from Ryan, each in a separate envelope, which I took as an indication of both his intent that only Abby's eyes see her letter and his new status as trustee—extra envelopes were a luxury. I placed Abby's on the kitchen counter and left it waiting for her, wondering when she would be home to receive it. Upon reading mine, I tried to recall what I had said in either an email or letter that may have been too much, but as I read, he made it clear.

May 2, 2017

Dear Ms. Colleen, I reckon the first thing you'll notice is that I sent Abby a letter, too. I have to tell you why, and I hope I don't sound disrespectful when I do. When I read your last letter and you said that you almost lost her back in January, that really got in my head bad. Considering both my parents committed suicide, that was not fair to say to me. It even made me call her once, but she didn't answer. That's when I wrote the letter she got. I know you weren't trying to upset me, and you might not know how Mama and Daddy died completely, but I'm telling you now because even though I'm dealing with a lot, that one's still too damn hard. It upset me bad. Like I said, I hope I don't come off as rude, but I wanted you to know that.

I did know about his mother's death, at least the rumors of its nature and the doubts, and I suspected his father's, but no one had ever confirmed either. Now, I knew. As I read the words, a wave of heat washed over me, reminding me that I have rarely worn self-assertion well. It's funny in an unfunny way: I have always censored myself for the comfort of others, having learned early that I can withhold my feelings more readily than I can contend with the adverse reactions they might elicit, but here was a reproach for a sentiment I did not know I should hold. I'm still that silent little girl in so many ways. I was angry at myself then, not for expressing myself, I realized, but for feeling wrong in doing it. I wasn't wrong. It was true. Abby was always wild and eager, but rarely depressed. She came home from California changed. It was a truth that unsettled all of us, including Ryan. Having said what troubled him, however, he changed the tone of his letter as it continued, almost contradicting himself and the boundary he had just established, which told me how bothered he was.

Besides that, I really love your letters and emails. I look forward to getting them. All those questions you sent got me thinking, and that's something I appreciate because there ain't much else to do most of the day. Please don't feel like you are overstepping any boundaries when writing or talking to me. I am a sponge for wisdom and advice, so I appreciate realness and deep conversations more than your average "how are you doing?" So, with that said, I'm an open book. Fire away! To answer your questions, I do hear from people back home more than I did at first, but it's only girls and no dude friends. It's funny because they all vent to me about every problem they have and ask for advice. I find that ironic considering my current residence. But I do offer whatever I can for them and encourage them to make decisions based on what they know and feel, not on my advice. My days go by pretty well now with being a trustee, but my nights are still crazy. I'm working on solutions for that, like starting a dream journal and wrapping my hands. (I had a really messed up dream the other night and busted my hands up on the wall in my sleep.) I will fix it before I'm out though. I know it. I've come further in the last two months than ever, and it excites me. And the question about life being better with Abby in my life or out, I honestly don't know. Easier? Definitely without her. I don't think about the betrayal daily anymore. I don't wonder if she's living right. I can focus on my issues instead of hers. I don't feel guilty about her spending money just to talk to me. My friends don't write or tell me sketchy things they see or hear about her when I call them. And I don't worry about being betrayed again because the person who betrayed me the worst in my life isn't in my life anymore.

Reading that last sentence struck me hard— "the person who betrayed me the worst in my life." She did a horrible thing, cheating with his friend, absolutely horrible, but the worst betrayal of his life? Was he talking about Abby or Derrick? It had to be Abby. But Abby was still in his life, even if only through me? And could something so common as cheating really be the worst? That made me think. Experience is so subjective, yet we are supposed to go out into the world and live collectively as individuals in a coherent society. But, we become individuals through our interactions with others who are equally unique and common. We are all wired the same way, for the most part, yet we have such trouble recognizing, understanding, and forgiving what is worst in ourselves, especially when we see it in others. How ironic that our own experience is the lens through which we must understand everyone else.

I wondered what emotions, what memories from his young life Ryan might have attached to Abby, like crossed phone lines, misdirected. I know Abby and Ryan had a deep connection. Abby felt truly seen by him, understood more than by anyone else, perhaps other than me, she said, which gave me far too much credit. Maybe he felt equally seen. Their childhoods could not have been more different, though. Really, I wasn't sure that Abby's had ended. She met him at seventeen. Was Ryan and all that came with him just that—an adolescent heartbreak, a lesson in growing up? Accepting that was difficult. Just as difficult was believing that their year-long telephone romance and handful of days together resulted in a connection whose break could hurt worse than the tumultuous past Ryan had lived before Abby arrived in his life. Worse than anyone in his life? Something in him, in the situation, something somewhere was misplaced.

The letter continued:

That is so much easier than attempting to fix something that hurts so bad physically and emotionally. I don't really feel wrong or right without her, just numb. But better? That's a question time is gonna have to answer for me. Love, to me, is measured by how much you have been through with a person, yet you continue your journey with them. Is it worth all the pain and suffering to get a treasure so scarce in life that lots of people die without it? Shit, I don't know. What I do know is that I'm willing to find out the only way I know how, the hard way. If in Abby's eyes I'm the person that she portrayed me to be in that letter you sent a while back, I believe a love like that may be worth it all. Thinking about that, I'd have to have lost myself as a person and forgotten my morals not to pursue that possibility. So better, easier, harder, worse, those aren't characteristics I can say just yet. But worth the struggle, I believe so. And thank you for telling me I'm a good man, even after everything and from your own opinion, not just what Abby said. You have gotten to know me a good bit, and I've always been honest with you. So, with that said, I'm letting you know that the letter I sent her asks if I can write to her again and if we can talk here and there. Like I said, I don't have answers yet, but I'd be crazy not to look for them. One last thing, my separation from the military is coming up in June, and I'd really appreciate it if you could send a copy of that character statement you sent my lawyer to my C.O. I told Abby all his information in her letter. Ms. Colleen, I appreciate you more than I can say. Love, Ryan Freeman

In the margin was the tiniest of postscripts. It explained that he might have the opportunity to take college classes once he was sentenced and in a federal prison—an opportunity I could hardly believe—and he wanted to know what I thought he would be good at in terms of a profession. I had no right to be proud of Ryan. I find the expression, "I'm proud of you," a bit odd, really, asserting some strange ownership or control over others, as if they owe you a certain decision. My influence in his life hardly entitled me to pride in him, but I was pleased to see him thinking about what life could become for him after all this. I was pleased that he saw past the day.

Chapter 28

Collective Magic

During my first semester of college, before I met Scott, I carpooled to U.N.O. with two friends who were also commuting. Greg had a 1979 Supra. It was 1987, and the little silver car, tiny rust spots along the hood, had seen better days. He called her Annie, after Annie Lennox, whose music we would sing along to thanks to the then-modern wonder of the cassette player.

Annie was temperamental in her old age, and would stall often at inconvenient places. We never knew if we would be stranded at the St. Claude Bridge, the train tracks on Claiborne, or any given corner where shady things happen in the glow of the city's traffic lights. We—me, Greg, and Katie, our third carpooler—took to chanting "Annie, Annie, Annie" as encouragement to the car whenever the engine died in hopes that it would start again. There was so much starting and stopping. We'd all pretend to be astonished when it started, as if some magic had occurred through our collective will.

That is the only way magic happens though, when people set their minds to the impossible, continuing to believe.

Greg kept that car for six more years—through college and graduate school. When he began working as an environmental research scientist, he finally bought a new one, but when I'd visit home after I got married, I would see Annie sitting in his mom's driveway, a monument to belief in impossible things.

That's how I felt with Abby and Ryan, too—as if I were part of some potential magic that needed everyone's attention now but would eventually settle into a well-earned rest. I knew time would change things, but I did not know how.

Abby's reaction to receiving Ryan's letter was nothing short of astonishment. Her eyes filled upon seeing it, and she reached for the envelope hesitantly, shy like a child who had been scolded before for snatching cookies but could have one now. Going upstairs to her room to read it, she called Opal, asking in her dog-voice, "Opes, what does this mean?" Not long after, Abby came down, Opal bounding behind her, no longer dressed in her black work clothes, but in her USMC sweatshirt, a show of commitment Ryan would never see. She told me that he did not suggest they rekindle a romance or commitment, but he did say he missed her, that whenever he recovered a new memory, she was the first person he wanted to tell, so he thought that must mean something important. He suggested they write and talk now and then. The prospect of it lit up Abby's eyes as she told me.

Ryan also said that his May court appearance, just days away from his writing the letters, seemed no more than a formality since his lawyer already knew the D.A. would not accept his plea of three years. The D.A. wanted no fewer than seven. The cop wanted the full thirteen, which seemed so ridiculous to me when rapists and murderers are out in fewer. I could not fathom how young men can serve their country, and in doing so, suffer events that create or exacerbate tremendous mental struggles, then when those disorders manifest, be abandoned by the system. We already knew Ryan had unknowingly suffered from PTSD since at least age fifteen, but I wondered, when he enlisted, were the screenings so superficial that his experience raised no red flags in terms of his emotional stability? Were the numbers rather than the fitness of recruits the primary concern? How did a disorder that has become so largely associated with military service go unnoticed at recruitment?

Later, after we had been writing for over two years and Ryan was applying for an upgrade to the character of his discharge, he explained to me that the enlistment process made sure he was a legal resident, passed a physical exam, took the ASVAB, and had a high school diploma. After that, they took him at his word, which included a brief history of family life. They thought he'd be fine. I suppose, given the horror stories they encounter in combat, his domestic struggles posed few concerns. Besides, at the age of eighteen, having navigated three years with little guidance, Ryan believed he was fine. What strong-willed eighteen-year-old doesn't?

In any case, he had asked me if I would send the character witness letter to his commanding officer for his military separation proceedings in June. Just shy of fulfilling his contract, his civil arrest would likely result in a dishonorable discharge—a felony and a dishonorable discharge, all for a night he couldn't even remember. It seemed so wrong. His service was unimpeachable according to his CO, at least as far as Abby found out. Ryan had asked her if she would write something, too, if she wanted to. Of course, she did, and she wrote honestly, almost blatantly, about all that had happened, not just according to what she knew of the night of his arrest, but also between them. Reading her words reminded me that so much of my opinion of Ryan came directly from her love for him, and her love for him was obvious in every word she wrote. It broke my heart to hear her believe in someone else so much more than in herself, and now, I am overcome with guilt in knowing that I fostered that lack of belief.

Abby, as I've said, has always been such a handful—my wild, compassionate dark-haired angel. How many nights did she wish to lose all that she felt too intensely within a haze of forgetfulness, the relief as ephemeral as the smoke? And how often did I know and berate her rather than pry to discover the pain, the real cause of it. Once I uttered words so hurtful I cannot now recall how I summoned the anger through which I spit such venom.

Abby had always said I was her best friend, a role I'd now accept with hesitation, knowing that being her mother puts me at odds sometimes, but she said it, I think, as an expression of her love for and trust in me—words meant to go beyond "I love you." Children are not obliged to befriend their parents, after all. After one of her late night, no-call, no-text episodes, she came home to my ire. I told her that we would never have been friends if I were her age, and we're not friends now. Her habits were nothing I wanted a part of, and, most regretfully, I continued with this: "With the way you are going, you better hope you are good enough for Ryan when he gets out!" Writing that, hearing it in my mind as I tap the words across the keys, hurts so badly. How could I have said it? How could a mother be so hurtful? How does anyone ever love correctly? We can't recapture those bullets. In the end, if anyone loves us, it is clearly despite our failings.

Reading the letter Abby wrote for Ryan reminded me of all she had been working so hard to suppress over the last six months. Her words did not capture past feelings, though. They were as fresh as the moment in which she wrote them.

May 2, 2017

To Whom It May Concern,

My name is Abby Hildebrand, and I am writing this character witness on behalf of Ryan Freeman. I have known Ryan for almost two years. I am well-aware of the charges Ryan is facing, as well as the potential repercussions of his actions. I believe it is in your best interest to know that I was his significant other—well, as significant as I could be, considering the circumstances-of distance and casual commitment-at the time of his arrest. Ryan came into my life in December of 2015 while on leave after he had returned from an eight-month deployment with the Marine Corps. When I met this man, I was dumbfounded. We met at a local gym, then went out for sushi later in the week. He was a complete gentleman to me and the server, an important detail to me, and offered to pay for my meal, which I didn't allow him to do. I truly did not believe that people like him still, if ever, existed in this world. He lights up any room he's in. He was polite, yet playful. Sensitive, yet strong. Stern, yet still so loving. And above all else, he was unapologetically himself. That is ultimately what made me fall in love with him.

Ryan and I continued to contact one another when he went back to California, where he was stationed, for the next few months. During that time, he opened up to me about some of the events he had gone through growing up in what would become a literal burned down, broken home. He told me things humbly, genuinely wanting me to learn who he was, never in hope of my giving him sympathy. From finding his mother shot in the head on the kitchen floor at age fifteen to holding a mattress over a bathtub full of people while a tornado destroyed the house around them, Ryan has suffered from more extreme trauma than I've ever heard of a single person experiencing. The craziest part? He smiles, laughs, and cares more than anyone else I know. He does his best to turn every situation into something positive, whether that be a lesson learned or making someone smile just because he loves them and is good at doing that.

In mid-March of 2016, I got a phone call from Ryan one Friday morning. I remember being confused as to the chosen time; he knew my schedule, therefore knew that I was in class. I told my teacher it was important, and she allowed me to answer it outside the classroom. "Hey darlin'...I'm goin' home," I heard him mutter. Not knowing exactly what he meant, still slightly puzzled, I replied, "Oh, well that's good. Maybe you can catch up on sleep!"

Ryan has always had problems sleeping since I've known him, and apparently prior to that as well. "No, like I'm goin' HOME, Daddy's dead," his voice broke, then all I heard were sobs. I had no idea what to think. I felt so sorry for him. I felt his pain so deeply, and although I had never met his father, tears streamed down my cheeks. Ryan is the strongest person I have ever met, and I had never heard him cry before. It was the saddest thing I had ever heard; this guy's world just never seemed to stop falling apart.

The week and a half of his time at home, Ryan did his best to be strong. He stayed at my parents' house the first night and a few nights after that, despite never making their acquaintance before. The March flash floods in Louisiana really damaged his home, which was in bad shape already, and he had nowhere else to go. I was more than appreciative of my parents' hospitality. I cannot explain how much of a relief it was to know he was safe, comfortable, and able to sleep after being awake for a consecutive 72 hours. While he was home, Ryan had a gathering mainly of his close friends one night. The next morning at the gas station, I discovered all my cash had been stolen from my wallet. Without hesitation, Ryan went inside the gas station to the ATM and came out with the whole amount I was missing. He said it was his responsibility because it happened at his house with his friends. He gave me money of his own that he really couldn't afford to give away and refused to accept it when I tried to give it back to him. I had never met someone so generous and so quick to take blame for others' mistakes. He continues to be the most thoughtful person I know.

Our relationship continued throughout summer and early fall, with my California trips on occasional long weekends and his homecoming in October. Each time we were together, I saw so much love in him. He is truly the most compassionate person I know. He will talk to absolutely anyone without judgment yet isn't afraid to stand up for his beliefs or convey his positive attitude when he's given the opportunity. His confidence is so inspiring. He encouraged aspects of my personality that I had hidden away because I was afraid. He tested me. He genuinely wanted me to grow into my potential. He loved me in a way that cannot be described as anything other than Christ-like. The way he tells stories, the way he genuinely loves teaching people how to do things, the way he looks at the people he loves are all evidence of how—despite his rough past—Ryan continues to try his best. I came to know Ryan in a different way from how anyone else has known him, and I know he will attest to that. Little did I know what was to come.

When I received news of Ryan's incarceration and the allegations against him, I felt more emotion than I ever had in my entire life. Ryan was, and continues to be, the strongest person I know, but he was not and is not perfect. He used alcohol and sex as coping mechanisms in order to maintain his pleasant composure. He was always "the life of the party." The lifestyle he had lived for eight years and had become so used to led to his poor decisions that night. Obviously, as his semi-significant other, I was heartbroken. I did forgive him, though, and tried to continue to be what he needed, as his actual girlfriend. Unfortunately, awful circumstances of my own led to Ryan's breaking up with me. Ryan had one other girlfriend before me, a high school sweetheart. Although I have never met her, I have heard that she was incredibly abusive. From breaking bottles on his head to putting cigarettes out on his face, she scarred him physically and emotionally. I've heard stories of her punching him as hard as she could, and Ryan would just stand there and take it, never laying a finger on her. She eventually left him and married the guy who was always a problem in her and Ryan's relationship. Ryan has trust issues when it comes to relationships because of this, and I was not strong enough to prove his hesitations wrong. We broke up because I had been careless with his feelings. Since then, our relationship has completely changed. Ironically, it has become stronger.

Since February, I have seen Ryan become the true definition of a man. He chose to forgive me for what I had done—not easily, but he has. He has given at least our friendship a second chance after I gave him the same. He turned to the Bible, humbled himself, and sought guidance as to how to live and love according to Jesus Christ. I am aware that everyone has their religious preferences, but I honestly believe despite this, love and forgiveness are the ultimate messages. Being a firm believer in Jesus Christ, over the past 9 months, I have seen God work miracles through Ryan. He has given himself fully to what he believes is right and just, regardless of the consequences. In doing that, he has been able to recognize blessings when they come and has developed great spiritual maturity. Ryan has been able to overcome so many of his greatest trials, mainly stemming from his childhood. He has opened up his heart to what hurts and has received the help of God's word and love. He has been able to put pieces together and come to understand himself and the denial he had lived in for so long. Frankly, I couldn't be more proud of him.

Ryan is clearly not perfect, but I do believe he has come further, regardless of his circumstances, than most free men do in a lifetime. The wisdom he has gained and the self-reflection he has done is incredibly admirable. He sincerely wants to be successful and receive any help he can. I talk to him *weekly, if not more, and know that not only has he become a better man, but he has also helped the men he lives with better themselves. He began a workout plan for them. He reads them scripture. He teaches them how to play guitar and draw. Ryan is a true leader. He understands the impact he has and could have on this world and wants nothing more than to fulfill that potential. In the time that I have known him, Ryan has demonstrated an uncommon ability to accomplish what he says he will. He puts thought into his actions and can truly achieve whatever he sets his mind to. We all have that ability, but he utilizes that quality more than most. He is genuine. He is rare. He is exceptional.*

I have been completely honest in all that I have said, and I pray that you take my words into consideration when making the decision on what to do with Ryan's life. He trusts you with it. I am not making excuses for what he did, but I do believe in mercy. A person is not defined by his mistakes, but by how he reacts to them. Ryan has and will continue to become a man of integrity by being accountable and always seeking improvement as he has proven over the past nine months. I have nothing but faith in him. Thank you for your patience in reading this. Please do not hesitate to contact me if I can answer any questions.

Sincerely,
Abby Hildebrand

As I finished Abby's letter, I knew that she had written it from a place of such emotional complexity that I could not bring myself to offer a single criticism of it, not that it deserved any. It was perfect. I could not hold my emotion, though, and as I spoke, my voice cracked, and I know she thought I was overcome with feeling because of him, because I had learned over the last six months that the seemingly impossible description of Ryan she offered was true, but that wasn't it at all.

It was because of her.

There, in that letter, were all her best qualities, too—her insight, her humility, her eloquence, her honesty, even hints of her joy, robbed from her by circumstances none of us understood. I wish, even today, she could see herself the way I do. I know all the other things, the less flattering things, too, but what does scripture say? Love covers a multitude of sins? Perhaps I am romanticizing her—them. Perhaps I am too involved. But, even now I recognize that Ryan was the single fact of Abby's life that brought her back to purpose. I wanted her to be that fact for herself. I wanted her to value herself so much more, but the hope and energy that hearing from and writing for Ryan rekindled in her was good to see. Seeing her come to life again, even momentarily, was a small miracle. It affected me oddly. I was thankful and uncertain, relieved—the kind of joyous relief you feel when a car that's stranded you at red lights in sketchy places suddenly turns over.

It made me believe in their magic.

Chapter 29

Snakes

As the end of the school year approached, life changed again. Abby lost her scholarship, as anticipated. Despite the financial loss, she followed through with the move, with Riley, into an apartment just off campus, increased her hours at the restaurant, and got a student loan for the fall. Needless to say, I was disappointed in the grades and her need for a loan, but something about the assertion of her independence seemed promising.

Scott, Jenna, and I moved Abby into her apartment—with its chipped countertop and sheetrock crumbling around the frame of the sliding glass door—on June first. It had two large bedrooms and a spacious living area, though, and the tile floor was certainly more pet-friendly for the small menagerie she would collect than carpet would have been. Of course, I'm not sure snakes care one way or the other.

That's how summer began—with the snake incident. It was ridiculous. I was at a curriculum workshop in mid-June when my phone began vibrating incessantly. I had deferred the call twice already, so on the third, I declined yet again and texted Abby to tell her would call her at lunch. She responded that she needed me "NOW!" So, I excused myself from the intriguing discussion of ACT-aligned texts and went outside to call my daughter back.

"Hey Mama. Oh my god, you aren't going to believe this," she began.

"What happened, love?" I could tell by her tone that whatever it was, was upsetting but not in the soul-crushing way some things affected her. I thought I might even hear amusement in her voice. I did.

"Okay, so you know my friend Vincent?"

"No."

She continued, "Whatever. Well, he has a ball python, and his girlfriend came in from Georgia this weekend, and she's afraid of it, so he asked me if I'd keep her here for the week—"

I cut her off, asking, "Wait, why would he want his girlfriend to stay—"

"No, Mom, not the girlfriend. The snake. She's a girl. Melody. Isn't that a sweet snake name? He's had her since he was fourteen." she digressed.

"So, you are babysitting Melody the ball python because Vincent's girlfriend from Georgia is afraid of her?" I clarified.

"Yes but wait. I have a big problem, like an almost five-foot long problem."

"Oh no, is it dead?"

"I hope not. She's loose in the apartment. At least I hope she's in the apartment. I can't find her."

"Abby! How do you lose a five-foot snake? Oh my gosh, the things that happen to—"

"I know, Mom! I don't know what to do!" She sounded somewhat desperate, but also somewhat entertained by the ridiculousness of the situation. I know I was.

"Well, clearly, you've looked everywhere—under beds, in cabinets, behind the washing machine and dryer, refrigerator—"

"Wait, actually I haven't looked there. Good idea... nope. She's not there." She continued calling "Melody" in a sing-song voice, as if a ball python would come slithering like a dog eager to get a treat.

"Abby!" I interrupted. "You have to tell Vincent. Maybe he can help you find her. You cannot sleep there tonight if you don't. I don't need you waking up in a python sleeping bag!"

"Mom, she's not going to eat me. Ugh, and I will. I'm gonna look more. I don't know how she got out of her aquarium last night. I put it in the bathroom and rolled up towels under the bathroom door, too, just in case she could flatten herself to get under. Do you think she could fit down the drain in the tub or sink?"

"I'm not well versed in snakes, love. I have no idea."

"Ugh, okay. I'm going to look a little more then call him, I guess. I'll let you know what happens. I love you. Bye, Mama."

"I love you, too, sweetie. And be careful!"

I wish I could say the snake incident was the most upsetting thing that happened that summer. It was resolved, though, just over a month later. After hanging up with me, Abby searched again, more thoroughly, and in the bathroom found a two-inch hole under the vanity cabinet along the baseboard.

She called her friend, who was surprisingly unupset by the ordeal. He explained that the lovely Melody had escaped before and would turn up in a few weeks when she got hungry. Meanwhile, she had probably slinked into the hole in the baseboard and snuggled up inside the wall, he said, which Abby relayed to me without a shred of the horror I felt. I wasn't scared of snakes. I'm respectful of them, knowing from which to keep my distance. My brother's snakes were the small varieties—king snake, corn snake, rat snake, snake from the canal across the street, but Melody was a Big Snake, a constrictor at that. The whole thing—a secret snake in the wall—seemed like a B-horror movie: The Co-ed in the Python Sleeping Bag. Or, as Michael put it, "That's some Harry Potter shit right there."

After a week, Abby bought two feeder mice to lure the snake out of the wall, but that went badly. After the mice survived the first night, she named them—Cotton and Lydia—and bought a cage, from which Lydia promptly escaped and was never seen again. Cotton lived to the ripe old age of eighteen months. And Melody, well, she surfaced in the corner of the den one night in July, about a month after her escape. She was coiled up and deflated on the tile, Abby said, looking more like a mottled green ribbon than a movie monster.

After the snake-phone-call curriculum workshop, I had no work-related responsibilities, and summer ended all those springtime social obligations, too. With my free time, I felt Abby's absence, though she had seldom been home while living here. Moving her was easy, having just a few items of furniture to bring to her new place, but not having her at home was harder than I expected. When Jenna moved out, I still heard from her nearly every day. Even now, she calls on her way home from work, when I get to hear her uncensored vocabulary explode into passive road-rage as she launches ineffectual obscenities at the Lulu lemon-wearing moms who cut her off on their way to yoga. No one would expect Jenna to be so foul-mouthed.

It's funny.

I often wonder if the parents of the teenagers I teach believe they do not use or hear foul language. I hear them hear it and use it, which is why, when a well-meaning, church-going mama calls me wanting an alternative novel for *Slaughterhouse-Five*—and that happens at least every-other-year—all I can do is shake my head and suggest *The Red Badge of Courage*, because, clearly, that mom wants the lie. I can always trust that parent's student to list *Slaughterhouse* as the best book he read in high school. I read and teach Vonnegut's novel differently now. Post-traumatic Stress Disorder became an official diagnosis of the American Psychiatric Association in 1980, eleven years after *Slaughterhouse's* publication, and after centuries of soldiers suffering from a condition once classified only as "unsteady nerves" rendering recruits unfit to serve. But, PTSD is not a condition confined to the military. Ryan's, like so many other cases, began at home.

Childhood trauma is too often disregarded, but people who have suffered abuse, neglect, abandonment, the death of a loved one, divorce, or any combination of the ten indicators on the Adverse Childhood Experiences test can count on additional difficulties as an adult—anything from addiction to cardiovascular disease, according to Harvard Medical and so many others. And we still don't take it seriously.

Ryan had lots of time to think about his life in jail, and at one point, after he completed his second round of court-ordered psychiatric testing, I sent him another book, Bessel Van der Kolk's *The Body Keeps the Score*. He had asked for something that would help him understand PTSD better, so I googled and read reviews of several books, but most were either too combat-oriented or too self-helpy. This one, though, seemed to cover everything from history and science to therapy. I ordered one for myself and another for Abby, too. Through reading it, I began to understand not only Ryan, but everyone I have ever known better, myself included. I had never considered myself a traumatized person, but I realized through reading that trauma is not dependent solely on what happens to us. Sometimes it is what we do to ourselves. It is the story we tell ourselves about what has happened, or it is the story we fail to tell, allowing experience to settle into our bodies and be remembered in sudden sweats, racing pulses, flushed cheeks, cramped stomachs, and vagal responses.

When I was six years old, my mom left my father in charge of me while she enjoyed the day at the ballpark playing in a ladies' recreational softball league. He and I both loved animals, so we mostly spent the day outside with our two dogs, Bandit and Midnight. Midnight was a Labrador retriever, and Bandit, Midnight's son, resulted from a tryst with Daisy, the neighbor's golden retriever. No small dog, Bandit allowed my six-year-old self to believe I could control him—most of the time. On this day, I convinced my dad to let me walk him outside of the yard, just on the porch and carport, on his leash. I wound it around my tiny wrist, pretending Bandit was a horse on a lead rope as I walked in circles under the carport, pretending to give an imaginary friend a pony ride. What happened next did not register with me as trauma until I read *The Body Keeps the Score*.

I think the phone rang, so my dad went inside. The neighbors had just gotten a new puppy, and they had just let it outside. Bandit must have lunged and run toward their yard, and I couldn't untangle the leash. All I really remember is tasting the blood in my mouth, going in through the side door, seeing my dad drop the phone, and saying, "I'm sorry, Daddy." The next thing I remember is the emergency room, the shots to deaden the pain, which were excruciating as they pierced my gums and inner cheeks, and the almost-numb feeling of the stitches as the needle weaved in and out of the inside of my lower lip. I was not allowed to look in a mirror for at least two weeks, not until the swelling from the broken nose and black eyes went away.

Because of that accident, I no longer have a lower frenum, that little line of tissue that connects your lips to your gums. In 2016, I learned that the head injury I suffered in 1975 may be the culprit behind a tiny unruptured brain aneurysm I have now, located just behind my left eye. When it was diagnosed, the doctor wanted to be sure it was not about to burst, so I had a post-dural puncture, pretty much the same as a spinal tap. I passed out. Then, I had an epidural blood-patch procedure to stop the massive headaches caused by the loss of cerebrospinal fluid through the puncture. I passed out again. I also passed out when I had epidural cortisone shots for a slipped disc when I was thirty-three. After the dog-fiasco, I suddenly became anemic from ages six to eight. Once a month at first, I had to have a finger-prick blood test. Guess what would happen. I'd pass out.

I am not afraid of dogs at all, quite the opposite, and I am not consciously afraid of needles, but my vagus nerve is. Trauma isn't always what happens to us or what we do.

It is what the body remembers.

It is the fingerprints of one nurse squeezing your chin in her hands to hold it still while the other injects foot-long needles into your jaw. It is the same nurse saying, "Don't cry," as the doctor sews your mouth back together. For some, it is the imprint of the open hand across a cheek, a closed fist to the gut, the churning of the hungry stomach in an empty house, the last look or word of a brother, a father, a mother before the life goes out. It is the story we tell ourselves—or fail to. It is how we internalize it.

Even before receiving the book, Ryan put a lot of thought into his PTSD. He saw a therapist, whom he described as willing to listen depending on the day. If there had been no attacks or suicides among the inmates that day, he would have a more productive session. He actually made more progress through journaling. He uncovered memories, made connections, and thought through his life with a sober mind. I continued to email him, periodically checking in about his sleep, asking questions about his motivation and hopes, telling bad jokes—Why shouldn't you hang out around trees? They're shady— and offering to send reading materials of whatever kind he'd like. I found and ordered *The Body Keeps the Score* after receiving this letter in response:

May 14, 2017

Dear Ms. Colleen, First off, I want to apologize for this yellow paper. It was white but I laughed so hard at your joke, well, you get the idea. Haha, that's kinda gross, huh? But you're right. You do have an excellent sense of humor. Secondly, if you can find a book on mental illnesses, PTSD, symptoms, triggers, dreams, and anything similar to what I'm going through, I'd love to read that. The novel you sent me a while back, is on the inmate favorites list now, by the way. Third, what motivates me? Negativity. That may sound crazy, but it's true. People telling me "it'll never work, you can't have that, you can't do that, it's harder than it looks, you'll just be a statistic, the odds are against you, you can't afford that, it's impossible" has always driven me to prove them wrong in the most perfect way. Maybe I'm just stubborn, but I'll never admit defeat to anything. I'll just keep trying everything I can until I find a way that works. Then I'll find a way to perfect it, plus some. As for my hands and my sleep situation, I am working extremely hard to figure out what triggers me at night. When I'm awake, I've noticed a few triggers. Digital green numbers, doors slamming, lights flashing or flickering, the outside phone ringing. The other day I freaked out because I walked into the day room, looked at the T.V. and saw a girl shoot herself directly in the face with a shotgun. I accidentally flipped my chair over and started shaking really bad. That's happened three times, the flashback type things when I actually lose my sense of what's happening in real time around me. Unconsciously though, I believe that dates, times, daytime experiences, tastes, and smells are triggering my nightmares. My mama died on the eighteenth of August, Daddy on March 18, I got arrested on November 18, and 18 has pretty much popped up in horrible life memories many times. I notice I have bad dreams around those days of the month. I found Mama at 1:58 (green digital numbers on the stove), and I usually wake up around 2 a.m. on bad nights. The smell of dry wall or wet paint adds in because I hit my wall after finding Mama and it had just been painted. If I have a busted lip, I have nightmares, too. I'm certain that's because of the smell of all the blood, so much that you could taste iron in the air. So, I'm trying really hard to figure it out and avoid the triggers that I can. Please let me know if I'm oversharing because I know it's not an easy subject considering it's not a movie. You are the only person I've shared that with because I feel crazy trying to figure out ways to stop dreaming and keep my thoughts from drifting. But I guess that's that. That's where I am for now. I know you didn't ask, but I bet you are wondering about me and Abby. She wrote me back. I miss her so much, but I got so much figuring out about me to do right now, I've been waiting to call her til I feel a little steadier. But tell her I think about and pray for her every day. Thank you for complimenting my insight on love. Did you and Mr. Scott have any big problems? Maybe I shouldn't ask that. Sorry. I remember all the problems mama and Daddy had. They had big ones. From drugs, cheating, beating on each other, emotional abuse, trying to turn us against the other, hiding in hotels, women's shelters, Daddy pulling a gun on everybody, patching bullet holes in the car, and finally getting divorced when I was 12. They had issues. But I sure as hell loved them. Although I loved them, they 100 percent taught me how not to be an adult in a marriage. Haha, I'm too much of a romantic type for all that Bonnie and Clyde shit. You and Mr. Scott were great examples for Abby by the way. I'm glad her knowing me helped her appreciate y'all more. It was funny when you said that. I laughed hard because I wasn't expecting how you said it. And honestly, Ms. Colleen, thank y'all so much for not hating me for everything that's happened in the short time you've known me. For all the bad between me and Abby, you've offered nothing but good advice for both of us. Thank you for all the prayers, emails, letters, drawings, books, character statements, advice, insight, and entertainment over the past ten months. I know my parents would thank you if they could, but I'll do it for them. I've hit the reset button so many times in my life and you kinda helped me realize I just need to move forward with everything instead of restarting and trying to leave it behind. I don't know if that's what you were trying to do, but that's what happened anyway. I may have less right now than I have ever had in my life, but things I do have are worth more than any dollar amount. And I'm learning how to deal with it without my parents' weaknesses. Haha, that's crazy to me. They were the strongest people I know, but they gave up before God could show them how their life's achievements would become themselves. I'll never give up. Whoa, that was intense to write. Anyways, I love you, and I will find a way to thank y'all for everything y'all have given me. From a place to sleep to a hell of a lot of hope, y'all have given me so much. Love, Ryan Freeman

Reading Ryan's letter broke my heart, too. He hadn't said anything I had not already known, but he said it all for the first time. I couldn't imagine his life, or more accurately, I couldn't imagine how he could emerge so positively from that life. He was an exception, not a statistic. I believe it was Einstein who said that there are only two ways of seeing the world: as if everything is a miracle or as if nothing is.

Ryan saw miracles.

He saw the necessity of finding connections, of revisiting the past to find present meaning, of finding beautiful things deep in the pain of memory to protect him from feeling it all again and again. He already understood what I wanted Abby to learn for herself—that everything is connected, that our own experience is the only lens through which we can understand others. I wanted her to understand that ignoring experience would leave her less prepared for whatever came next—ignorant. She was pretending to do well, with work if not school, which had become a slow slide downhill since her first semester. But, she still was not ready, not to talk, not to me, anyway. She still would not talk about December beyond saying it was too complicated and hurt too much. Even as she expanded the parameters of her physical life, moving out and meeting new friends, she constricted her emotional self. I knew her broad and shallow meanderings could not shield her from pain.

That is what Ryan was learning.

He had not plumbed his own depths until the circumference of his life had been reduced to the size of a dime.

I did not want such forced reflection to teach Abby. I wanted her to choose it. I wanted her to breathe life in knowingly, intentionally, and not be coiled so tightly in self-deception.

Chapter 30

Saying I Love You

We all come into ourselves at different paces as we discover who we are. I have always felt grounded in myself, never really succumbing to the crowd, in fact, feeling quite excluded most of my life. That was okay with me. I have always been more of an observer than a participant. Observing is its own form of participation.

I myself have been my chief subject of study, so I know when I married Scott, I was just a girl. I may have been more emotionally mature than my years suggested, but I was as green as clover in experience and more intuitive than wise. I am fortunate that Scott tolerated my learning through mistakes. Fear, then, kept me quiet about so much. I don't know what I believed would happen if I spoke up, asking to turn the car's air conditioner off so I wasn't freezing or sending a too-rare steak back to the kitchen, or other, bigger things, but I didn't speak up for a long time. I was a quiet, compliant child and teenager. It was the memory of my father's anger or the risk of rejection or humiliation that kept me silent. But when I found Scott, I found my voice, too. In many ways, he drew it from me. He will laughingly tell you that I am not the shy girl he married—still reserved, but also a "ball buster," as he endearingly describes me. He says I'm blessed with the ability to invoke guilt simply by telling people the truth about themselves. I don't make a habit of it, at least not with strangers, but sometimes it's necessary.

A man who lives in the neighborhood has made a habit of speaking to—well, yelling at—me when he sees me running. Usually, he calls "Why so slow?" or "Fail any kids lately?" Once, he made a comment about his daughter-in-law's body fat percentage in comparison to mine. Hers was lower. Another time, as I ran past him and another neighbor talking outside their homes, he quipped, "Pick up the pace!" and started clapping, punctuating his specious encouragement with a whistle, not a lewd one, but the type a wrangler might use as he shoos cattle through a chute. So, recently, as he slithered up, slowing his car and rolling down his window to launch what he believed were completely innocent words at me, I told him that sometimes, just waving would be fine, that more often than not, I found his comments negative and offensive, and that I was telling him this because I knew he was unaware of it and that although he meant to be friendly, he was a bit behind the times. The sight of me was not an invitation to bravado. I said it nicely but firmly, and he understood. He apologized and was embarrassed. I saw it in his eyes. I felt rather bad for him, but not too much. He has not said more than hello to me since, which is fine. Years ago, I would not have said a word—didn't say a word in worse situations.

I know who I am today, my worth, but learning it was filled with missteps. Does anyone grow through success? I know we grow toward it, but it seems that any value in learning comes through adversity, proving all the platitudes true. I wanted Abby to know, as Ryan was discovering, that meeting adversity head on—revisiting it on your terms—could settle months of restless nights, but I knew she would have to discover that for herself. No one can teach anyone anything. Learning, while not a completely singular act, depends far more on the learner than on the teacher, and often the most meaningful lessons occur when the dialogue between teacher and learner occurs in a single mind.

Summer moved along at a clip too brisk for me, always reminding me that August would bring back imposed responsibilities and schedules. September would bring a sentence, or so we thought. Once again, Ryan's sentencing was delayed, but this time, it was because of his decisions. He finally called Abby, which I learned when he called me one afternoon as I took Opal on her second walk of the day. Well, technically, her first, since her first "walk" was really a run. Abby became even more scarce in my life when she moved, and I tried to respect the space between us, but occasionally, a letter or rare phone call from Ryan would fill me in on occurrences I had not yet learned of from her. When I saw the San Diego number on my phone, I answered expecting the recorded message to play, but after saying "hello," I heard Ryan's voice immediately. I was so confused.

"Ms. Colleen! Hey! It's Ryan. How are you doing?" he asked.

"Ryan! How are you calling me? Where are you?" I replied, ignoring his question and hoping that he was inexplicably free.

"I'm in jail," he laughed. "My supervising officer is letting me call from his office. I guess it's a perk of being a trustee."

"Wow, that's allowed?" I asked, thinking I'm sure it wasn't, not officially.

"I don't know, but he's in charge and said I could, so here I am. Listen, I was hoping to talk to you and Mr. Scott about two things, well you about two, and I wanted to get his opinion on one, too," he explained.

"Okay, I'm out walking Opal right now, but I'm not far from home. He's there, so we can talk about the one now and when I get back, the other. What's going on?"

"Have you talked to Abby recently? As in the last two days?"

"I have not."

"Well, I have. I called her Thursday night and we talked for forty-five minutes before some other guy had to use the phone. It was good. God, I miss her." He paused.

"I think she misses you, too. But as you know, she doesn't ask me much and I don't tell unless she does. I'm glad that it went well." I said, not really knowing what else to say.

Then he asked, "Ms. Colleen, do you think I still think about her so much because I haven't really seen another woman in the last, what, nine or ten months? Or is it because of her, just her?"

I hesitated for a moment before saying, "That's part of it, I'm sure, not meeting anyone else in so long. But, you have known and heard from lots of other women before and during the last ten months. It makes sense that she's the most prominent in your memory because she's the last relationship you had begun, but as far as what you feel for her, I can't say. It isn't my place to, but you know what you've felt for others before. Only you know how it compares."

"You're right. It doesn't compare. I reckon I just have to figure out why. Ms. Colleen, I've got so many things to figure out, it ain't even funny," he said. Then he laughed.

"I know you do, and I am completely confident that you will. You've done so much of the hard work already. Most people avoid it all their lives. Always running," I offered.

"Well, ain't nowhere to run in a cell," he quipped, sounding more Southern than usual. Then more seriously, he added, "Being locked up gives you lots of time to think, and I think about Abby a lot. I just wish that stuff wouldn't have happened."

"You mean with your friend, ex-friend, right?" I clarified.

"Yes, ma'am. Did I tell you he came to see me?" he said, with a note of indignation, maybe annoyance, in his voice.

"Oh my gosh, no! You didn't tell me," I reacted.

"Yeah, this guy comes in here and I'm expecting an apology or something, but he starts talking about how we, me and him, were always the alphas and it was inevitable that something like that would happen, like if she liked me, she'd like him better or something. It pissed me off real bad."

"What did you say?" I asked.

"I told him to get the fuck out of my life, excuse my language. I mean, when Abby told me, she was crying and sorry and owned her part of it. He, I don't know what he was doing, but it wasn't apologizing or taking responsibility. It felt like a competition. That dude is fucked up."

"Sounds like it," I said. "But let me ask, where does that leave you with Abby? I mean, in trusting her? You had said once that you didn't think you could again. Is that still the case?"

"That is something I don't know yet. I do know I trust her a hell of a lot more than him, than a lot of people. We talked about it a little when I called her, and I told her he came here. She got kinda quiet then called herself a slut. Then I got quiet," Ryan said. He went on to confess that right after it happened, he had called her—not just once—and said awful things to her. Then, he continued, "Ms. Colleen, she was just repeating what I said months ago, and I'm sorry. I was so hard on her, and I was even more wrong for making you think I wasn't," he admitted. "I can't believe she never told you."

"She didn't," I paused, thinking quickly of how he must have berated her, and some of her behavior of the last six months made more sense. I know my tone became colder. "I'd be lying if I said that doesn't upset me now. She hasn't been right since that episode. I hate hearing you were part of the mob, but I, I should have known. I mean, you were the victim in all of it. That explains a lot. I wish I had known. She must not have had anyone there for her through it. How didn't I...." My voice trailed off a little.

"I'm sorry. I should have told you. I really thought she would, but then you never said anything to me, and I reckon I was being selfish. I really liked having you there for me. I thought if you knew, you wouldn't be there anymore. I've told her I'm sorry, too. I think I was just so angry, not just about that whole thing but about being told I had so much making up to do for things I did before she told me. And about things that have nothing to do with her if I'm honest. I'm working on lettin' all that go," he finished.

He was right. It would have changed my attitude toward him.

Thoughts rushed. After what seemed longer than the second it was, I said, "But Ryan, I thought you said it was a good conversation?" I spoke flatly, feeling blindsided by my own naivety.

"Oh, it was! I told her it was over, that I forgave her, and I reminded her of all the amazing things that make me love her, because I do. I just don't know how I love her yet. We even talked about her coming out here again after all that," he said.

"Really? When?" I asked.

"Well, that's the other thing I wanted to talk to you and Mr. Scott about, my sentencing. She wants to come for it."

"Well, I am home now. I've been sitting on the porch for the last ten minutes. Do you want me to get him?" I asked, not sure I wanted the conversation to go on.

"Wow, we've been talking a while, huh? I should go so I don't get anybody in trouble or something, but I'm gonna call back soon. Is there a good time?" he asked, to my relief.

"We are home every day, sometimes all day in the summer. He goes to the gym but is back by three o'clock, so any time after that. Or in the morning. We're up early." I explained.

"Okay," Ryan said, "I'll give y'all a call next week. Thanks for talking to me, Ms. Colleen. Thank you for everything." He sounded so sincere. "And Ms. Colleen, I love you."

I had read those words from Ryan many times, but I had never heard them. His saying them jarred me slightly, especially because I was upset with him.

The words "I love you" had never come easily to me, though the feeling they expressed did. Ryan said them effortlessly, almost too easily, being the kind of person who believes they should be dispensed liberally because so many people need to hear them and because love can take so many forms, but I was never like that. My love was partnered with my trust in a person, and I was skeptical of most people. I, even in my fifties, was still learning to say "I love you" to people outside of my immediate family. My mom was remarried for ten years, yet I never said, "I love you" to "Papa," the only grandfather my girls remember. But I do love him. I rarely said it to my sister, though I love her dearly. I tell my mom, Scott, my girls all the time, maybe too much. It never occurred to me that I would say "I love you" to anyone else.

In that moment, when Ryan said, "I love you," my entire emotional history—from the origin of my difficulty expressing love to my need for recovery from it—became clear to me.

"You're welcome, Ryan. I'll be looking forward to hearing from you again. Stay safe and be smart, okay?" That was the best I could do at the time.

"Yes, ma'am. You, too. Bye now."

"Goodbye, Ryan." I wondered if he noticed I had not said it. I felt bad, but I was upset with him for allowing me to believe he had behaved more selflessly toward Abby than he had. I later emailed him to explain my disappointment and my lack of response to his offered love. When speaking fails, me, there is always writing.

Before he had a chance to call again, Abby told Scott and me that the other issue Ryan wanted to speak to us about was his plea deal. She came over to visit after her brunch shift the Sunday after he and I spoke. I told her he had called and even told her he talked about the Derrick situation. I also

173

told her about his confession, but she asked few questions and volunteered little commentary on that subject. She did confirm that he said some hurtful things. She also fully explained his court date in September would probably not be a sentencing because he was considering rejecting the plea deal and putting everything in the hands of the judge, "pleading the sheet," as he said it is called. She said he would tell us more when he called, and although he wanted to know what we thought, he was fairly certain he had decided to do it. She added that she respected his reasoning in making the choice. She also told me she wanted to go see him, that in the months without him she had met no one who interested her beyond a night, and she just felt empty without him.

I didn't know what to think. I didn't know what was right or wrong to say. I just knew I believed her, believed the intensity of what she felt, of what he felt, too, in all its confused emotion. I had no advice for anyone, having lived so differently, but I empathized, quite literally feeling the pain of the situation and wanting the outcome I wanted but also wanting to leave every decision to them. In my stereotypical-mom moments, I knew how crazy my hoping for a son-in-law with a felony was, but with every letter or phone call, I grew to respect—to love—something new about Ryan. I grew to love him like a son.

That proved complicated, but I managed. Mostly, I wanted Abby to know I understood. We talked that afternoon. She even walked Opal with me in the July heat, and she and Scott watched a scary movie together before she went home to her apartment, where the long-hidden constrictor would be waiting huddled in the corner, having finally emerged from the interior.

After she left, I sat with my thoughts, imagining her thoughts, and wrote a poem in my notes on my phone. I read and reread it before texting her:

> Hey love. I'm so glad you came over today. I hope I wasn't too intrusive when we talked. I love you so much, and I want what you want for yourself, which I hope is what is best for you. Thinking about all you said, I wrote this:

Pagan
I see and understand yet am powerless
To control a single choice
Except my own
I see myself standing by
Humbled by the intensity
Between you
And holding tears behind closed eyes
Because I know,
Because I have already seen—
Because I feel— too much.
You are the story I want to write
The raw experience of life unrestrained
Wild in your need to know what there is
That will satiate your craving for
All there is
And keep you hungry—
An appetite made more intense
By what satisfies it…
And I know the answer,
As do you
It is him.
He is the wild in you that calms
Your soul
He is the loneliness
Of being in any other's arms
He is the urgency of every epiphany
And the only comfort in any wrong
He is the truth
That renders every other an idol—
Hollow and able to draw no more
Than a pagan Hallelujah
From your lips.

After sending it, some time passed before a response came. All it said was, "It's perfect, Mama. I love you."

Chapter 31

Empath

As promised, Ryan called the next week and explained he would submit an open plea. He told us he had no question about his guilt, but he didn't think he deserved seven years for it. He thought his chances would be better with the judge's decision, but he also realized that thirteen years was still the high end of his possibilities. He was willing to risk it. We listened and agreed that with his time served and good behavior his chances were good. Then, he thanked Scott and me for talking to him, and before hanging up, said, "I love y'all." Scott, cut from the same cloth, said, "We love you, too, man," without hesitation.

Abby absolutely wanted to go to California in September, but as I'm sure you can understand, I had reservations about it. In the weeks well before she went, not that Scott and I could really stop her, she lobbied that she would not be going alone, but with Ryan's aunts, one who lived here and one who lived in South Carolina, and his brother. For Abby, the idea of seeing Ryan again fell somewhere between encountering the Ghost of Christmas Past and witnessing the second coming of Jesus. One afternoon as we sat at opposite ends of the daybed with Opal between us, she asserted that she knew nothing like before could ever happen again. Her saying that led me to probe. As gently as possible, I asked, "I know you didn't plan to have a lapse in judgment the last time. And, I am not trying to upset you by asking this, but how can you be sure you'll be okay?"

She didn't look up at me, but at the dog, petting her speckled coat, but she said, "Mom, trust me. I am sure. Positive. I am not that naive anymore. And, I would be staying in the same Airbnb as his aunts and brother, so no one would even be there to do something like that."

I replayed words in my mind—"naive," "do something like that"—I found them odd choices, so I asked her, "What about the last time made you see yourself as naive?"

All she gave in response was, "Lots of things I don't want to talk about."

With her reluctance came her impatience. I was always pressing for more than she was willing to give. I learned to curb that. I told myself that she was here spending time with me, for which I was thankful, so I had to learn not to nag. I did not want to make her anxious about coming home to visit, dreading an always-waiting interrogation within minutes of walking through the door. I resisted my impulse to delve into her word choices further, and let it go, saying, "Just promise me you will call me every day you're gone."

"I will," she responded, dragging a rather large Opal into a bear-hug, asking her with her most annoying dog-voice, "Who's dat bihggg gurhl?" repeatedly.

Once Abby made her San Diego plans for September definite, she and Ryan began writing again throughout the summer, tightening the knot that had never really been released between them. My dad used to say there are silver cords that pass through the air unseen, tethering souls to certain other souls. I had not thought about these cords much growing up, not until I felt something electric flash in me when I met Scott, surrounded by that halo of perfect light—which he later told me was smoke (He dropped his cigarette when he saw me). I was absolutely struck. I fell so hard and fast and later felt, even through troubled times, that I could never let him go. For all the ways in which we are total opposites, we work together. He is my match, attached by an unseen, silver cord. At least he is in my mind, and if I believe that, it just might make it true.

I know how odd that sounds, but as I've said, I only masquerade as normal, like everyone else. Sometimes, I really do think there's something to all the theories and conjectures, that the phenomena of science—quantum entanglement, for example—play out in human interactions. Too many coincidences occur for me to believe they have not been directed by our own energy. Since my crazy is beginning to show, I might as well tell you: I felt a little flash of something the first time I saw Michael, too, before I knew he was Jenna's Michael, when I was on campus completing my masters' courses and he ran by. I went to visit Jenna in her dorm after class, and not having met anyone of interest since breaking up with her first boyfriend over two years before, she whined to me that there were "no cute boys at this school." I told her, "I just saw one."

They met the next week. They are engaged now—and I swear, that's a true story.

As much as I did not want to admit it at the time, I felt the same small flash with Ryan, not when I saw him, but once, when Abby was still in high school, just after they met. She was sitting in the computer lab as I passed through, and instead of working on MathXL, she was drawing in her sketchbook. I looked over her shoulder and saw her filling a colored-pencil eye with shades of blue. That's when I felt it. I'm not even sure I realized it was his eye at the time.

I don't know if those little electric nudges in my mind mean a thing, but I feel them now and then, impulses from the ether. Who knows how who is connected to whom and what. There is, indeed, more between heaven and earth than we can imagine, connections unseen. I thought about Ryan's name: Y-A-R-N. Funny, he became a thread between me and Abby. Occasionally, he would send a letter for Abby to our house rather than to her apartment just so she would have to come get it. He knew I would enjoy seeing her.

Abby did go that September, and it was as good a trip as it could be. She said Ryan's aunts were lots of fun to be with, and they made her feel welcomed and appreciated. Travis, too, she said. Abby had always spoken well of Ryan's brother, saying that although Ryan could play the guitar and sing very well, it was Travis who was jaw-droppingly talented. She described him as a sweet guy, but she noted that on this trip, although they hiked and rented bikes together and had a good enough time, he was slightly cooler toward her. She knew why. Sometimes, people hold on to grievances in defense of those they love—even after those they love have forgiven.

They saw Ryan at every opportunity within the established visitation times over that weekend, going two at a time and trying to share the phone, but she also said his family gave her and Ryan some privacy, simply meaning that she saw him alone once (because true privacy is nonexistent in jail). Considering the guards and whoever monitors audio have more serious things to watch and listen for than a strained romance, she said he spoke freely to her, and she to him although there were a few topics she just didn't want to bring up. What that meant, exactly, I guessed at, but upon her return, they did stay in closer contact, with weekly phone calls and sporadic letters.

The Monday of her visit, the day of Ryan's court appearance, went well, according to Abby. His lawyer, Peter, as she referred to him, had consulted with Ryan about his plea deal, which he had indeed decided to reject, and told him that although the judge had not stated it directly, he believed she respected his decision.

Shortly after Abby returned from California, my weekly email to Ryan straightforwardly asked if the trip had been as good as Abby said it was. She had received just a few nasty comments from some of Ryan's social media crowd when she posted pictures, provocative silhouettes, from her San Diego hotel room. The pictures were artsy and edgy, but in truth, I wasn't thrilled about them. They were also immodest, Abby's specialty of late. She had become quite good at hiding her thoughtful, inquisitive self behind her body. She made it easy for others to make assumptions, and I wished she didn't.

Regardless of appearances, I will never understand how some people believe they have the right to condemn what they do not know so harshly. They knew a single story about Abby: She was Ryan's girlfriend. She cheated, and they knew that from a short-lived cyber-attack on her. As far as I knew, Ryan stayed in touch with few, if any, friends from Louisiana. But Abby had been right. After all the trouble in January, he did receive several letters, mostly from girls at home who were more than willing to lend their ears and other body parts as comfort and consolation to help him cope with Abby's egregious and public wrong. I have no idea whether he wrote back to any. As for Abby, she deleted the ugly comments and messages and blocked some users from her accounts. I thought it best not to include that gossip in my email.

September 19, 2017

Well, Ryan, how are you?The last week must have been just a little exhausting for you, emotionally at least.I probably assume too much,but I imagine seeing your brother and aunts, let alone Abby, must have been pretty far out of your regular routine,but I hope in a good way.I talked to Abby several times while she was gone, wondered if she was leaving things out, and was ultimately thankful that things seem to have gone well and that she made it home safely.Really, though I'm asking you:are things between y'all good?I certainly do not want to encourage delusions in her. She said she was buying a fake engagement ring! I told her not to be crazy, but hey, maybe you don't mind or even like the idea. And the crazy.Not my business—except maybe a tiny bit because I may or may not be paying the bills when she has to see a therapist about the possibly false reality she is building.Unless it's ok.She should see a therapist anyway. She always says no; she has me.You see how well that has worked. Ok, so new topic, sort of: this book still has me in amazement. When you get the letter I'm still writing (school has been so busy) you'll see my own brand of crazy. I'm full of theories. I think I somehow know things, which I probably don't, but thinking about possibilities and noticing synchronicities is fun to me. I will be a neuropsychologist eventually if reincarnation is real. I'm not smart enough for at least 2 or 3 more lives. But I'm working on it!So right now in school I'm teaching two of my favorite things: *Life of Pi* and *The Crucible*. I'm sure you've read those, but I seriously suggest another look with grown up, post-*The Body Keeps* eyes. I try my hardest to make 15 to17 year-olds get the depth of these works, but now I realize there is even more to get.Here's the gist: *Pi*—the miracle that should make people believe in God isn't that he survived; it's that he went on to live a peaceful life. It is his recovery from trauma through the story he tells. *The Crucible*: Abigail Williams has PTSD from childhood trauma and has histrionic personality disorder and John Proctor mildly traumatized himself by betraying his own values. He is the ultimate illustration of the difficulty of forgiving oneself and the importance of integrity. I know those ideas aren't lost on you. I've done pretty amazing things with that play some years. Maybe one day you can ask me if we're ever sitting somewhere not knowing what to say :) I know you're not a fan of any more fiction books, but sometimes fiction is more true than nonfiction. Good fiction is the truth of the human condition and always offers something valuable to think about. Of course, nonfiction does that too, but differently. Ok, I am just rambling now like I haven't done in a while, so I'll spare you the rest. I hope you are feeling encouraged about the future. I want a great one for you. <3 Ms.Colleen

The email didn't specify deeper reasons Abby might seek counseling, and I did not ask about my more serious worries concerning him, those that revolved around life threatening possibilities. The outcome of Ryan's "pleading the sheet" required yet another round of psychiatric testing, more thorough than the battery of tests conducted at the county jail. It required that he transfer to California Institution for Men, more commonly called Chino, after its location. Chino had a reputation. It had been the scene of riots in 2009 that left hundreds of inmates injured, and was a popular setting for films, most notably *American History X* and more recently *Shot Caller*, both movies that capitalize on the prison's culture of white supremacy. That wasn't good. Although Ryan had never given me a single reason to believe he had even a hint of racism in him, his blonde hair, blue eyes, and stature made him a poster-boy for the Aryan Nation or whatever such awfulness is called. I had so many concerns for him, I could not even bring myself to put them into words.

My concerns for Abby were also numerous—and constant. She was managing well on her own in terms of work and financial responsibility, but school continued to slip. She changed majors twice, from biology to education to psychology, but still, she had no idea of what she wanted to do. When she was a child, she was certain she wanted to be a vet, always collecting kittens, birds, dogs, once even a flying squirrel to save. I'm not sure of what became too hard: the reality that being a vet required so much education or that it required putting animals down sometimes. Abby has always been soft-hearted. In fact, as she's grown older, that compassion has extended to people. In high school, she loved volunteering at the Special Olympics events held in the football stadium each fall, and even when her friends, some of whom seemed so superficial to me, would gossip about or directly challenge her about anything—like Ryan—she needed little more than an "I'm sorry" to forgive them. Maybe I'm just mean, but I think she still forgives far too easily sometimes. I've never met someone who works so hard to have empathy for the "enemy," if those who attack are indeed enemies. Sometimes they are just injured friends.

Because of her ability to imagine another's pain, I should not have been surprised when, eventually, she told me that she had not mentioned Ryan's vituperative phone calls months back because she knew he was alone and angry, but angry about so much more than her behavior. She knew he just had to get it all out, and she thought she could bear it.

I doubted that.

Chapter 32

Clerical Error

Abby refused to talk to a therapist. She said she was fine, and I let myself believe her. She adopted a black and white tuxedo kitten she named Bingham from the shelter and still had her mouse, Cotton. Her apartment was cute. She frequented flea-markets and second-hand stores and found cast-off treasures to fill it. Some of her own art hung on its walls, and Riley had contributed an overstuffed sofa, donated by her grandmother, and a pet rat named Edmund. On the few occasions I visited her during the fall semester, I was always pleased to see how tidy she kept the place—a far cry from the disaster that was her room at home—and the evidence of academic life that lay on her coffee table.

She seemed more diligent in her studies. Maybe psychology would stick. She had spoken to all her instructors about her absences before going to San Diego, and only one gave her a hard time about it—ironically, her criminal justice professor. She was also taking an upper-level English course, the first since she had earned credit in high school for college composition and critical reading. Although the loss of her scholarship still stung, I was proud of her. At the beginning of her second year, she was just six hours shy of junior standing. By the time midterms arrived in October, she was on pace to graduate a semester early. But, that's when things began to change again.

She and Ryan had been talking and writing, and I heard from both of them that the plan was for her to finish school then move to California and live with a childhood friend who lived just outside of L.A. At least they would be in the same state if Ryan were still serving his sentence. She would find a job in either social work or education and begin to build a foundation for them, a place for him to call home. Of course, the hope was that when he went before the judge again, she would give him only probation, considering his time served and good behavior. If that were the case, they would live in San Diego until the probationary period was over—about eighteen months—then they would be free to go wherever they pleased, to come home.

None of that happened, though.

In early October, Ryan transferred from Vista to Chino for the court-ordered psychiatric evaluations. There was some trouble with his paperwork and personal belongings arriving at the reception center, an office error, which turned out to be very bad, not administratively, since information exists digitally in the system, but socially. Long after the fact, he explained that without his paperwork, he could not prove to the other inmates, those who really "ran things," what his charges were, and that made him a target of suspicion. His time at Chino was terrible although he became a trustee there, too, during his short stay. While he underwent the mandated testing, he was dodging threats and attempting to navigate the complex social hierarchy without becoming affiliated with any faction. Constantly vigilant, he grew exhausted, and the effect of the place showed in his few letters to me over that time. He no longer had the privilege of making frequent phone calls or receiving email, so both Abby and I wrote to him—until he asked us not to.

In the beginning of his time at Chino, I found it odd that neither Abby nor I had heard from Ryan in over two weeks, sufficient time for mail to find its way if it were not lost along the route. Abby began searching for Ryan through the CDCR's inmate locator system. She was able to find the general information for mail at Chino, but we did not know the facility in which Ryan was housed. Searching deeper for a contact number, she found the prison's Public Information Officer's name and number, which she passed on to me, asking if I would make the call. I did. Lt. Manny Ortega was kind, providing me with an update on the receipt of Ryan's belongings and with a specific facility address and list of approved items to send once I gave him Ryan's inmate number and explained my relationship to him—since mine was not the name on his emergency contact list. That task that left me momentarily at a loss. What was I to Ryan? I couldn't say "fairy-godmother." Was I his ex-girlfriend's mom? Girlfriend's mom? Friend's mom? Friend? I found myself saying, "He's very close to my daughter and has become something like a son to me." It still sounded strange. Lt. Ortega asked for my daughter's name, which I gave him, and he informed me that Ryan listed her as one of his primary contacts, so he guessed he could give me the information. Abby was still a primary contact. What did that mean?

Before Abby's trip but after they had begun to talk regularly again, Ryan and I exchanged letters only once, though emails were weekly. I eventually sent the letter I had been working on as the end of school approached, but it was mid-July, after his military discharge hearing, by the time I dropped it in the mail—practically a different letter than the one started over a month prior. Some of what it said will sound familiar since I've told you so much already, but here it is. It was also the last one I sent before he was transferred to Chino.

July 11, 2017

Dear Ryan,

I know I've emailed you a few times since receiving your last letter and speaking to you, but somehow correspondence feels incomplete to me if a letter is not answered with the same handwritten care in which it was sent. Maybe that's illogical since words typed and words written originate in the same mind, but whatever. Sometimes the rules I impose on my life clash with the logic of the world. Anyway, here's ink and paper and thoughts. I certainly hope your case's outcome improves with your decision to plead the sheet, as you said. I understand how having the judge review all the details herself rather than rely on lawyers' presentations could work in your favor. You cannot be the typical defendant she sees. I mean, what inmate makes Father's Day cards for the incarcerated dads?

Anyway, I have to confess: I'm not sure I should be writing to you. I certainly don't want corresponding to be a mistake! I have actually rewritten this letter, realizing that some of what I originally said has been covered in either our few phone conversations or in relayed messages through Abby. I feel that as you and Abby re-establish whatever y'all have going on, I should fade into the background. I don't want to be where I don't belong, but then, my concern for you gets the best of me and there I go—writing or asking away. I really do try to think of the two of you as separate parts of my life. That sounds dumb. What I mean is, I try to think of you not as Abby's boyfriend-not-boyfriend, but as I would a student with whom I've stayed in touch. But you aren't that either. Labels might be useful most of the time, but some things, I guess, just have to "be" –to exist unnamed.

Abby is so thrilled to be going to Ca. in September. Ah, see, I shouldn't say that! You know, part of the problem is that I don't share many of my mom-

feelings with others, only my own mom and Scott, sometimes, but he can only hear so much before it all sounds the same to him. And I don't want to burden my own mom with more worry than she already has. So, when I have a blank page in front of me, my journal-mind kicks in and I just start writing what I think. For a year now, you have not seemed to mind my ramblings, but I shouldn't impose them on you. I have lots of emotions, especially about Abby. Jenna, too, but those emotions are different. Jenna's approach to life is more responsible, though Abby is really trying. My concern for Jenna is that she puts too much pressure on herself. Can a person have too much order in her life? Abby has been the opposite for so long. Everything she loves seems to arise from spontaneity and impulse. I know that isn't completely true, especially lately. I can't explain it, but in some ways your presence in her life brings her back to order. When we last spoke, you asked what I thought daily life without her would be like. I miss her since she's moved out. I also worry, but I know being on her own will be good for her, a test of her responsibility and maturity. She will be financially responsible for everything except her car insurance and phone, which is pretty indulgent. Lots of kids have to pay for that starting in high school. I hope the distance between her and me allows her to find herself more sincerely. She's lived on her own terms for a while now, often to my disapproval, but I hope being on her own reveals choices that have roots in some substance, some values we've tried to impart. And I really appreciate your perspective on her decision making. I'm glad you do not believe in ultimatums. Any genuine change in behavior should come from a freely made choice, not a forced one. She knows which habits of hers have to change. She always knows what she should be doing, but knowing it and finding the will to do it are entirely different matters. Honestly, I don't need her to listen to me. If she would just listen to herself, that ever-present little voice inside, that would be enough. She would be better. There are things I wish I could say... but I do believe she's learning to be more of an asset to herself than a liability.

So, empty nesting. So far it's good! Although, our grand-dog, whom we are raising as our own child, demands more attention than Jenna or Abby ever did. I run or walk the little beast twice a day just to get some rest at night. She has far too much energy, and I realize I'm creating a monster by improving her cardio. Opal—who names a pit bull Opal? On a serious note, letting go is ridiculously hard. I miss Abby terribly. It's strange, Jenna's leaving home seemed less traumatic for me, I guess because Abby was still here, and I worried so much less about Jenna's decisions. I miss Abby's squishy little feet tucked behind me on the sofa. I miss seeing her exaggerated satisfaction when she'd take the first bite of a turkey sandwich I'd make for her. I guess I miss her need for me. It's funny. The goal of parenthood is to raise independent adults, but allowing children, even grown ones, to challenge their success in autonomy is like ripping your heart out and watching it walk through a maze on legs you didn't know it had and being unable to reach out and steady or redirect it. You just keep watching it beat as it walks in wrong directions, into walls. But, she has shared her location with me, so I can be sure she gets home or wherever she is supposed to be going. That gives me some peace of mind. I check it every twenty minutes...

Wow, I did not begin with the intention to ramble so long about Abby, and that after I announced that I wasn't sure I should even write to you because of your relationship. Am I even a grown-up? Anyway, you asked Abby to ask me what I thought you would be good at in terms of a profession, so I'll give that my best shot: (Keep in mind that I'm working with limited resources—a handful of letters and even fewer face to face conversations, along with my own observations and intuition—so please forgive any inaccuracies.) Given your eye for balance, proportion, and design in art and your mind for understanding abstract concepts, I could see you in graphic design and advertising. You also read people quickly, I bet. So, there's one option, given that skill set. Another option might be engineering, drafting, or mechanical work—given your understanding of how things work and/or are put together, but you don't have an engineer's personality, which might make an office more interesting! You are also a charismatic storyteller, a people person, which would suit you well in business or sales. And you are compassionate and growing wiser by the day, so some sort of counseling or psychology work might be fulfilling to you. And Ryan, I have to tell you, the honesty with which you've looked at your own life and begun to figure things out nearly moves me to tears—not of sadness, though so much sorrow has surrounded you so young, but of ...I don't know, meaning? I am just so pleased to see you confront yourself, your past, and emerge stronger. Your last letter was a little different from your previous ones, more transparent maybe? That isn't right. You are always open. I think the difference shows in your own understanding of self, really. You've looked at your life differently over the past several months. You have had realizations. You're still having them. Your own experience would be a valuable resource in helping others. I really believe deep self-reflection is ironically the greatest tool through which to develop compassion. When we can see the "other" in ourselves, we become more humane. Most people do not want to look that deeply. So, yes, the field of psychology might be a meaningful option, but that, like teaching, can pay notoriously low (social workers) and doesn't offer tons of on-the-job encouragement. Obviously, you'd have to get a PhD:) I also think you should write. You have too much history at such a young age not to, and you can write. Blogging is a real job for some people! Don't think I didn't send my memoir and story about my brother to you a while back as subliminal encouragement. Turning pain and tragedy into art that can help others see what is important in their own lives is the most healing therapy there is. Crafting beauty from raw, painful emotion is a job few want, but I am so thankful that people do it. That's why I love literature—the ancient works to modern read like an emotional history of humankind. Whatever you feel has been felt before. The human condition doesn't change much, but every new voice can offer an audience a perspective that echoes centuries of prior wisdom. We must relearn with every age.

Ryan, you are one of the rare ones who can do whatever you choose because you are so diverse in your talents and intelligence (what about science, the medical field?), so maybe you should focus on your interests. What do you love? Music? What can you talk about for hours? When you have hours—and more options than your current situation offers—where do you like to go? Do you enjoy the presence of others? Solitude? Do you want to make decisions or follow directions? Do you want to create or reproduce or restore? Would you prefer to be outdoors or in? Do you want to work with your brain or your hands more? A combination—all work is really a combination to some degree. Culinary? Wildlife management? Service? Ministry? Unfortunately, for all my questions, your options may be limited because of your situation, but laws vary from state to state and charge to charge. Background checks will be a reality of whatever you pursue, and in some cases, very limiting, but I'm certain that if you can get a foot in the door you'll be able to win your way in once people get to know you. Ultimately, Ryan, be someone who makes your small space of the world better for the others in it.

As ever,
Ms. Colleen

I'm not sure when Ryan received that letter, but I know he did because he told Abby to tell me thank you for all the questions about his future, but he did not write back for a long while. With his court appearance, Abby's and his family's visit, and subsequent transfer, he had his mind on more important matters than a response. Come to find out, though, there was another reason. He had no paper. After getting the proper mailing address from Lt. Ortega, I sent Ryan a brief note explaining how Abby had tracked him down through the system and with it, several sheets of blank paper, and a few postage-paid envelopes, stamps not being allowed in Chino jail mail:

Dear Ryan,

I momentarily hoped they didn't have you anymore when we couldn't find you in the system! I'm glad we found you. I'm glad Abby found you. Wow, I mean that in a bigger way than it may appear. I hope that isn't bad to say! Put this paper to good use!

After receiving the package, Ryan responded.

September 18, 2017

Dear Ms. Colleen,

I don't think you understand how much I love you for sending the paper and envelopes. I can't believe I was so restricted because some office didn't do their job right. I was driving myself crazy not being able to write my thoughts out in my journal or letters. I actually acquired a ¾" piece of lead that I used to write a poem on the one sheet of paper I could find before obtaining this pen, well, the ink part of the pen. The poem is pretty sloppy, and the letters are small, but considering what I was working with, I think it's legible. I included it with this letter, and you can share it with whomever you would like to—in fact, read it to everybody who will listen. But its content isn't something I want to discuss anytime soon.

This place is hard. Being locked down for 23 hours of the day alone in a cell caused me to do something I've never done before, at least not as badly: I genuinely felt sorry for myself and upset about my life (sigh...) Glad that passed. Re-reading my poem made me realize how lucky I am to have my brother and sister, so I'm glad it happened. Not to mention the other people who care about me. After reading it a few times, I got slightly disgusted at how weak I felt when writing it and made a miraculous discovery within myself that Abby will agree with 100%. In fact, she's said it directly to me before. This is what it is: I am Ryan Freeman. No matter the outcome of all of this, I will fix my mistakes, my life, myself because that is what I do. It's crazy when the simplest answer fixes the most complex problem. That isn't saying I don't need help though—even professionally, haha.

I also know you want me to read, so I am (lots of time for it). This is what I have read so far: The Rare Coin Score, The Prison Angel, Mutant Message from Down Under, Brimstone, Gai-Jin, The Last Kingdom, The Pale Horseman, Lords of the North, *and another one I can't remember. That's a lot, right!? And some of them have really powerful messages and are amazing. With all that reading, I've also been doing a lot of pushups. A lot. I think I'm at 30,000. As far as other things, there's just doctor's appointments with weird diagnoses, social experiences I can't really describe, and some tricky sleep patterns on my 5' mattress for a 6'man.*

Now, to reply to your note... I love your wish about them not having me when you and Abby couldn't find me in the system for a minute. I think that's one of her best qualities, she's persistent, haha. I am glad she found me here though. I tell her she's crazy, and you might agree just a little, but I love that in her. And I'm not talking psycho bitch (excuse the language) crazy. I mean crazy in the best way. She has put herself out there for me so much. I miss her and would love to hear her voice more. It always calms my nerves and excites them at the same time, but calls here are really limited. Going way back to your other letter, I love the fact that you obsessively keep tabs on her location. It shows how good of a mom you are. My mama always knew where I was. ALWAYS. And that was before GPS. She made sure I knew it, too. Abby said she wanted another tattoo when she was here. Did she get it? A snake? I actually drew one for her a while ago. Did she show you? Maybe I wasn't supposed to say that. Dear lord! I don't know how you feel about all that, but I have 12. Too late to change it now. She described what she wants for the whole sleeve to me. How do you feel about being represented as a cicada? Haha, that girl's mind is something. I know I'm jumping all around but thank you for the paper and stuff and the prayers. I pray for y'all, too, at least 4 times a day. I'd like my brother and sister to read the poem I wrote one day, but that will happen in good time. I want them to read The Body Keeps the Score, *too, especially the Eye Movement Desensitization Reprocessing, but I know they won't even if it's sitting in front of them. How do your students like the content that you are presenting from it? You know what? You and Mama have almost the exact same penmanship. Another random thought: talking on the phone with you these last few times has been really nice, not awkward like the very first time I talked to you when we didn't know each other at all and talked about the most personal thing ever, haha.*

Thank you for noticing my efforts to improve and position myself for the future. It is hard without resources. But I'm doing my best. Haha, that reminds me, I'll have to tell you what happens here on Friday nights one day. Don't worry, it ain't bad. And thank you for the end of your letter. I have too much time in here to challenge every thought I think, and I'm scared I'm backtracking on some progress I've made. So, just to be told that you can see how hard I'm working on myself drives me toward my future goals. All in all, I just realized that for the first time I'm pushing myself beyond normal limits without the help of medication or even really professionals, unless I count you. So, to do nearly 20 years of healing in almost only a year is something to be proud of, right? Obviously not the circumstances that caused it, but the overall effort since. Either way, thank you for reminding me that I am strong. And for all the paper. Now I can write like a normal person. Also, tell Abby that even if we both end up in straitjackets, I'll find a way to hug her.

Love,
Ryan Freeman

The poem he included covered every centimeter, front and back, of flyleaf from a paperback. With slash marks and rhyme at fairly regular intervals, ballad-like, I could hear the rhythm pour from the page. The poem's lilt contrasted its content, seeming so carefree yet disclosing so much pain—like the young man himself. In time, I typed it and sent a copy back to him.

Ryan's Pandora's Box

You walk into a room and in the middle of the floor,
there's a box with a sign on top.
It reads "Ryan's Pandora's Box"
And unfortunately, the urge to peek inside won't stop.

So you open it up and there's an explosion of colors,
but the room you were in is no more.
There are the strangest creatures, beautiful scenery,
and memories, so you decide to go explore.

Drive-in theaters are everywhere
playing scenes of somebody's life
that people just love to watch:
Fight scenes, skydiving, racing, drinking, and
X-rated scenes with repeated use of this guy's crotch.

IN THE ETHER: A MEMOIR OF HOLDING SPACE

It's an amazing place, but in the middle of a field
there's an out-of-place door that just doesn't seem right.
You walk up to it and there's a sign on the front that says
"WARNING: THINGS THAT COME OUT AT NIGHT."

The sign is ignored, and you walk inside
and everything around is pitch black.
The door slams shut, the handle is gone,
and you realize there's no turning back.

You trudge through the darkness and find three kids
who seem to be hiding behind a door.
One boy says, "They're fighting again"
and the girl says, "I can't take it anymore."

She heroically runs out the door
and you hear the slap and pain that wrenches your heart.
You run out to help because these are just kids,
but remember, this is only the start.

The kids are older now, but they are crying and sad
because the middle one just found his parents' drugs.
The bullet holes are patched; he's covered in paint,
and the car looks different now due to the bad deal with the Fourth St. thugs.

Now you're in a car with the kids and their mom
driving fast and frantically looking side to side.
She pulls into a motel because dad's upset
and we all need a place to hide.

The chase goes on for months and months
and you wonder how much more these kids can take.
But they all seem brave and comfort their mom
because the stress is making her visibly shake.

Next thing you know, you're in a house
and you see a fifteen-year-old boy run by with a gun.
You run right behind him, he's aiming at a new man now,
and with blood on her face and in a raspy voice
the mom says, "Please don't do it, son."

You follow the boy as he unloads the gun
and goes to his room that doesn't even have a door.
Time goes by, there's a flash and a bang,
and horrified you find this boy's mother on the floor.

Brain and blood are everywhere, the gun is there,
and the clock on the stove says 1:58 a.m.
Your heart drops when the boy and his brother walk in
because you know the sight they see will haunt them.

You run out with them only to find them a year older
and both sitting sadly on the ground.
When you look back to see what all the new fuss is about,
you see their house is burning down.

The dad's there now, but he looks kind of high
and he leads the boys through yet another door.
You walk through with them, just shaking your head
thinking there can't be anymore.

The smell of burnt flesh and a hospital greet your nose
as you see the dad fried and on a stretcher fly by.
The girl and the boys are crying and praying
that today they don't see their Daddy die.

Everything's black now and you see a tornado
and it sounds just, almost, like a train.
You run into a brick house
to find the boys hiding some kids in a tub,
and as the roof goes, you start to feel the rain.

The storm jerks you up and you land on a ship
with a bunch of United States Marines.
You find the boy crying in sleep flinching from gunshots,
and you realize this boy suffers from all his dreams.

You follow again only to find him drinking
out behind a funeral parlor.
Daddy was paralyzed, so he took his own life
with so many pills— "help" was a word he couldn't holler.

Drinks every day and new drugs to cope,
you can only watch this man destroy his life.
He goes to jail blacked out after hitting a cop
and disappointing a girl he wanted to call his wife.

While in jail, he fights in his sleep
and faces every nightmare he drank away.
Lost everything he owns, and ashamed of it all,
while his best friend and girl did their best to betray.

You look up to God and ask for a way out
because all of this sadness is too much to take.
You find the door that leads back to the room
and you finally found your escape.

Your thoughts are racing to warn everybody about the box:
curious kids, a homeless guy, even your best friend's wife.
Then your eyes snap open to see a familiar prison cell,
and you realize...this was your life.

The poem and the letter made Ryan's troubled life clearer to me than it had ever been. With all the tragedies arranged into stanzas, the story brought him to where he was. I wondered if he had realized he had written dissociation into the verses. Although taking in all that it said overwhelmed me, two lines, the two most closely related to me, I am ashamed to say, stayed with me: "the girl he wanted to call his wife" and "his best friend and girl did their best to betray." Did he really, at some point before prison, want to marry her? And, doing one's "best to betray" sounds so intentional. It wasn't. It was a mistake. Still, it happened. Still, it felt unresolved.

Chapter 33

On Being Asked What Advice I'd Give a

Son

The time from October 2017 to January 2018 continued the roller coaster pattern of Abby and Ryan's relationship, and I held on tight–too tight.

Maybe I still am.

I have yet to figure out how to do what I know is necessary: *How do I let go?* Honestly, I am uncertain of what I am holding on to—hope, I suppose. But, it is a hope so divorced from logic that I cannot think it through to the root. I feel one thing yet think—or *realize* may be a better word—another.

I already knew that I couldn't control anything, that people must make their own lives. I tried to be rational, to keep my emotions quiet as a shadow, say all the proper things to both Abby and Ryan, but I knew I was failing. Somewhere beyond understanding within me, I thought I knew something important simply because of how I felt. How arrogant of me to think I had answers to questions that they had not yet thought to ask.

I still have much to learn about humility, about myself.

After his time at Chino, Ryan transferred back to Vista in San Diego, where his next court appearance would not be until January. After a tumultuous November, the one-year mark of his arrest, Abby arranged another trip to California to attend the late January sentencing. Prior to that planning, however, came some low moments. The isolation, the hostile atmosphere, and the intensive evaluation at Chino left Ryan in a dark place for several weeks. He was in a straitjacket at one point, thought to be a possible harm to himself. One early December evening, he called Abby, having found phone time, and relapsed into his anger over her behavior, almost a year past. All the awful names, all the accusations remembered, his own painful childhood conflated with memories not so remote—he unleashed his ire on her. She told me this time.

For the first time in a long while, I brought myself to say the obvious: "Sweetie, maybe this is just too much for either of you to fix. Maybe it should end."

Her response echoed the usual, but with a bit less conviction. She said, "But Mama, you know it's because of his situation right now. We were doing well before he went to Chino."

"Were you? You said you've had so much anxiety recently," I countered.

"Well, yeah, my ass sweats so bad I hate to stand up after class, but that isn't because of Ry!"

"What is it from then?" I asked.

"Life! School, work, money—"

I cut her off. "Money? What's going on with that? You said you were fine."

"I mean, I am. Everything is just so expensive. I had to take Bingham to the vet for his shots and to get fixed, so that's where it went," she explained, leaving other, less legitimate expenses out, I guessed.

"So, you are telling me that his calling you and rehashing everything since last December hasn't affected you?" I asked.

"I mean, it has, but not that I can't manage it. I know he just needs to vent. He's got so much going on inside, so much to be angry about, but I'm the one who's here. I can take it. I sort of deserve it."

And there it was. I had to say it.

"Abby, you know I have been as supportive of you and Ryan, together and individually, as I can possibly be throughout this whole ordeal, and it is an ordeal—painful, protracted, the works—but I want you to listen now: It might be time. It might be too hard."

"But Mama," she began, "I—"

I cut her off, knowing she was going to say, I love him. "Sweetie, I care about him, too, more than I ever thought I would, but you are my priority. I can't watch you prioritize your love for him over your own well-being. It's almost like an excuse or penance. It isn't healthy. You can't live in a cycle of guilt and forgiveness completely triggered by someone else's mood, especially a bipolar someone else."

Then the tears came. I know it was harsh, but it was true. While I wished that he could completely forgive her—that she could forgive herself—that they could call it even and begin fresh, I saw the impossibility of it. Each had too much to learn individually. The truth was that I was heartbroken, too. I loved Ryan. I was ready to accept all his difficulties, his past, into my family, but he was not willing to accept my daughter as she was.

I wrote to him shortly after the conversation I had with Abby. The letter was more direct than my usual meandering stream of consciousness, but still too long.

December 12, 2017

Dear Ryan,

Coincidentally—but you know I don't believe in coincidence—I had just ordered and sent a book on EMDR to you two days ago. I know that is the therapy you found most promising when you read TBKTS. *You will have gotten the new book by the time this letter arrives. I need to tell you why I sent it. First, it is designed as a self-help approach complete with exercises you will not need to adapt or improvise in your situation, and second, well, that angry phone call. Abby told me about your most recent. Needless to say, I am disappointed, for both of you. You and Abby are struggling with such a tangle of problems that I am unsure y'all will be able to sort the strands out. I am still trying to get her to read* The Body Keeps the Score, *to talk, and to face herself honestly and to listen. And you, I understand that 23 hours a day of nothing but memory could and obviously does drive people to dark, angry places, and I pray that you find your way out of that, even in physical confinement. I recall our conversation about EMDR not all that long ago, and you're telling me you focused on Abby at the beginning but ended in a memory of your own mother confessing infidelity. I cannot imagine how such a memory would complicate a boy's perceptions. Ryan, do you think it is possible that you could be projecting some of your childhood pain onto Abby, subconsciously associating her unfaithfulness to that moment in your past? I am not defending Abby. Her actions bring pain of their own to both you and her, but sorting that out is between the two of you, if and when you both deem it worthwhile. I simply want to help you both through this, so I sent the book.*

This paragraph won't be any more fun than the last one, so skip ahead if you want to avoid some of that open-book honesty to which you've invited me. Last week was the first time I've told her (since your arrest) that this relationship should probably end. And the reason is not because of her behavior or yours. It is your perception. You seem to have difficulty seeing the good in Abby, believing the selflessness underlying her desire to help you. You cannot see her greatest quality—her altruism. She forgives too easily, sometimes to her detriment. She values her own feelings too little, risks her own well-being to placate others, believes she deserves less than she does. I want her to overcome that, to realize she is worth so much more, and because of that, I do not want to see her constantly reminded of her greatest failure. While I sent the book to you, I cautioned her to understand that the two of you have a very tenuous relationship fraught with obstacles to overcome, and you have spent less than one month in each other's physical presence. I am not saying it could not work. I have grown to care so deeply for you that I, in fact, hope it can. But I do not get to decide. That is up to you and Abby. I am simply calling for you to recognize that the nature of trauma suggests that even you are not aware of the connections between past and present made in your own mind. And, the nature of being Abby suggests running head-on into a situation believing everything will be fine with complete disregard for her own injury.

I am not trying to preach or chastise. I intend to reassure you, actually—I know you struggle and it's okay. I know you get angry and it's okay. I know you want a beautiful life, and it's okay if it is not with Abby. You will find someone, who has not done what Abby has, or at least, not done it to you. People are human, after all. I—and Abby—want you to be happy. Just please do not drive her cruelly and slowly away if you determine that her past and your perception of it cannot fit into the future you want.

Love,
Ms. Colleen

The letters I received in response were hard to read, both literally and figuratively. Ryan's handwriting was so small, yet lines remained unfilled at the bottom of the page. He noticed the change in his penmanship, too, commenting that it reflected his distress. I received two, postmarked with two consecutive days. The first was frustrated—with himself because he felt himself losing control, with the prison situation that he could not disclose, with whomever else he was writing because no one was honest, with Abby because he didn't want to hurt her but knew he was doing exactly that, with everything.

He told me that he loved Abby, but he did not want her to be the first person he disappointed when he was released--, admitting he was not emotionally or morally mature enough to be with her that soon. He acknowledged that his own actions may have cost him the person he wanted most during this difficult time in his life, and he knew his feelings about her were warped. He admitted to wanting revenge for her cheating on him. It was four pages of uncensored emotion that ended with a thank you, a compliment, and questions: a thank you for the December twelfth letter; a compliment for being direct and honest; and the questions…were huge.

Had I ever felt such things or fought my "selfish wants"? Did I know any "secret ways" to change how one's mind works? Had I ever known what the right decision was but made the wrong one anyway? How does a person know when to let go or hold on? What's the perfect medium for gaining on both sides? When should a person put someone else's needs and wants before his own "because that seems necessary, too"? He explained, "The only thing I know about women is what they like, how to make them fall in love, how to keep them around, and what not to say to them. Well, at least it seems like I know these things. Mama only taught me how to treat girls properly. We never really got that far." He concluded his litany of questions with this: "I apologize if this question isn't fair, but nobody else is honest with me, so there's no one else to ask, and I know it sucks because she is your daughter, but what would you advise your son to do, if you had one?"

Upon reading that question, I thought, I'd give the advice I've already given you, and I meant it. When Abby asked me to stay in touch with him a year prior, I did not envision the relationship he and I have now. I didn't imagine Ryan wanting me in his life, continuing to ask for my help, and seeming to respect both Scott and me so much. I thought I'd write a few letters here and there, and he would stop responding out of disinterest.

That would have been easier.

After reading the first letter, my mind was already working, mentally addressing each concern, but then I read the second letter. The second letter was short:

January 3, 2018

Dear Ms. Colleen,

I've decided I shouldn't write to anyone anymore while I'm in prison. I should have seen it when I wrote that poem that I'm not myself. I'm sorry for all the crazy bullshit I've written to you and Abby, my brother, Lisa. Please tell Abby I'm sorry, but I need everybody to leave me alone until this is over. I don't have much longer here, and I don't want to keep saying dumb things that hurt feelings. I don't want to sound rude, but writing puts me in an awkward hole I can't get out of. I need to stop. I love y'all too much. This is weird. I will call someone when I'm at County again. Thank you for being patient and helping me and being so nice to me when you don't have to be.

Love,
Ryan Freeman

There was a postscript, too, just as long as the letter. Essentially, it said the same things, with the additions of, "Tell everyone you know never to get arrested;" "I'm tired of putting things in the mail that I regret as soon as they drop. Dear God, I hope this isn't one of them;" "Your last letter was very kind;" and lastly, "This should help me stop messing good things up." I wasn't sure of what the "this" was, so I assumed "this" was all of it. "This" included not getting more mail, my last letter, the lessons he'd learned from the whole ordeal, and the time between his letter and when he returned to county jail.

How we re-established contact is honestly a bit of a blur now. I sent him not a letter, but a list of ideas, typed and clearly marked "Not a Letter" at the top of the page, and an article that addressed his concerns about revenge, about how he couldn't stop himself from wanting to hurt Abby in the same way she hurt him. In my mind, he had already done that, but I didn't say it. The article was from *Psychology Today* and asserted that revenge causes more harm to self than to the target, and that made me think of Abby, wondering if some unacknowledged resentment motivated her indiscretion last December.

The not-a-letter was lost in the mail. Ryan never received the information I sent, making me seem to honor his request not to write back, but it gave him the advice I would have given a son.

January 4, 2018

THIS IS NOT A LETTER

1. "I do not understand what I do. For what I want to do, I do not do, but what I hate to do." So, this is sometimes true for everyone, whether they believe Bible stuff or not. The book is full of insight to human nature. Sometimes metaphorical. Not in this case. This is Romans 7:15, if you are curious. Worth it to read Romans 8:28. Just saying.

2. Secret ways to change how one's mind works: I don't know. I have a completely different mind from yours or anyone's. We all do, so I can only say how my mind works and might change. I have a natural capacity for mercy and service. I do not have revenge fantasies. I have apology fantasies. They never materialize. Anyway, my pain, confusion, or anger tends to decrease with (1.) communication, because it fosters understanding and compassion and (2.) prayer/meditation (sort of the same thing), because when communication is too scary or logistically impossible, conversing with God and contemplating my speck of self within the universe keeps me humble enough to be open minded and realize that I have no right to determine anyone else's penance. (3.) Time, because it magically heals. It numbs the pain without your noticing how. The clock's sleight of hand, I guess. And (4.) My mom's advice: The best revenge is living well. I try to focus on what I know to be good and true of myself and trust that God, Karma, the law of reciprocity— whatever—will address the offending party's conscience. I also remind myself that I've been forgiven for some crappy things, so maybe I should extend that kindness.

3.   I have fought my own selfishness and lost. Probably more than once, like every time I eat a handful of Jelly-Bellies, but definitely in a Big Way once. Because I know that feeling, and it is terrible, I know nothing I say will matter. People must come to choices on their own. All I can advise is this: The right decision is one that does not cause greater grief in the lives of those involved in its carrying out. Innocent bystanders should never be hurt.

4.   On women, of which I am one: Knowing what they like, how to make them fall in love, how to keep them around, and what not to say seems like a Machiavellian romance manual that could be titled "How to Get What You Want and Make It Seem Like It Wasn't Your Idea." Maybe a little manipulative? I think men believe it's harmless to allow a woman to think a relationship is more than it really is, but it's not. There is a twisted way in which honesty can be manipulated into deception. I think it happens within two things: in the discrepancy between words and action and in the understanding of that discrepancy. A guy can tell a girl they aren't "serious" or "official," but if he seems to prioritize her—calling her regularly, spending time with her, cultivating intimacy through conversation and physicality, telling her he loves her—she isn't going to believe him. It looks and feels serious to her. If he knows what she believes, despite what he says, are his words or his actions the lie? Are either? How can you account for the discrepancy? And it can't simply be "because she's crazy." I mean, maybe, but did he have a part in driving her there? And it can't be miscommunication if he is aware of it. Or she, it can work both ways. It's a terrible game and not harmless. Games are seldom fun when one is unaware of the rules.

5.   The perfect medium for gaining on both sides: It's communication. Honest communication. Best if it originates from shared values and mutual respect for each other's personhood.

6.   On other's wants and needs being prioritized: When one's own desires and needs are out of line with the values and beliefs he claims to hold, he should defer and evaluate where the other person's morals fall. Are they more...untainted? Defer when you know the other person is right, even when it hurts your pride. When another person's presence in your life makes you thankful and letting them know that is important, prioritize them. Do it when not doing it is just selfish. Do it when your conscience tells you to do it, when what they want is more important than what you want, when it is more beneficial to you both, when it is morally aligned with what you know is right—in short—when you love them. But, you should never do it when it causes a moral violation of self.

All of this, I would say to my son. I'd also tell him that he must live his own life, but in doing so, he must determine what he believes and why he believes it. I'd say, don't be careless with your life or the lives of others. Don't be reckless with people's hearts, or yours. I would tell him to have the grace to allow others to be who they are becoming, even through the awkward stages. I'd suggest that he avoid doing anything he would be too embarrassed to explain to me, and that he never assume to know anyone's full story. What people leave out is often the foundation for the rest. That is what I would say to my son. It is what I have said to my daughters.

The first time Ryan saw those words was when he read the first draft of the book you are reading now. Revisiting all of it here on the page in conversation with Ryan jogged my memory. With his help, I recalled how we resumed writing. I received a letter from him, one I have here now as confirmation, like all of them. In early January, after Christmas had passed without our wishing him a merry one, a short note arrived announcing that he was back in San Diego at Vista, resuming his role as a trustee, but at a higher level that placed more men under his leadership. He told me that his aunt got him a gift package of candy from the commissary, which he shared with as many of the inmates as he could, winning their esteem. He apologized for his "craziness" and asked if I would begin my weekly emails again, along with an occasional "rant" in the longer letters I sent. I obliged.

Abby, too, heard from Ryan, who called without revisiting his anger again. He told her, and she told me, that the book I had sent on EMDR was incredibly helpful to him, and that he had begun practicing the therapy daily. It helped him not only to uncover but also to process emotions and memories he had not faced in years. He even suggested to Abby that she learn about it and give it a try.

She didn't.

Their reconnection seemed strong, so strong that once again Abby would fly to California for Ryan's sentencing in late January. This time she was going alone, though a friend of his—a female friend whom Abby had met on her trip before his incarceration—would be in town, too. Although they were not sharing a hotel—her mother lived there—they made plans to see each other and attend court together, which was some comfort. Unlike her previous visits, the time between planning and going was short, barely a month, and once again it would be at the start of a semester. She would leave on Wednesday morning and return Sunday evening. Court was Thursday.

The few weeks leading up to her departure were typical, as far as she told me, filled with the start of school, the attempt to concentrate on classes that made her feel like the odd-man-out. I found her saying that odd and asked her why she felt that way. All she offered as an explanation was that she just wasn't like other college girls, with their Lilly Pulitzer binders and sorority t-shirts. I attempted to reassure her, saying I knew she could hold her own intellectually against the best of them, and that her appearance simply made her prominent in a sea of pastel-wearing blondes. She told me motherhood obligated me to say such things. I thought about reminding her that I was well-aware of less supportive things I had said despite my role, but decided just to smile, letting her have this kindness toward me and trying to allow myself to accept it.

We talked slightly more than usual in those weeks, mostly about the logistics of her trip, but she did tell me she was more nervous to see Ryan this time than she had ever been. I think his time at Chino left both of us—affected. I was concerned for his mental stability, as she was, but she was also concerned for her own, although I didn't know it. She told me, tearfully, that she loved him, but sometimes the weight of that love was crushing. She had been waiting for him, waiting out this whole criminal ordeal for over a year, and there was nearly a year before that. She reminded me that she met him when she was seventeen. That sounded young even to her now. She was about to be twenty, and she said she couldn't even remember her first two years of college. She asked me if life was supposed to feel "this way," but I wasn't sure of what that way was. It could hurt a lot sometimes, I told her, which everyone already knows, but what do you say when you see the conflict and pain in your child's eyes?

Chapter 34

Hard Decisions

The Tuesday night before her 8:00 a.m. flight, Abby slept at home in her old bedroom, though the twin bed with which I had replaced her platform was not as cozy. She came to the house immediately after her classes, beating me home from school and letting herself in much to Opal's delight. When I got there, she and the dog were sitting on the back porch in the evening sun. I decided to ignore the faint whiff of marijuana in the air and focus on keeping Opal's paws, wet from chasing egrets away as they landed along the shore of the bayou, off my pants.

"Hey, Sweetie," I said, closing the back door behind me and sitting on the bench next to her, Opal sprawling at our feet after greeting me.

"Hey, Mama."

"So, you are all packed and ready?" I asked.

"Yeah," was all she said, then offered a soft smile.

"What's bothering you, love? You seem a little sad, not that you don't have reason to be, but I thought you'd be more excited to be leaving."

Abby smiled and said, "I am excited, just a little scared, too."

"Of what, that you're going alone?" I asked, realizing this was the first time she would be traveling alone again since December a year ago.

"I mean, a little, flight nerves, you know, but don't worry—I'm not taking anything," she reassured me. "And, I just, I'm worried about his sentence. The time, how long."

"What do you mean, love? Last I heard, with his time served, it seemed likely that he'll get probation. That's what his lawyer told you, right?" I clarified.

"That's what he said, either probation or maybe a three-year sentence, which would become a little less than two with his time served."

"Hopefully, he can use however long it is productively. I did some reading. He can also earn time through good behavior and completing other programs, even taking classes. I sent him some information on college courses he might qualify for. Most of the education stuff is for G.E.D. programs, but, I mean..." I rolled my eyes to indicate the absurdity of Ryan's need for a high school equivalency diploma.

"I know. And I'm sure he will. I'm just nervous," she said.

We sat quietly for a moment and, now that the dog was lightly snoring, watched an egret, stand statue-like just before plunging its beak into the water. It came up with a small fish.

"Mom," Abby said.

"Yes?"

"What if I can't wait?" she asked me, leaving me a little caught off guard.

"What do you mean, love?"

"What if he doesn't get probation or even a year or two? What if it's a long time?" Her smile was gone. She huddled into herself, put her head on her knees and continued, barely audible, "I don't think I can wait more than that, Mama. It's already so hard." When she lifted her head to look at me, the tears, those perineal tears, slid quietly from her eyes. I said nothing, holding back my own as I pulled her close.

I understand the temptation to lie in the name of reassurance, especially to your own children. I could have said to her, "His sentence won't be that long," or "if you love him the time won't matter," or even "you might have more patience than you think." All of those were lies. I had no idea of his sentence, and time, the magician that it is, can transform life so seamlessly we don't know it has happened until we stand before something new, wondering how it materialized.

And, I knew my Abby.

Patience, she could have, but it required discipline, and discipline required strength. The young woman in my arms was already so exhausted by the last year that in some ways I was surprised she had not already given up. I didn't know if she could be that strong either, at least not then, but I didn't want to confirm that. In the end, I did not respond to her worry with a lie. I simply said, "Things will work out as they should, Sweetie," not understanding what it meant myself.

That night, not very late, Abby came downstairs while Scott and I watched the evening news, which was all bad, as usual. Four Baton Rouge police officers were ambushed, leaving one dead. Abby had been on the phone with Ryan, who asked if he could call back to speak to us. She said he just needed reassurance. Of course, we said yes, and she informed us he would be calling shortly. Within fifteen minutes, her phone rang, and after answering and going through the automated instructions, she pressed five and handed me her phone. I pressed speaker.

"Hey Ryan," I said almost in unison with Scott's "hey, man." Scott continued, asking how he was feeling about everything.

"Nervous. A little overwhelmed, I think, if I'm being honest," came the answer.

I tried to reassure him, saying, "That's completely understandable, Ryan. You've been waiting for this for over a year, so now that it's finally here, I can certainly understand how emotional it is. Does your lawyer have any idea of how things might go?"

"Oh, yes ma'am," he said, sounding like himself. "He thinks I have a good chance of getting probation for two years or maybe six months in prison and then probation, but I'm just not sure I did this right."

"What do you mean?" asked Scott.

"Well, y'all remember the last time I talked to y'all? When I told y'all about pleadin' the sheet and all?"

"Yeah, man," said Scott. "Sounded like you had good reason to. Seven years can't be the best deal."

"Yes sir," Ryan said, "that's what I thought. But I've been sittin' here wonderin' if I'm seein' it right. Like, I know the lawyers saw all the evidence collected in discovery, but it's their job to present it a certain way. I don't think that's good. I mean, I saw the cop's body cam, and I didn't know who I was lookin' at. I mean—" He paused for a minute and made a sound that could have been the beginning of laughter or crying before composing himself and continuing. "I didn't know I had that in me, that," again he paused, "rage."

Scott looked at me, hoping I would speak. Abby sat on the floor next to me, near tears herself.

"Ryan," I said, "listen, you have learned enough about yourself over the last year to understand it, if not completely, at least better. Your behavior and progress since your arrest speak for themselves. The judge will see that." I hoped it was enough to assuage his turmoil.

"Yes, ma'am. That's just it. I saw how I was. I don't remember it. I don't know what I deserve. I don't think the D.A. knows or my lawyer. They just do their jobs. I figured if the judge had everything to look at for herself, she could make the best decision." His voice was emotional but controlled. "I mean, I don't want more time. Shit, I don't want the time I have, but if she goes through it all and decides—." He stopped again before saying more calmly, "I know it might turn out I get even longer, but I just want somebody to look at everything that happened and be able to tell me what I deserve. Because I don't know, and I want what's right."

Scott and I were speechless for a beat, then Scott said, "That shows a lot of integrity on your part. I hope the judge—"

The automated voice broke in, "You have sixty seconds left on this call."

Scott continued, "I was saying I hope the judge knows what you just told us. I'm sure most people she deals with don't think like that."

"Yes, sir. She knows, I wrote it all in my statement."

I said, "That's good. She'll be able to see the kind of person you are despite the charges. At least, it seems like she will."

Ryan said, rather quickly, "It's gonna cut off any second. Thank y'all for talkin' to me, and for everything. I love y'all so much."

Scott replied, "We'll be here when you need us, man, and we love you, too."

I quickly added, "Bye Ry—" and the call ended. I handed the phone back to Abby, who had sat quietly listening to everything, things she already knew. I bent down and kissed her head.

"Sweetie, he's worth waiting for," I told her.

She broke up with him two weeks later.

Chapter 35

Prisms

Ryan's January court date proved to be another misfire. Abby and Ashlyn, Ryan's friend, were there, along with Ashlyn's mother, who lived in San Diego. Just before the proceedings began, Peter Blair walked over to Abby and gave her the bad news: There would be no decision on sentencing today. Again, it would be postponed, one week—something about the officer, the victim, having a medical emergency and being unable to attend. I sincerely wondered if it were theatrics. The new date was set for February 7, 2018.

I vividly remember when I received the call. Abby had come home from San Diego the previous week having lost some hope that Ryan would get probation in lieu of jail time, and she was upset that without her there, only Ashlyn would be in the courtroom to show support for him. On the day of his hearing, Ashlyn called her immediately when it was over. She told Abby that it was ridiculous. News cameras, every cop on the force, and every nurse who had so much as looked at the officer packed the courtroom. She said even Judge Naziri seemed surprised by the showing.

The cell phone girl read a statement, and she cried talking about how guilty she felt. I wondered about that. Did she realize Ryan had not stolen her phone and she, no doubt in a drunken stupor, had acted rashly? Did she feel guilty because she had since learned that the Marine to whom she was initially attracted had already overcome so much tragedy in his life? Or did she feel guilty over the officer's injury?

The officer also read an impact statement, a lengthy one, according to Ashlyn. Standing before the judge, he looked down at his paper as he explained Ryan's family history, which he felt was evidence that Ryan was, indeed, a man doomed by heredity never to amount to anything. He also told the court that he "lost everything, everything because of this man." He went on to say that in addition to the physical problems, he suffered from memory loss, depression, and PTSD from the single punch. Ashlyn told Abby the cop talked about the comfort animal his therapist recommended. He had chosen an owl, a comfort owl. He had to work at a desk now because "no one would give him a chance." His girlfriend broke up with him. Ashlyn said he went on and on, while Ryan, in his tan jumpsuit, sat looking remorseful and pained. Then, Ryan addressed the judge and the victims. The local news filmed much of each person's statements, and sure enough the video is on YouTube.

I watched it—and heard each speaker.

The girl, through tears, apologizes to everyone. She had the least time.

The cop, reading from his statement, speaks like an injured bird. He said he forgave "Mr. Freeman" but believed, given his "propensities," he should be sentenced "to the full extent of the law," thirteen years.

Hearing that enraged me. His propensities—did he mean having a difficult childhood, losing his mother, having PTSD? The justice this man called for would convict every child of his father's crime. Did Ryan's service to his country count for anything, or was that, too, a detriment considering his Other Than Honorable discharge? There was no forgiveness, no belief in redemption. The comments beneath the video attest to the public distrust of police, some saying quite disparaging things about the officer, whose on-screen demeanor certainly did not represent him well.

Ryan spoke, too. His voice quaking, he looked at each person—the officer, the girl, and the judge—as he offered no excuses but thanks. He thanked the officer for not shooting him. He acknowledged he was on a "wrong path" and because of that night, has had the opportunity to change it. He thanked them for that, too. He also said he hoped whatever his sentence was, that it would include the opportunity to serve others, to make up for what he had done that night in November. The judge listened. The next clip of the video showed her addressing Ryan, almost in a motherly way, though scolding, saying, "You must have known that you couldn't drink." She concluded by telling Ryan he would have to live with his guilt. When Abby called me as I walked through the parking lot of St. Andrew's Hospital to see my niece's newborn on February 7, all I heard through wailing cries was, "Five years! Mama, they gave him five years!"

Ashlyn also told Abby she said "some things" to the cop outside the courtroom about how "shitty" he was for using Ryan's childhood against him. Abby had already emailed Ryan and left a message for Peter Blair, asking him to call her "just for a few minutes," to explain the decision. The lawyer had seemed so certain Ryan would get little more than probation. He even said the judge had seemed sympathetic, but believed the news cameras, courtroom packed with police officers, and recent publicity of retaliation against cops had swayed the judge from her earlier sentiments. The only hope in the situation was that the judge had recommended Ryan for the inmate firefighter program, which would provide him with training as both a firefighter and emergency medical technician, but he would have to be accepted, despite her endorsement. Peter also told Abby that five years was already three and a half because of time served, and it would be further reduced, especially if Ryan made it into the program. All that said, it was still too much for Abby to bear.

Ryan called Abby the next day, and I received a text from her telling me he had requested an "entertaining" email. Given the situation, I was at a loss for humor, but I tried. I think I told him the unfortunately true story of my mixing up the initial consonant sounds of the phrase "felt smart" in class. Maybe it made him smile. He also explained what would happen next. He would remain at Vista for several weeks more before being transferred once again to Chino. I hated hearing that. He would know by then if he would be accepted into the Calfire program, and if he were, he could be placed at any one of the numerous fire camps throughout the state. Having read what I could find about the program, it sounded like the best scenario for him. It came with many opportunities.

While Ryan was still at the county jail in Vista, I emailed him a combination of foolishness and words of encouragement, short little missives, every few days, even after February 15, when Abby arrived at her decision. She had reached the conclusion she could not promise him her physical faithfulness for three more years. She told me that, too, and I hated hearing it. Her carnality always seemed to rule her reason, but at least she was honest, and she was determined no one would ever call her a "cheater" again. So, she told him. She told him she wasn't strong enough. She told him they had to move on. She told him she was sorry. Afterward, she told me she loved him, and she always would.

I believed Abby then, and I still do, but she did move on, too quickly and indiscriminately at first, and every so often she would step back a few paces, toward him in her thoughts and longings, only to rush forward again. Today, she is no longer in a rush, but I still wonder if her backward glances will ever direct her path. I probably shouldn't. There is more to understand of the past before I can begin to glimpse the future or show you the present. Since the second official end of Abby and Ryan, I have reinstituted the Don't Ask/Don't Tell policy, which I usually maintain, and they routinely break, but circumstances sometimes make contact between them unavoidable.

During the most intense time of their break-up—still such a strange way to characterize the end of a romance that really never was—I vowed to myself that I would not say his name to her or hers to him. I would exist not between them, but with them—each, separately. I tried. I really did. It was impossible.

Immediately after Abby's post-Valentine's Day phone call, I emailed Ryan, simply telling him that Abby told me, and saying that I understood if he would rather not hear from me, that I'd leave any further contact up to him. I also told Abby I would not bring him up to her if he did continue to write and call.

Two days after she ended things, she called me. She had just received a Valentine's Day card from him. It was postmarked February 8, and she sobbed, "He was just sentenced to prison for five years, but he wrote a poem for me." She wanted me to tell him she received it and that it was beautiful. I did not email him. I didn't know if he wanted to hear from me, and I did not want her message to be the purpose of my email. Then, a letter came for me.

Ryan's penmanship had changed.

February 26, 2018

Dear Ms. Colleen,

I'm not sure of how much you have talked to Abby about everything, but we haven't talked in about two weeks. She told me some things that hurt to hear, but I appreciate her honesty and completely understand. I know she has spent way too much time worrying about me and too much money on trips and phone calls. That poor girl is stressed out because of me and should be spending her time and money on better things like traveling to places other than the San Diego County Jail. I don't want to be the reason she misses opportunities in life. I have had some great experiences, already been around the world, so it's her turn now. All of that, with our last conversation just solidified me knowing that the right thing is for her to move on. I know there are a ton of guys out there who are so happy she's available. If there's someone else who can give her what she needs right now, then let them, because I can't. And this isn't self-pity. I fucking love Abby so much, but certainly don't benefit her right now and will be a while before I do. I hope she's learned a little from me and maybe I've raised her standards in what to expect from a man. She has definitely raised mine. I hate that quote "if you love something, let it go," but it's true. I think this is the first time I ever understood it. Abby is so beautiful inside and out. Ms. Colleen, please make sure that whoever her next guy is, he knows that. I'm here where I can't touch, talk, love, help, kiss, or just see her when I need or want to, but that's being forced on me. That kind of pain shouldn't be forced on her. That's the right thing to think, isn't it?

This is a weird journey. I feel like I've gone through a transition that has been like a color wheel or rainbow that started with white light and ended in black. I started as a color that's made of every color, so I got along with every color, and every color needed me to help them shine. Even the colors I helped be more vivid have forgotten me, but I'm still here. Unfortunately, I used up all my energy focusing on others instead of helping myself, noticing my own loss of color. Now, I'm sitting here in the black darkness, but you know what I just realized? In the dark there are stars. They are way out there, but they're there. And even if I can't touch them, some of them shine their white light back to me, kinda like an invitation. Haha, transformation and light, I'm a moth! Butterflies are too fancy. Moths are more real. I don't know if that makes any sense at all, but it felt right to say.

Letting Abby go is real hard because I hardly ever was able to let go when it was necessary, but I've accepted a lot of hard things this past year, and if she shines when she's gone, it will make me happy. Ms. Colleen, do you know you're the only one who has been with me consistently this whole time? Other people don't even answer when I call. Nobody writes but you and Abby. And I understand if not, but if you don't mind, I would still like to write to you. I love you so much for making room in your life for me.

Haha, and how do you like my new handwriting? I thought I'd try to improve my script, but I think I'm doing some of the letters wrong. Thank you for listening to me. Please tell Mr. Scott and Opal I said hey! I love y'all to death. All of you. And thank you for always being here ready to give me advice. Lord knows I need it.

Love,
Ryan Freeman

He was forming some of the cursive letters wrong, but it didn't matter. His words sank within me, anchoring me to a hope.

I am the one still having trouble letting go. I guess the irony is fate's little joke, the same one she keeps playing. I've told you that I think I'm crazy sometimes, the kind of crazy that flies under the radar, the kind that notices patterns that aren't there, immediately theorizes conspiracies as explanations to shocking events, and thinks that synchronicities in one's life mean something, though what is anyone's guess. I have the everyday sense not to broadcast my offness, and mostly I'm just humored by it, but the level of coincidence—in which I do not believe—that occurs between Abby and Ryan is almost too much for even me.

How can it mean nothing?

Their timing is synchronized, always close enough to make me wonder if they've spoken and just aren't telling me. Maybe a day after I got the letter from Ryan, Abby texted me a picture of her apartment with the morning light shining in. Sunlight passed through the beveled glass of her back door and fell across the white tile in patterns of color, while in the shaded part of the room, she sat with camera aimed toward the ribbons of light just past her, her toes—painted a nacreous pink—barely visible on the ottoman. The text that followed said, "Little rainbows everywhere, but none for me."

I responded to Ryan's letter with an email, the last I was sure he received before being transferred:

March 3, 2018

Ryan, your letter arrived today, and I must say, the handwriting is on-point! One constructive criticism though: the tops of your lower-case F's should be as tall as the upper-case letters. Otherwise, what a change! This handwriting has a sophistication about it. I'm sure it will only improve from here. Honestly, you sound better than you have in a while, as if you've liberated yourself, too, by letting go. I agree that both of you need the freedom from worrying about the other at this point, and while I don't want to say much about all that, I will say your reasons for letting go are noble, but more than what you've mentioned, I know that Abby has to learn her own capacity for resilience. She got your poem and asked me to tell you it is beautiful. I loved your rainbow analogy. Have you ever explained that, in that way, to Abby? You have come with lots of lessons, Ryan, and while you've been good for her in many respects, your situation exacerbated others. But that's life. And learning. I hope you have both learned and that life doesn't take either of you toward any more chaos than you've already invited in. And of course, you are more than welcome to stay in touch with me. Please write to me as soon as you are settled. I hope they don't lose your things this time. And here's the stuff I probably shouldn't say, but if it offends you, I don't think I'm sorry. I think you should think about it: Your friends sound fickle. I mean, not even answering! No one writes? Do they at least email saying, "Hey, sorry I missed you"? I know you are not asking for my advice, but downsizing or changing your circle of friends might be a good idea when you are out. I wrote to you once about people who see and use others as entertainment, fodder for gossip, click bait. I have no respect for such superficiality. In genuine friendships, any relationship, there must be reciprocity, at least a mutual respect if other aspects can't be equal. People who show their love, not just say it when it is convenient or easy, are the ones I value. And with

that, much love, Ryan.<3 Ms. Colleen. P.S.I know March is a sucky
month for you, dates and memories.You are in my prayers.

March is the month it all begins again, a month riddled with rain,
memories, and birthdays Jenna, Abby, and I would celebrate together.
Sandwiched between the dates Jenna and Abby were born was a day new to
me, Ryan's mom's birthday, and the day after my birthday, which I share with
Abby, was the place this all began, the day his father died. I remember more
than I wish I did sometimes.

The spring of 2018 was quite different from the previous year—the
previous two years. Without the endless wedding and baby showers of the
year before, only Easter remained after March, and everything was calm,
except for Abby's decision to quit school when the semester ended. She had
junior standing but couldn't imagine two more semesters. She resumed
keeping a distance as she pursued her life, calling me on occasion, stopping
by unexpectedly, but not often. I couldn't help wondering if, although I never
mentioned him, if she avoided me because of Ryan, because she knew I
would know what was happening in his life. I wondered if she was scared to
risk hearing his name, or worse, if the sight of me reminded her of everything
she wanted to forget. The thought was excruciating.

I loved Ryan, but I wasn't willing to sacrifice my relationship with Abby.

I remembered, though, that Abby had kept a safe distance from me since
age twelve. Only when she met Ryan did she want me so much closer. Now,
Ryan was gone, and my place, my role, grew less urgent and again remote.

It hurt.

I know I've twisted all the feelings. Ryan had become a conduit between
Abby and me, and I guess I was the same between her and him. No one
intended that. Some part of it seemed wrong, given the way things worked
out—maybe my sister was right. But, I had grown to know him, to see him
not as "that" kind of guy or a charming renegade or a sad story or a felon,
but as a person fully fleshed out in his humanity, as full as any of us. How
could I walk away?

Keeping people simple keeps us from caring about them–it keeps our
lives more convenient. We reduce others to a single word and think we
understand them. The words we choose are seldom kind. To acknowledge
that another has experienced the same emotions as you is humbling. At least
it is if you ask how and why.

I read in an old psychology book about the painting of Narcissus staring
into the water. People assume he falls in love with his own reflection and
eventually dies right there on the spot, but what if that's not it? The author
suggests Narcissus stared so long that he stared right past himself, finally
seeing "the other" within him. Overwhelmed with sudden compassion, he
couldn't look away. I can't imagine how debilitating a rush like that might be

if you had never felt it before. It might kill you. What if, somehow, we were able to meet ourselves as older or younger, richer or poorer, a different race or gender—would we recognize ourselves?

We should treat everyone as though they are iterations of ourselves—because they are.

I did not want to believe that Ryan was just someone who would pass through my life on the way to his own, like the kids I taught. I thought all the terrible things, the strange things that happened, all the tears I had seen Abby cry—the tears I cried—meant something. But the older I get, the more certain I am of what I know, and that is nothing. I can't explain what I feel sometimes. The impossibility of saying what I mean overwhelms me. The loss of what never was overwhelms me. I know how illogical I am, and I understand the need to let go, but it doesn't lessen the difficulty, the sadness. In front of Abby and talking to Ryan, I try my best not to let them see. I work to keep the sorrow in, but it's there, sitting on my shoulder, cawing at me like a morbid angel, accusing me of never knowing the right thing to do.

Chapter 36

Doves

Time performed its vanishing act, and March became May, which became August, then December. Time moved, building a different world and making what seemed important recede into memory so deep that to dredge it up might shift the earth on its axis. From March to December, our "Don't Ask/Don't Tell" policy worked pretty well. Although there were occasional queries and declarations, no damage was done. I received and sent monthly letters to Ryan, who had survived another stay at Chino and narrowly earned his way into the fire camp program.

Within the prison system, inmates are assessed for the risk they pose, and the resulting scores determine where they are housed, what jobs they may perform, and what privileges they have. Their behavior within the system determines much of that, but the nature of the crime begins the process. Ryan's history on the inside was exemplary, but as a violent offender, his risk assessment score of nineteen should have disqualified him from the program. Because of the judge's reference, however, he won an interview, at which he ironically did not speak during the first half. The lieutenant in charge simply said, "Sorry son, but blah blah blah…" After the interview, Ryan called me to say they initially turned him down. But then, he explained, as he walked out of the room, he audaciously turned to the officer and asked if he could have just five minutes to state his case, which they gave him. On his second departure from the room, he was shaking hands and being congratulated on his new position as an inmate firefighter at the California Correctional Center Firehouse in Susanville. He was transferred to the northern California facility in July, underwent training and classes, earned certificates, and eventually saved lives—at least two in addition to his own.

I saw Ryan's growth in the letters we exchanged. They acquired a different nature. He rarely asked about Abby, as seldom as she asked about him, but more than once, I'd retrieve a letter from the mailbox just as my phone would ring. It would be her. Their timing was still in unison, but they were separately moving on.

I hung comfortably in the balance for a little while.

I focused my attention where it seemed appreciated. Abby had found someone in whom she was interested, but she was not very forthcoming about the new relationship. She seemed happy, though, so I did my best to be happy for her.

Ryan's letters became more interesting in a few ways. He had begun to decorate his envelopes with drawings. Once, I had frivolously described my excitement over finding a tiny, forgotten box of unopened Jelly Bellies, a student's gift to me left over from Christmas, when I cleaned out my desk in May. The next letter I received was adorned with a wizard holding in his hands the "offering" of a giant jellybean. Another was of a chicken on crutches eating a fried chicken leg with the caption "Worth It." Another was a dove. There were several illustrated envelopes, and I laughed aloud at their wit sometimes, but other times, the letters he wrote nearly drew tears from me, not from sadness anymore, but from joy—maybe meaning is a more appropriate word—from seeing the change he had undergone. Each one— in his new handwriting, complete with proper "f's"—conveyed clarity in his voice and eagerness to learn everything he could. He was full of insight and questions, and in my responses, I told him as much.

June 12, 2018

Dear Ryan,

I am so glad you have heard from your family! I confess that I thought about anonymously sending them stamped envelopes addressed to you, complete with blank paper inside. I figured they could find a pen. But, alas, I realize it is not my place to do such things. And I am so impressed that you have read Dante's Inferno! Do you know that most people's ideas of Heaven and Hell come from The Divine Comedy *and Milton's* Paradise Lost, *not the Bible? True story. I haven't read Dante since I taught gifted English I years ago, but what stays with me is the concept of degrees of sin, each circle being a gradient that escalates as the malicious intent of the sinner becomes more intentional, more psychologically intrusive and damaging to others. It seems like knowingly causing someone to violate his or her own conscience is worse than lust or violence, like a betrayal of the divine part of self is a betrayal of God. Are you also reading* Paradiso *and* Purgatorio? *I'm so impressed with your choices! Seriously, I think all your reading and writing has been so beneficial to you, not just personally, but academically, too. If I sent you the first letter you wrote to me and you compared it to this one, you would see some differences, and not just the penmanship. You should be so proud of yourself. There are lots of reasons, too many to list, that I see that growth. Aside from your wit and honesty, which have always been there, something else has emerged—a sense of peace or acceptance, resolve, and intellectual curiosity. Maybe shedding the social worries you cannot control anyway made room for the mental energy I see in your writing now. Whatever the difference, the depth of your letters to me has definitely reached a lower zone in the best of ways, like how all the terrifyingly beautiful things live past the level at which sunlight penetrates water.*

Your thoughts, from a while back, on coincidences and embarrassing revelations definitely resonate with me. And yes, I've had a few brave souls bare their feelings to me in moments of awkward teenage innocence and idiocy. I attempt to handle those with grace enough to preserve the dignity of the confessor. And none of the confessions have ever been obnoxious. By the time any student is comfortable enough to confide misplaced feelings in me, they know who I am and how I am. They just need a minute to speak their truth and test reality, which is how a person matures. Haha, you have me remembering some stories. But, far more than the silly crushes, I appreciate the ones who really confide in me about their lives, their troubles and hopes. I have adopted a few students along the way. Most stay in touch until their mid-twenties, until life becomes more demanding with their jobs, relationships, babies, just life in general. Being a teacher reminds me of a revolving door, with people cycling in and out of my life. And that's okay. A few pop-up years later with something nice remembered or that just-then made sense, and I love that, but I don't expect it. So, anyway, you had a crush on Ms. Reynolds and told her. That's hilarious. And understandable. She's great.

Figuring out the secret to lasting relationships, huh? Having started that at age twelve, you were ahead of the game, I think. I think I knew it, forgot it, and later remembered in a way that seared it into my mind by age twenty-six or so, which isn't so bad considering I know people in their forties and fifties who are still fumbling around. I think humility is at the base of good foundations. And, you will discover that humility finds new ways to present itself throughout life. I think I've learned to spot it from a fair distance, so now, when I see it approaching, I nod in acknowledgement and check myself. Really, I know nothing in the grand scheme of things except that under certain conditions, whatever they may be—but usually they are not "right" ones— anyone will do anything. And denying that makes people more vulnerable to their potential weaknesses. Everyone has weak moments, though, so the best we can do is know ourselves well enough to recognize situations in which we should not put ourselves. I'm not sure I understand the question you wrote in the margin of your letter, but my thought on it is that one person's venting becomes the other person's gossip sometimes, so I guess if you've been a listener who has not turned other people's confidences into your own small talk, that's good! If you've sought advice from those who make you the topic of their conversations or who use you to fuel their own discontent—well, that's not so good. Chances are we have all been on every side of that situation at some point. Just learn—that is the best anyone can do.

Hmmm. Do I actually think I am crazy? Do I think I see the world, define reality, and comprehend God the way most people do? No, but being aware of that probably means I am fairly sane. Also, knowing that I am probably not right about much of my theorizing and that the next person's ideas are just as important as mine suggests mental clarity. My "crazy" is my willingness to entertain the unusual and accept possibilities that defy empirical evidence— to embrace the metaphysical, I guess. I am not afraid of questions about unanswerable things. I love those, so bring them on! I've worked out my beliefs pretty well, and realize they will change until I die, maybe even after. I like to think of myself as a Transcendental Christian, a cult of one. Here's an example of my kind of crazy: When I was little, I'd go to my grandparents' house often since they lived only two houses away. My Pop-Pop was the kindest, gentlest man I have ever known (and talk about a guitar player!). I'd sit with him in their yard and listen to him sing or tell stories about when he was in Germany after WWII or about growing up in Yazoo City, MS. The yard had a mimosa tree right in the middle of it, and he'd scatter seeds or bread crusts around it for the birds. Where I grew up, there were mostly sparrows, a cardinal here and there, a few blue jays, but in his yard, grey doves, mourning doves, would come in pairs. I rarely saw them anywhere else.

Anyway, he passed away much later, in 2001—thirteen years after my brother and almost a year before my father. After he died, I began to notice doves again, in pairs, then in threes. I've been seeing them for decades now, and I know they are just birds, but they are more than that, they are a sign or at least a reminder. I know the doves are real, and I know the associations I make are just in my head, but still. Maybe there's something to it. And that's what makes me a little off—that I entertain the "maybe." Besides, there has been a single dove lately, not exactly a fourth. She just chills near the house or flies past me on a run. I don't know if she's a "she," but that's the vibe I get. Anyway, I know how to keep my oddities in check and that I'm in good company when I don't have to.

New topic: you are a logophile now. If you do not know what that is, you will soon since you are on the K's in your dictionary reading. And Southern Gothic, you already understand that; you just don't know it yet. Have you read "A Rose for Emily" or As I Lay Dying, *or anything by Flannery O'Connor? Or how about this—do you know "Goodbye Earl"? By the Dixie Chicks? (I pair music with literary stuff all the time in class. See also:* Beowulf / *"Immigrant Song,* The Scarlet Letter / *"Take Me to Church," lots more!) Anyway, Southern Gothic always involves some twisted, dark, disconcerting tale revolving around damaged characters (isn't everybody damaged though?) whom you feel you shouldn't laugh at but kind of, sort of are disturbingly entertaining in the most unfunny, horrible ways. It's pretty sick stuff that taps into the foibles of human nature to leave readers delightfully unsettled. Or just disturbed, depending on their tolerance. Unfortunately, when Scott and I used to run the summer camp, we engaged in a bit of Southern Gothic flair in telling campfire stories and even getting the local teenagers to help out on a "haunted hike" complete with chainsaw and ski mask—the chain was removed. Today, we would probably be sued. More than one camper peed himself. (Disclaimer: these were twelve to fourteen-year-olds, not little babies!) Ahhh, the good old days.*

One last thing, well maybe two: You have figured out my strategy. I am a dealer in self-fulfilling prophecies. Everything I said in the letter about you all those months ago was not what I knew, but what I felt was true about you. I am easily able to see the good in others, along with the other stuff, but people often become who they are told they are. Isn't that the root of so much? I know lots of people are told the wrong things. (Oh my, what a weight just fell on me as I realize I have said the wrong things—but...) The joy of it is that you get to choose whom you believe. It's nice to believe those who believe good things about you. Secondly, I've also figured it all out, not that it devalues any of what I have ever done for anyone, including you, but it's probably mostly for me. Inspired by TBKTS and what you've further told me about EMDR, I've been doing some thinking about all this, about my savior complex, which I know I have. I'm trying to save my brother, and he's been gone for thirty years. Since I began teaching, I've been drawn to kids who fit his profile, whether they are male or female—tall, attractive, funny, troubled, sweet but close to going off the rails. I can't believe I have never made the connection so clearly before. Realistically, I know I can't save anyone, and you have to be careful when extending a hand to a drowning man, to use an appropriately inappropriate metaphor. I know they can take you down with them. Some of Zeke's friends did go down, whether they were with him that night or not. The collateral damage of others' poor decisions has a wide reach, but so do the lessons learned from them. I hope discovering my motive does not make my effort or my concern for you or anyone feel like less. As I see it, it is driven by a love I feel at my core.

Well, I should probably stop writing before this becomes a novel! And please, stop saying you have to find a way to repay us. Anything I or my family has done for you was done because we wanted to do it. You are in no way obligated to us! All I want is for you to live a meaningful, productive life, preferably one that does not involve prison ever again :)

Love,
Ms. Colleen

That was my response to the chicken letter. The next one I received was the dove.

Doves.

They still follow me when I run, or I find them along the way, a sudden fluttering from tall grass as I pass. Sometimes, they will be waiting on my roof's peak just over the front door for me when I return. I guess they've always been there, but seeing them now without thinking of Ryan is impossible.

June 23, 2018

Dear Ms. Colleen,

I only get to read the classics when one shows up on the book cart, but you're right about the sins being worse when they betray your own values.

Those are worse than the physical weaknesses. And what a compliment! You still have my first letter? Without a doubt in my mind, I believe I have changed for the better, and not just in my writing. I'd love to read that first letter one day, so I could see the difference for myself. You've also changed, you know. You don't censor yourself anymore or worry about overwhelming me with too much information. That's impossible anyway. I'm a sponge. Your willingness to share more openly makes me happy. And it makes me laugh sometimes, too. Your humor has gotten funnier and way more out of the blue. I love that. I can only imagine the hilarious moments of teenagers pouring their broken hearts out to you. I could never teach seniors. I'm way too naturally flirtatious and too much of a smart-ass. My actions wouldn't get me in trouble, but my words would.

I don't really think I figured out anything about lasting relationships at age 12, more like my mother needing someone to listen and God putting the right words in my mouth at the time. I'm just lucky enough to have retained the knowledge. Retaining and applying, however, are completely different. Applying requires wisdom. Otherwise, it's just good advice. Lots of people can give decent advice, but not many can live by what they tell others. Too many people fail to learn from their own mistakes, much less from other people's. They have no concept of a real struggle, and they lack God's eyes, so they live without really knowing how to live for too long. I never want to do that. Do you know that sometimes I annotate your letters? I'll circle words or underline some sentences to go back to and really break them down. You should write a novel. Hopefully, this isn't too weird to say, but if it is, I don't care. Losing people my whole life has caused me to keep "memories" of them, useful for everyone. Obviously, this question is 70 years too early, but if you die before I do, do I have your permission to bring some of your letters to Abby and Jenna? I'd choose perfectly. I myself plan to make a 20 second video every year until I die to play at my funeral. It might entertain my family. In fact, I know it would. I'm extremely comfortable talking about death, but if you're not, I'm sorry, and we don't have to speak of it again.

Ok, you are definitely not actually crazy. In fact, the definition of your "crazy" is what I thought life was about... looking for answers to explain the unexplainable, thinking outside the bun. Just entertaining the "what's next" thoughts broadens my scope of understanding for what's now. Are we dying literally to be born—the light at the end of the tunnel is being the last and first experience? Are we all living every life so that when God asks, "What have you learned?" we have answers. I pity those who don't. Does that explain

221

Deja Vu? Dreams? Connections we feel immediately to some others but can't explain? One life is simply not enough to gain all the wisdom we need to live successfully, but if somehow, we are all living each other's lives, think of how wise we could be. Retaining wisdom and applying it is key. The people running around the Earth confused about why they're here, why they're dying, why they didn't learn anything. The why is to see ourselves in each other. It's to love. At least that's one way to look at it, haha.

Ready to be freaked out? I wasn't, but at least I'm warning you. Honestly, it probably won't freak you out. It will make sense. Because you're crazy, haha. I don't believe in coincidences either. Have you seen the tattoo I got after my dad died? It's 4 doves. Travis, Marissa, Mama, and Daddy around praying hands and rays of light. Mama used to make cooing noises to us, and we all learned how to do it. Doves are the only birds I notice, other than exotic ones, and obviously, they remind me of my family, too. I see them every day in here in pairs and they seem to look right at me. Oddly enough, you mentioned sparrows, too. I have one tattooed on my thigh to represent me. Weird, huh?

Well, enough of peaceful doves, how 'bout chainsaws? I have a history with them, too. And I think my life is a Southern Gothic story, by the way. My parents used to play those kinds of practical jokes on us as kids. It messed us up a little—gave my sister anxiety, and me nightmares. I think it screwed up my perception of reality, not allowing fear to kick in when it was actually supposed to because I didn't think what I was experiencing was real. Like when my dad actually put a shotgun to everybody's heads, I wasn't scared because I thought it was fake. And when mama—I thought that was fake, too, at first. I get scared of things that shouldn't scare me and don't even react to things that I should. I remember this one time when I was really young, probably 4 or 5, Daddy noticed I slept with my feet uncovered, poking out of the blanket. So, he told me an elaborate story about a guy who slept that way, too, said he was a college football player, and jealous teammates possessed by demons snuck into his room and hacked off his feet one night with a saw. Now, he prowls the night in a wheelchair and does it to others for revenge. Well, that really scared my four-year-old ass, but I forgot about it eventually. Then one night when he had some buddies over drinking with him, I fell asleep. I woke up unable to move because his friends were on each side holding a sheet tight over me with my feet out. Dad was at the foot of the bed, covered in thick red Kool-Aid mix, in a wheelchair, with a chainless chainsaw going full throttle coming slowly down at my shins. I screamed until the saw touched my legs. Then I passed out. To this day, I sleep with my feet covered even if the rest of me is butt-naked. "The good old days" is right. Haha, but really, I haven't had nightmares and have been sleeping well since November or so.

Ms. Colleen, I am so happy you made that connection between your brother and wanting to help people like him. When I read, no, when I studied that book, I realized so much about the reasons for so many of my behaviors, good and bad. I thought about exactly what you said about your motives and even asked Abby if she thought staying in touch with me was good or bad for you. She said good. She actually said you have way too many thoughts and emotional energy, so your having some other people to distribute those on besides her was definitely good, haha. But seriously, it seems like your brother's death was a catalyst in your life, and I, having benefited from what it sparked in you, am certainly thankful for it. I am sure many other young people are, too, and in a way, I guess we are his legacy. That should make both you and him proud. No one knew then, but that's how it happened. I think my own life has given me the same fire you have—wanting to spare others whatever pain I can. I've tried to do that since the first time I saw my mama cry. But I know I caused some pain, too. Isn't it weird how we can be most kind to people when we don't really know them, but we are terrible to the ones who love us and we love most sometimes? I am terribly sorry for the collateral damage you have experienced from my bad decisions, and I am really very, very sorry to Abby, too. I might be over-estimating the effect of things I said and did on her, but I don't think so. I was horrible, and I'm glad we've finally stopped hurting each other. I have definitely learned a lot in this life.

Alright, three last things: 1. I think I would have loved your class. Led Zeppelin and Anglo-Saxon literature sounds perfect to me. 2. I am a logophile! How awesome is it that there's a word for people who love words! And 3. I drew an ugly, cross-eyed Barbie-looking woman named KoKo and wrote "BAE" with a bunch of crooked, little-kid hearts all over it and hung it on my bed. The cops see it every time they inspect my cell. I thought you'd find that funny. Oh, and I guess 4. This one needs a drum roll (which tells you even though I just made it seem like an afterthought, I've been saving it the whole time. Ready?) Before you write to me again, check to see if I'm still here because...I WAS REFERRED TO FIRE CAMP! I should be there in three weeks.

Whoa, that's a lot of stuff we talked about, huh? I'm gonna try to give you a call before I am transferred because there's a good story about how I got *in. Anyways, I love you Ms. Colleen, and as always, thank you for keeping me in your life. I hope you and Mr. Scott are enjoying your summer and appreciating every hug you get from your girls. And tell my mama "hi" for me if she flies by!*

Love,
Ryan Freeman

Chapter 37

Revelation II

That's how it was for nearly a year. Ryan and I continued to write back and forth while he was at fire camp, finding all sorts of other-than-Abby things to talk about. Often, conversations from my classes would spill onto the page, so I am quite sure that during his incarceration, Ryan had his fill not only of lame jokes, but also of unsolicited grammar lessons, literary commentary, philosophy, and obscure observations he never needed to know. He was too polite to act uninterested.

I had not really known Ryan before he was alone in prison, so I occasionally wondered if the interest he showed in the barrage of topics I heaped on him resulted from his isolation and lack of other opportunities or from a genuine curiosity. Once I rambled on about Michelangelo's The Creation of Adam and synapses—I decided that the space between God's fingers and Adam is a synapse since God is lounging in a brain—because pointing it out to every class was not enough. I get too caught up in looking for meaning, creating symbols, noticing synchronicities sometimes, but when they happen so obviously—like the book, the song, and the birds—it's hard to believe life is just chance.

The search for meanings—reasons—can drive you insane. Once in a while though, I do think we get to see the purpose of the design, all those intersecting lives we walk past unaware of how our own tangles with them.

I saw the purpose once.

When Zeke drowned, he was working for the gas company. Remember that. Anyway, about nine years later, my sister and brother-in-law were going through a rough spot, and they turned to a local Church group for encouragement. Their marriage survived, and my brother-in-law, Jason, became very active in the men's group there. He was on a weekend retreat once, and another member gave his testimony. Jason only knew the man casually, and as we all do, assumed he was just an average family guy because that's what he looked like. You can never tell from looking, though.

The man told his story, saying that he and his wife were at their lowest point—living off the charity of others, with his mother- in-law, and without knowing what new disaster the next day would bring. He said he was at a breaking point, suicidal. He looked for jobs, but no one was hiring. Jason grew more attentive as the man spoke, realizing that no one's hardship looks the same. The man explained that the gas company was his last interview, but even they said they had no immediate positions, but that he would be first on their list. That was a Friday. On Tuesday, he got a call. They lost an employee over the weekend and had a position available. The man said that job saved his life and has been providing for his family for nine years.

Jason knew.

The lost employee was my brother.

Life hardly ever shows you its machinery, but I know it is there, unfathomable in its operation. Events coincide for reasons beyond those we can understand, and we seldom discover them, but that once, my family glimpsed a thread of the fabric woven by the cosmos.

That's how I see even small synchronicities, as a clue that something beyond now is in motion, and the moment you notice it, you know you're in the right place, playing a role in a larger plan. That is how everything with Abby and Ryan felt. He called once when I was driving, and Abby was with me. She sat silently, not wanting him to know she was there, while he told me that he had gotten a dog to train as part of the Pups on Parole program. Another time, she had just walked into the house, and my phone buzzed, nearly migrating off the kitchen countertop by the time she—a bit freaked out—called me over to answer it. They spoke briefly on that occasion. There were others, too, but they all make the same point—and that is, I don't know how it was possible. If Abby visited frequently, I could dismiss it as chance, but she rarely came home, once a month, maybe.

Sometimes, a week would pass with little more than a text from Abby—usually in response to one I had sent. Sometimes she didn't respond at all, which hurt. My relationship with Abby had definitely changed from late 2015 to mid-2018, and beyond, moving from strained to close to painful, close again to I don't know what—available, or maybe understanding, intuitive?

We don't talk often, and she doesn't always text back. She does not openly share her personal life with me anymore, which may be good, but we both know how much we love each other.

I miss her—us—the depth of us.

She allows me occasional moments, inviting me in when I least expect it.

Near the same time as Ryan was accepted into fire camp, Abby began a new relationship. It was late July, and she had called me to say she and Riley were going to Destin for the weekend. I professed my jealousy, not having been to Florida's beaches in years, and asked where they were staying. That's when she told me. She met a man. She actually met him in April, when she and some friends had taken a weekend trip to the beach. She had been talking to him since, and he had come to New Orleans twice, once in May and once in June. It was her turn to go there, they decided.

His name was Tristan Waters. He was thirty years old to her recent twenty, and he owned his own business, had served in the Navy, and was the son of a deceased father and estranged mother, and he had a three-year-old son. He was never married. I could go into it all—the miles she put on her car, the difficulties leaving her pets caused with Riley, the time she had to testify against his ex-girlfriend because she was stalking him, the trip to Amsterdam, and the worry all of it brought me. But, in the end, it doesn't matter. It didn't last. He was a bundle of sorrows and did not know how to recover from them. He thought her youth and beauty and kindness might be his answer. I think he still does, but I'm thankful she knows it is not. Their relationship lasted from April, I suppose, to December. They broke up just after Amsterdam. It was over before, but the trip had been planned.

Abby came over one Saturday in early November to tell me about the trip and to get her passport, which was still at our house among the important papers. Scott was walking out the door on his way to the gym just as she arrived, so they hugged hello and he asked how long she planned to stay. Hearing her say "a while" delighted me. Opal, always excitable but more so when Abby was around, danced on her hind legs waiting for attention. We decided to take her for a walk together although I had run two miles with her earlier that morning.

The weather was still warm and Black-eyed Susans were blooming along the trails. Abby pointed them out, saying, "Those are your favorites, aren't they?"

"They are," I said, smiling. "All sunny and bright with a dark center."

"Oh my gosh. You are so dramatic," she said, rolling her eyes.

We walked and talked about school—mine—and raccoon tracks and parallel dimensions and Brett Kavanaugh, who was recently in the news. I suppose that laid the foundation for the conversation we continued when we got home. Comfortably on the daybed with the dog between us once more, we meandered in conversation through politics and scandals and relationships, which is when she told me that Tristan wanted to take her to Europe, either Paris or Amsterdam. She wanted to go to Amsterdam more because Paris was "so cliché," she asserted with an accent as she sipped her tea, pinky out. I told her such a big trip sounded serious and asked how serious she was about him. She said she did love him, which I understood as filial love, because Abby loves everyone too easily, but not the "in" kind of love. She said there was much to love about him, but she was not sure of a future. She said, "He just wants to take me, and I want to go, so it's simple."

Then she added, "His friend Chuck is going, too."

The look on my face must have given away my thoughts because her next words were, "Don't worry, Mama, he's nothing like Derrick was. Besides, I actually know him already. And I'm not stupid anymore."

Surprised by her willingness to mention it at all, I said, "I didn't say a word."

"I know, but you thought about it." She was perceptive, and I was not, am not, as opaque as I think.

"Is all of that still something you think about?" I asked. "I was willing to let that conversation rest forever."

She looked at me, saying, "I mean, I've just thought about it so much, especially with all the stuff in the news lately. Even if Chuck were a little sketchy, I'm just not so stupid anymore. It cost me too much not to learn a lot from it."

"I'm intrigued," I said. "Why the news, and what made you 'so stupid' then?"

She sighed deeply, then began, "Well, I mean, the news—alone with a guy in a room usually works out one way, doesn't it? And stupid—well, I took a Xanax for the plane. That was dumb. I can get through the nerves of flying without it. Then, when he picked me up, I mean, he—Derrick—said it should be a fun trip even though I was there for a sad reason, so he suggested drinks, and I said alright. That was stupid. It was more stupid when drinks became a bottle of Jack in my room. Nothing like that will happen again in my life. Ever."

"Abby," I said as she refocused on Opal, "this is the most you've ever told me about that night."

With eyes cast downward, she said, "I know. Telling your mom about passing out drunk and waking up with a guy on you isn't exactly what you do."

"What!" I reacted immediately, before I thought. "Abby, what did you just say? You were unconscious?"

"I mean, I drank too much—stupid—so, yeah."

I couldn't believe her nonchalance. I had to be sure I heard her correctly, so I clarified, asking, "So, wait, were the two of you...together, I mean intimately, before you passed out?"

"Absolutely not. I mean we were talking and having fun, but if you're asking me if I wanted to fuck him, no."

"Oh, my god, Sweetie, that's rape!" I blurted out.

Unshaken, all Abby said was, "That's what Riley told me."

"Abby, love, do you not see it that way? I mean, if you were passed out, how could he…"

"I was, but when I came to, I didn't stop him. I think I said 'Ry' at first, but then I saw the dark hair, and maybe I tried to get up out from under him, but he kissed me. Hard. I stopped trying. I don't think of it as rape. I didn't scream or even try to push him off. I just…let him. I was so dumb."

"Oh my god, love. No. No. It is rape. I mean, did you want to have sex with him?"

"I told you. No."

"And he, he…started while you were unconscious?"

"Mom, yes."

"Then the only thing that could have prevented you from having sex with him was if he would not have put his dick inside you while you were unconscious! That is rape."

"Mom, stop. I don't want to talk about this anymore," she said, her eyes wet.

I went over to her and held her. I told her, "This whole situation is not what it seemed. Sweetie, we need to talk about it. You need to. This wasn't your fault. Why didn't you tell me? I'm sorry. I am so, so sorry for everything I said, for what I thought. I knew it seemed wrong. Abby, sweetie—and everything that happened after—the jugs incident. Oh, I am so sorry, love. This isn't your fault."

Looking at me through silent tears, she shook her head. "But Mama," she began, "I did it. I let him come in my room. I drank with him. I drank too much. I let it happen. I wasn't strong enough."

"And you shouldn't have to be! Abby, consent and compliance are not the same! I understand that you complied, but I also understand that your intentions prior to the plane, the whiskey, the passing out were nowhere near where the night ended." I retorted, feeling the absurdity of her logic deeply in my past, and understanding it too well. "Abby," I said firmly, "listen to me. I know you feel like you contributed to this. Xanax, drinking—all bad choices. I understand that better than you know, but ultimately, he was in control of the situation, and he took it where you did not want to go. And what choice did you have? Is he the kind of drunk man who would have stopped? He could have let you sleep. He could have left while you were asleep. He could have acted like a friend should act! You were not the bad guy. Sweetie, you have been holding this in for almost two years! Oh, what has it done to you? Baby, still, you should really talk to someone, about everything, professionally."

She looked at me, as if to say, no, we've tried that. Then she said, barely audible, "But I'm talking to you."

I just held her. For so long, I had blamed her, said those terrible things to her then, assumed the worst about her behavior for two years, and now, I don't know how I didn't know. I have lived, wrote, and read this. It hurts. Not seeing what I did not know to look for feels like my biggest failure. Cutting her hair, losing all interest in school, losing weight, smoking so much, the depression, the boys' whose names I never heard, this man's name, so much older—it was all right in front of me, and I missed it. I had completely lost sight of her. Abby traveled through the truth of her pain alone. How strong did she think she had to be? I realized, just now: as strong as me.

Abby did not know then what I'm about to tell you, and hardly anyone else knows now: In July after my sophomore year in college, I went to Fort Walton Beach for the Fourth with friends, a trip planned since April, and though it was not spring-break-crowded, the hotels were filled and overflowing with alcohol. I guess I had my #metoo moment there. The story is so typical, and I'm not sure if that should make me feel better or worse about it; no matter how many other girls experience it, the memory of my moment still makes me want to look away. I had already had a few drinks that evening. Later, I was swimming—I know, a bad combination already—stupid. Anyway, as I treaded water in my wet t-shirt and bikini bottoms, a boy started talking to me. I remember not being interested—I had just met Scott—but I was being nice. I remember downing a shot of tequila by the pool, and another, and another. Things got fuzzy, but I remember saying I felt sick. I remember going into a room, a bathroom. I remember vomiting. Someone was holding my hair. I don't remember who it was. I don't remember his being there with me. I don't remember disrobing. I don't remember his hands on me. I don't remember anything. I remember waking up—or coming to consciousness—and wondering how I got there, naked on the cold tile of a bathroom floor gritty with sand and seeing him, shorts on, sitting there. I remember covering myself with a dirty towel then asking in genuine confusion, "What's happening? Are you trying to have sex with me?" He told me we already had. I didn't remember. I cried. I cried and told him I needed to go, threw on my still-wet shirt and bottoms, and walked out, walked past a small chorus of "Yeahhhh, get it, Cole!" So that was his name; I didn't remember. He followed me, asking what was wrong. He thought I wanted to. I had gone to his room. "Because I was sick," I spoke almost inaudibly. I told him I didn't remember, that I must have blacked out. Didn't I throw up? I asked. Did I seem like I wanted to? I asked. I asked if I said no. No, I hadn't said no. I didn't know what to think. He seemed like a decent guy, not a predator or pervert or anything other than a regular boy. I didn't remember anything, but there I was.

I hated myself then, almost as much as I'd hate myself later, much later, when a ring was on my finger. In the 1980's, no one had said "me, too" yet. I didn't think I was assaulted. People wonder why women wait so long to say anything. I think it's because we just don't know what to say in cases like mine, like Abby's. No one wants to tell a story of drinking, willingly "hanging out," and then waking up naked or with a man on top of you. Alcohol complicates everything. Blacking out isn't passing out. It's more like missing time, having time stolen from you. I don't know how I behaved. I didn't consider what happened to me a rape. The only violation I could grasp was the one I made to the commitment I already felt to Scott. But, I've let that all go. The pain I hold from it is my confusion that became secrecy, my selfishness, dishonesty—my delayed honesty. It happened before Scott and I were officially together, but by the time I told him, it felt like a terrible betrayal, not the act itself so much, but the silent lie that wrapped around it in the years that followed. I've learned to be honest with myself since then. It prevents me from deceiving those I love, even by omission.

People misunderstand behavior after sexual assault, expecting victims to be filled with righteous anger that drives them to report immediately. Instead, guilt, shame, anxiety, and sadness often overwhelm them, paralyze them into silence. Not having the option of flight, they are caught in a state of fright that they may not even recognize as such, being too confused about the details, how the situation evolved to what it was. Mindlessly, they might comply, "fawn," as obsequious, self-protective behavior toward an aggressor is now called. Consent is direct, an act of will. Compliance is passive, a reaction driven by some unspoken "or else," a fear of the possibly worse unknown. Sex should never be a compromise between what you want and what you think you can withstand—that goes for other aspects of a relationship, too. I know so many women willing to tolerate what they absolutely do not want simply because it is familiar.

A friend told me this story: She has a friend who would never divorce her husband. Her life is too secure. Despite his expectation that she work full time and manage the "womanly chores,"—which is everything except what the lawn service does—she knows what she has with him. To call him controlling is an understatement. He "micromanages." He is a man who uses her bath water after she washes to save money on the water bill. She secretly retaliates. She pees in the tub before she gets out. Resentment is not what anyone willingly chooses. Women resort to it because it feels like control, and sometimes control seems worth more than dignity. People believe rapes occur in dark alleys and deserted parks, but that happens mostly in movies. The everyday varieties occur in cars, on sofas, in master bedrooms, in hotel rooms—carried out by familiar faces, men mistaken for trustworthy.

Abby had to learn her own lessons, but I wanted to help her recover from the feelings of worthlessness that I knew had come, the confusion of how to be in a world that still told girls having a tiny waist, full busts and lips and hips, a pretty face would make their lives #amazing, told them that the double standard was dead, and then called them whores for flaunting their appearance and resurrected judgment when it was convenient. The disconnect between real-life interaction and media messages spans light years sometimes. No wonder even well-adjusted young women have difficulty navigating, much less girls who have been victims.

People think someone who is raped would avoid sex, might avoid men altogether, and they might, but that isn't always true. Often, they have more sexual partners than they would have had, had the assault not occurred. I wish I could explain it well. I can't. But, when you believe the worst of yourself, especially when you believe others believe it too, sometimes you claim it. It seems simultaneously a form of self-harm and false empowerment. It's about control, or the illusion of it, like the student who never tries because at least failing on purpose makes it seem like a choice. Like a self-fulfilling prophecy, some people adopt whatever negativity others thrust upon them— liar, thief, slut, thug—perhaps to avoid conflict, which might displease the name-callers even more, or to punish themselves, or to give themselves a sense of control by choosing the easiest option when options have been robbed from them. Victims of sexual assault have no choice. The soul-deep violation confuses their self-perceptions, and no wonder. When sex becomes an exercise of power, why wouldn't women, especially those who have been victims before, behave seductively, making themselves believe they have control? The only problem with that, though, is that I don't know if many men have ever felt subjugated by being brought to orgasm.

Abby had to have been suffering quietly through her memories, her own misplaced blame, attempting to escape in the wrong ways for nearly two years, and I didn't see it. She told me she wasn't sure if she had ever told Ryan in the same way she told me. They had not talked about it when she saw him last. When she told him in January of '17, she thought taking responsibility for it was best, that anything else would seem like blame and cowardice or—ironically—a lie. She saw no point in his knowing now. I completely disagreed but didn't tell her that. I knew I would tell him, but not when or how. I could not let him continue to think of her so wrongly in his memories. I did tell her that she was still denying a lot of feelings, that she had not really resolved the incident or some missteps that might have resulted from it. She sat with me, crying quietly, now and then letting out a sputtered breath as I spoke. She didn't want to hear any of it, but she did listen—more this time than any before. How could I have missed so much? The thought of Abby's emotional burden became too much for me to carry. I told Scott. He didn't know how to react. He, too, had taken Abby at her word: she just cheated.

People usually lie to make themselves look better or simply different because they are afraid of some consequence. Abby said, later, that being thought of as a "slut" was easier than labeling herself a victim. Too much comes with victimhood. People sometimes contort their own truth to avoid the hassle. Sometimes people lie unintentionally, because something prevents them from understanding the truth, or because they feel obligated to protect others. I wondered whether Abby misperceived the situation to protect this awful young man—or to protect Ryan's judgment of him. Derrick was supposed to be Ryan's good friend. He was supposed to be a "dark-haired Ryan." He was supposed to be trustworthy. He was none of that. He was an odd-scaled snake that twisted around Abby's body and mind so tightly that she was still gasping for air.

Chapter 38

Cosmic Irony

December of 2018 proved difficult for Abby, as were the previous two years. This year's tragedy, though at a slight distance from Abby, was for a family I do not know. A high school friend, Carson, with whom she stayed in touch through his girlfriend, Rachel, was killed in a collision on I-12. It had been raining, and his truck hydroplaned, spinning into on-coming traffic. An eighteen-wheeler hit him, sending him into the trees along the roadside. His death, the first in her memory of someone she really knew well, affected her deeply. She was with his girlfriend when it happened. It was just two days before Christmas.

Like death can, the tragedy drove Abby inward, looking for meaning, wondering what could make life, in all its impossible fragility, worth living. She spent time with friends with whom she had lost touch over the weekend of Carson's funeral, but when she spoke to me, they were not the ones on her mind. Maybe it was the funeral itself, the reminder of the last one she had attended, that made her think of him. Before school resumed from the holidays, she spent the night with us. While she was snuggled under her old Hello Kitty comforter on the sofa with me, she asked me about Ryan. I told her about his progress in fire camp; about Buck, his paroled pup; and about the certifications he had earned. She listened, but then said, no, she didn't want to know what he was doing; she wanted to know about him. How was he doing? How was he thinking, and did he ever ask about her? I told her he did, occasionally. And, I told her that he had, indeed, changed. She wouldn't even recognize his handwriting now. Of course, she wanted to see it. Pausing just briefly, I said okay, and told her to follow me upstairs. From my desk, I pulled a thick stack of letters. She noticed the handful of illustrated envelopes and smiled at the chicken one. She liked the tree that was really a brain, too. I opened one, took its second page, and pointed out this paragraph for her to read:

Well, I don't make New Year's resolutions, but I can tell you this, The Ryan Freeman going into 2019 is a lot more patient and reserved than the Ryan I knew in 2016. I cannot and will not waste anymore of my life with alcohol and meaningless relationships. I won't dwell on the past either. At 22, I held on to bad memories, but never acknowledged them. I thought I was "the Shit." And I believed too many people who acted like I was. I is so much smarterer now! Haha. Now, I know shit is just shit. And I am human. I need to use that humanity to make my life better so that I can make better lives for people I love, which is everyone. I don't know what the new year will bring or what the biggest change in my life has been or will be, but Ms. Colleen, I promise you, I will be ready when it comes.

She read and looked up at me. "Can I read the rest of it?" she asked. I handed her the other pages. She took them, went to her old room, opened her closet, and emerged wearing his jacket, one she brought home to keep safe for him after he was arrested. She crawled into the twin bed I put in the room to replace her own, pulled the blue blanket up around herself, as if to protect her from something unseen, and read. She stayed up there longer than four pages required. I knew she was in a difficult place. Maybe she thought she would find answers in his words. I think she thought for a moment that he was the answer. I can admit now that I did.

Just a week before Abby spent the night before Christmas, I had spoken to Ryan. His phone calls from Susanville had become regular at every-other Sunday.

I had decided to tell him.

Although I had rehearsed the words in the incessant conversations I held in my mind, the call did not follow the script I had imagined. When I answered, after the recording, Ryan sounded elated. He went on to tell me that he would be beginning college courses in January, that he just mailed a letter with "lots of self-reflection in it"—it was the one Abby read—and that he was finally putting on the muscle mass he always wanted, so "please tell Mr. Scott that my goal is to catch up to him." The conversation was as pleasant as the sun on my back porch on that brisk December day, but when the voice gave us the sixty second notification, I found myself saying, "Ryan, is there any chance you could call me back. There is something I wanted to tell you." I suppose my tone suggested the seriousness of the unspoken topic. He said that as a matter of fact he could and would be happy to. We disconnected and my phone rang again within two minutes.

I pressed five and said, "Thanks, Ryan."

"What's going on," he asked, his accent heavier than usual. "Is Abby okay?"

"Well, that is a complicated question, and honestly, I am not sure."

"Why? What happened?" I heard the concern in his voice.

"A lot, but at the same time, nothing recently," I said, making no sense. I continued, "What I am about to tell you is from a long time ago, and I just found out." I don't know what he may have conjured in his imagination from that vagary, but I stopped just long enough for him to break in.

"Oh, Lord," he said without a hint of playfulness.

"So," I began, "Abby and I were talking pretty seriously about three weeks ago, for the first time, about her visit to see you in December of '17. She told me something I don't know if you know."

"Ms. Colleen, we talked a lot about that when it happened, and she told me pretty much all of what she did." The flatness of his tone told me how badly he did not want to discuss the topic.

"Ryan, I don't know if she told you this, and I'm going to say it just like she said it to me. She was explaining how she had taken Xanax, and how they were drinking—"

He cut me off, "She told me all that."

I ignored him and continued, "I told her that was the most she ever said to me about what happened, and then she said, 'telling your mom about the time you passed out drunk and woke up with a guy on top of you just isn't what you usually do.' Ryan, she was unconscious when he started having sex with her."

The line was silent.

Ryan spoke after a second, "Um, Ms. Colleen, I—she—Ms. Colleen, what you just said really fucked me up just now. No, I didn't know that."

"Ryan, I'm not telling you this because I want you to do anything. I just want you to know what happened, and you already do, but how it started changes a lot for me. It might for you, too. I said some awful things to her then. I needed you to know it wasn't what it seemed. She's not the person everyone made her out to be. I'm sorry to drop that on you, but she's my daughter..." I trailed off.

"I get it. My—um—I know girls who went through stuff like that. That explains why he was so weird when he came to see me. And I should have thought about how benzodiazepines can cause disinhibition. And she was vulnerable because of... It makes so much more sense."

For some reason, I responded to that with, "She's telling the truth, Ryan. She still won't call it rape, and that's what it was. She still isn't holding him responsible."

"Wow, this is just so much," he said with that laugh of his that's almost crying, the sound that holds his pain.

"I would say I'm sorry for upsetting you, Ryan, but I'm not. I wanted you to know. What you do with it is up to you, but I can't let Abby continue to misrepresent herself."

"I understand, I really do. I know I'm gonna think about it a lot, but do you think she'd answer if I called her?" he asked.

"I do, but don't feel obligated to do that, okay?"

"I'm not. If I call, I want to."

"Well, Ryan, thank you for calling me back. I know that was hard to hear. I'm going to let you go now. You need to sort through your thoughts. I've been doing that a lot. Take care, okay?"

"I do. I will. Thank you. I love you, Ms. Colleen."

"I love you, too, Ryan."

Rather than call me when Ryan made his next other-Sunday call, he called Abby.

To notice others' presence depends on much: their energy and voice, their frequency in your life, your own mindfulness and patience, your need for and enjoyment of them. And to notice their absence, that ironically depends on much the same, but with a different depth. When Abby kept her distance from me, I felt the loss of her terribly, but all along, I knew where she was, at least physically, and usually, emotionally. I believed, perhaps wrongly, that the time she had spent with Tristan or with nameless company was not truly an attempt to move on, but to bide time until she could have Ryan in her life again. I thought I sensed that. She never said it. And, I thought her unwillingness to reflect on what happened to her, to sort through the rubble to make herself whole again depended on him. I thought his understanding was the missing piece. I thought what she was missing was him.

As it turns out, I thought wrong.

From January through February, Abby and Ryan stayed in touch, and I stayed out of their way as best I could, having become a confidant to both. I know that I loved when Abby was with Ryan most because it strangely brought her closer to me. When she was little, she clung to me. With deep, dark eyes, she would look up with outstretched arms and say, "Hold you." She was affixed to my hip for years. She would crawl into our bed at night until she was ten years old, and even now that she is twenty-two, when she feels the need and makes the time to be here, she will snuggle up to me on the sofa. Times like that happened most when she missed Ryan and knew that I carried a small part of him with me.

I remind myself now that it was initially at her request. She wanted me to "be a mother to him," too, but that seems irrelevant now. Now, I don't know how to hold both of them in my heart without wanting them together, but I'm learning. When I imagine them apart, two, five, or ten years into the future, I think in metaphors—of donating clothes to the Good Will store. I imagine that, for them, seeing each other with others would feel like giving away your favorite leather jacket, then seeing it on someone else. It would still crease at the bend of the elbows from your years of wear, but on the arms of someone else. You would remember its soft fleece lining and know how it contoured itself to the curve of your back. You might even be close enough to tell if it still had that familiar, warm smell leather has, and it would remind you of the days you wore it in the winter sun and nights you came home, tired, tossing it on your bed.

But it would not be yours. You could not walk up and take it.

You would stand there, cold, thinking it didn't look right on whomever wore it and wondering why you thought you had to get rid of it.

Abby and Ryan's reconnection didn't last long. There were phone calls and letters of which I knew, and a few of which I didn't, but the biggest factor of which I was ignorant was that when Carson passed away, Abby had reconnected with a boy she had known since ninth grade, Eli, who was now a young man. They had followed and friended each other on all the apps back then, so he knew her, her story, and she needed an ear other than mine. I now know that they talked occasionally, snapchatting each other foolishness in January and February, nothing serious, she said, just a friend. But by March, conversations that began as mutual commiseration over their mutual loss turned into solace over past relationships. I guess the exchange of unhappinesses sowed the seeds of their eventual relationship.

The end of Abby and Ryan really resulted from fate's warped sense of humor.

Abby wrote Ryan a poem for Valentine's Day. It expressed her hope that they would give a real relationship, one in which they could actually spend time physically together, a chance when he was released. She mailed it too late for him to receive it on the fourteenth, but he did call her on Valentine's Day. Unfortunately, she was out with her friends, and the call was short and unclear. He never responded to the letter. She assumed he was angry about the call, her going out, and she did not write again. He called me, still on the every-other plan, but with so much going on in his training and my attempting to respect boundaries, I did not ask about his relationship with Abby. They were free to talk or not talk as they wished. So, not until March, near our birthdays, did Ryan say that he had not heard from Abby in almost a month, but he wanted to call her for her birthday. That's when I asked, "Didn't you get the poem?"

"What poem?"

"No. I called her for Valentine's Day, but she was with her friends, so when I didn't get a letter in the next week or so, I just figured she didn't want to talk anymore. She sent me a poem?"

My heart sank. A letter lost in the mail determined the future.

On March 17, 2019, Abby attended a wedding, unusual for a Sunday, with Eli. She texted me a happy birthday that morning and told me she would spend the day in Crown Pointe at the celebration. Ryan called me twice— once to tell me happy birthday, and again, frantic, to ask if Abby was okay. She was not answering her phone. I told him where she was.

And that was it, the end, I thought, for all practical purposes.

Abby brought Eli to meet us on Easter Sunday.

Chapter 39

Things You Can't Tell by Looking

The inevitability of loss is something we attempt—constantly—to keep at bay. There are moments of success, when we do not feel the emptiness of our efforts, but often even in an embrace of hello-it's-been-so-long, we feel the end. Understanding that, I suppose we all know how every story ends, ultimately, but before the end, so much complexity, often of our own creation, swirls in and out of our lives, teaching us what we can withstand.

Maybe the resistance we initially show toward something is indicative of the degree of our eventual acceptance of it—if we truly accept it. Now that Abby was moving on from Ryan, he was the only one who made sense to me. He shared one final detail about the last of his letters to Abby. After the lost poem, after the frantic call, after she became reacquainted with Eli, Ryan wrote to her, saying that he would focus on his future when he was released, so he didn't think he could give her the love she wanted anyway. She was right to move on. But, he told me it wasn't true; he said it because he hurt so badly when she wasn't there. He knew it was a defensive response. But, it was done, and he asked me not to say anything to her. He said to let her have her happiness.

I guess Eli makes her happy. He's nice, has an admirable work ethic, and no felonies. He makes sense, checks most of her boxes, she says. He's great on paper. In person, I'm not sure. When I think of them together, I see a neon sign flashing: Fundamental Incompatibility! But what do I know?

Clearly, nothing in the long run.

A few months into their relationship, maybe six months, after they moved in together—because that happened very quickly and without a bit of input from me—Abby hurt her back at work. Eli was at work himself, and I was home because Scott had just had back surgery, and I was there to care for him. Abby called, frustrated because Eli couldn't take her to the urgent care office for an x-ray, and she could not drive herself. She wanted to know if I could. Of course, Scott was rather helpless, and I hated to leave him, but what could I do? Having to choose between those you love is never easy. I knew Scott was fine and comfortable for the moment, so I went to get her.

Eli did meet us at the office later, so I didn't have to bring her all the way home, and as he and Abby got into his car, he called to me, "Tell your husband I hope he feels better!" It registered with me, simultaneously, as an attempt at cordiality and an admission of disinterest. Abby caught it too. Even through the closed car door, I heard her as I walked away. She pounced, repeating, "your husband?" Then she yelled, "What's my dad's name, mother fucker?"

Eli now knows Scott's name, and mine, too, I think.

Ryan walked out of the California Correctional Center on August 16, 2019, facing parole until February of 2022, barring unforeseen good fortune. During the last eight months of his incarceration, I continued to learn things I never thought I needed to know as I investigated the likelihood of Ryan's being hired by Calfire after his release. It was not probable at the time.

Apparently, a felony conviction prevented people from earning the required EMT license, which firefighters must have, yet the inmate program established for convicted felons, trains and uses prisoners accepted into it as firefighters and EMTs. In fact, California's wildfires are first met by inmate fire crews who work for $1 per hour as they dig fire lines and risk their lives. In 2018, wildfires ravaged the state, yet legislation to clear a pathway to employment for former inmates with Calfire met resistance. It infuriated me to see the news each night and hear of the laudable job firefighters were doing, yet never hear that near 3,600 of the men at risk were inmates. More infuriating was a state that proclaimed its progressive values loudly but obviously had little faith in its own rehabilitative programs, especially when the programs actually worked. Thankfully, today that pathway to employment is being established through California Assembly Bill 2147.

I helped Ryan as much as I could with information regarding his military discharge upgrade, too, writing letters to congressmen to ask that they be aware of his situation with regard to his PTSD under the Hagel and Carson memos, which I'd never heard of before, and be available to check on the status of his upgrade request. I heard back from each office, which restored my faith in politics just a little. I also had a colleague, a retired Air Force colonel who had served on a Discharge Review Board during his service, and my uncle, a retired Navy commander, read Ryan's letter of request for his review and for the restoration of his benefits. It impressed both as Ryan had written it, but both offered a suggestion or two that proved beneficial. Ryan sent me his grades after each semester. He maintained a 4.0. He sent me a list of all the emergency calls he had been on. There were over sixty. Two of them, in particular, were genuinely lifesaving. One, though, resonated with him more than the other.

It was in late May. School was already out, and Scott and I were sitting on the sofa in the evening, probably watching *Game of Thrones*. When the phone rang, I was surprised. The moment I heard Ryan's voice, I knew something was wrong. I asked what it was, and he began to explain. It was an attempted suicide call, he said. They arrived, and a young man, twenty or so, was lying on the kitchen floor, his mother panicking above his body, covered in her son's blood. On the floor, not quite in his hands was a shotgun. He had put the barrel in his mouth but fired through his cheek, not his brain. Ryan didn't have to say it, but he did: It was a reversal of his own mother's death. But, this incident had a happy ending, largely thanks to his immediately recognizing the boy's fortunate misfire. He said, "He looked dead, but he didn't look like Mama." I can't imagine how hard finding those words must have been.

I wrote to Ryan throughout the spring and summer before his release, mostly about practical matters since he was so busy with his courses, training, and job, but I did manage one last, heartfelt note. I tried to keep it short, but as usual was unsuccessful. In it, I detailed the belongings of his housed in my studio closet since the summer of 2017, when his friend Chris brought them back to Louisiana after his own discharge, and Abby got them from him. I told him that the items in the closet included two guitars, two amplifiers, a garment bag of snazzy dress blues, a nylon guitar case with jingly things in it, bike parts, a skateboard, and "an undisclosed number of skeletons." I also told him that despite my strange perspective on people saying, "I'm proud of you," I was proud of him—so incredibly proud. I finally felt close enough and helpful enough to believe I had some part in his success.

I told him I was honored to be with him on the unpleasant journey it had all been, but despite the pain, I hoped he would not forget the strength he found in himself along the way. I promised him I would be there to celebrate the end of it with him, and that it was so close. I was proud of us both. I thanked him for allowing me to have a role in his life, for all that I learned because of him. I reminded him that one day he would be old and I would be gone, but I hoped he would keep it all—the books, drawings, letters, and journals—evidence of an inner life no one would suspect just by looking—safely tucked away. It was evidence of his own hero's journey. And I meant all of it.

I also told him that, although I might never fully understand the relationship between him and Abby, I hoped he would remember her more fondly than harshly. That is the hardest part for me, letting go of what never was.

I didn't tell him that.

This is his final letter to me:

July 21, 2019

Dear Ms. Colleen,

Well, damn, your letter made me cry. Don't do that! Seriously, I can't believe this is probably the last letter I will send you, at least as a prisoner. With that said, thank you. I can never say it enough. You, Abby, Jenna, and Mr. Scott chose to help me during the most fucked up time of my life, and you helped more than anyone. From teaching me how to loop my lower-case F's properly, to finding information I needed to fix my nightmares, to giving me honest feedback, and finally to just being there when nobody else was, you made three years of prison easier for me. Not being able to have a mom to talk to in a situation like mine would have been horrible. I might not have had mine, but Abby and Jenna let me borrow theirs. Please tell them thank you for me, and tell Mr. Scott, too, because I'm sure there were days when he was sick of me taking up your time. I really needed every minute though. You helped me more than years of drinking and random girls ever could, and I don't know how I will ever thank you properly.

You've said more than once that you don't understand what Abby and I had. I have no idea of what she thinks, but I'll tell you what it was to me. When I first met her, I knew I was fucked. Here was a beautiful treasure of a girl who had lived ten minutes away from me my whole life, and I actually enjoyed talking to her odd self. She hadn't been tainted by my one requirement to date a girl: She hadn't slept with any of my friends. She had drive, plans, intelligence, self-respect, and an open mind. I met her at a gym, not a bar. She didn't care about my tooth, which I was so embarrassed by. Yet I did everything in my power to push her away. But she persisted. She knew the exact number of women I had been with, knew my dysfunctional life, and nearly every one of my skeletons. With all of that, she accepted me as I was. After Dad's funeral, I was sitting outside my house crying in a boat, sharing a hotdog with my pit bull on Easter Sunday morning. I asked God for a way out or for just some type of happiness to come in my life, and at that moment, she put her hand on my knee and asked if I would let her help me. That was when I fell in love with her. Our amazing conversations leading to that moment helped, but she loved me, and I knew it. However, I was terrified to love anyone. My ex had really hurt me. In fact, at the moment a tornado was destroying my house, I tried to call that girl and left a voicemail saying I was sorry for any wrong I did and that I loved her. I really thought I would die in that storm. Later, I found out that at the exact time I called, she was hooking up with a guy I couldn't stand out of spite. That broke my trust in anyone for a long time. Because of my own stubbornness and unwillingness to trust, I ignored that Easter sign and tried to make Abby dislike me. I also didn't want to ruin her shot at a good life. She had such a better shot than me, with a good family, goals, intelligence, and beauty. So, I told her my biggest flaw, which I was scared to death to do, and she flipped out and got angry. I left her alone to think. I actually got my things ready to bring her to the airport, but she did the exact opposite of what I thought she would. Then, I knew I didn't just love her, I wanted to marry that girl and have a family. She was and is so much more to me than most people can even understand. For a minute, the future that I thought was lost seemed possible. It all felt so real. I wanted to stop all my bullshit whoring around and marry the perfect girl for me. She was everything I wanted, and her family even liked me. And I did stop, but had a hiccup, got nervous, and pushed her away again. The week before I got arrested I decided I had to man-up and ask her to be mine, officially. I bought her a ticket and planned to ask her to be with me forever. When I date a girl, I don't commit unless I can see myself marrying her. That's why I'm so picky. We talked so much, Ms. Colleen. Our relationship wasn't about sexual attraction, the need to be in each other's presence constantly, or some other bullshit. We had genuine conversations. Our relationship was based on honesty, overcoming hardship, acceptance, and love that could be felt from any distance. We had a future. That's what I felt we had. She might explain it differently, but I have never felt that for anyone else, probably never will again. I hope that helps you understand.

Love,
Ryan Freeman

Chapter 40

Cleaving

I sit here tapping these keys, tears rolling down my cheeks, wondering—why does this hurt so much? Nothing has changed. I've simply reached the end of the story I wanted to tell you.

Everything will change.

Already, something has shifted. I don't know what it is. How do you hold a vision of the future with such hope and then let it go? How do you learn to accept things as they are without being overwhelmed by the loss of what they could have been? How do you live with never knowing?

I guess, in finally reaching what must be the end, it's time to let go, to accept what is and allow whatever will be. I've been cleaving to the past. Now, I must cleave from it. It's done.

Sometimes letting go of the familiar feels like it will destroy us, and in some ways it does. Abandoning those realities we build in our minds requires us to create new patterns, to construct paths through our thoughts that leave memories—those once-real hopes on which we believed the future would be built—behind. It hurts so deeply to become something new. I should know better, but I keep learning the lesson, and it never gets easier.

I am so foolish to think I had any answers. I'm sitting with such sadness, wondering why all this happened and learning again that I don't know a thing.

It feels like grief, like mourning the death of something so deep and unspoken within me that it has not yet been named, a miscarriage of hope. For all the signs and synchronicities—ones that still occur—the meaning I thought I'd find isn't there. Birds are just birds and timing is mere coincidence. Magic only lasts as long as you believe in it, and I have learned that being the last one who believes is lonely and embarrassing, like still writing letters to Santa in sixth grade. I really thought they would be a love story, full of bright, earthbound magic. Now, at the what-I-guess-is the end of this ordeal, I can claim only that life continues to find new ways to teach us, to humble us, to expose us to what we do not think we can bear, and then say, "See, it has passed." I suppose in that way, time does work her dark magic.

Abby and Ryan are just living, finding and fixing themselves, looking for what they once saw in each other in new faces, those once-strangers now familiar to them. Sometimes I think all past pain gets heaped into one smoldering pile, a conflation of half-memories and whole emotion that twist together so that parsing the strands out is as tedious as untangling knots in a fine gold necklace. The work overwhelming, we leave it despite its value.

Ryan was able to visit home the November after his release. He and the friends who came with him spent a day with me and Scott, and it was lovely. I don't think I've ever been hugged so tightly. Abby stopped by briefly, for an hour or so. Seeing them together struck me hard. As we all talked around the table, their glances caught each other, a tangle of emotion like the dalliance of eagles in mid-air. Later, Ryan told Abby that as he flew back to San Diego, all he could imagine was his heart as a ball of yarn, one strand tied to her, unraveling across the sky so that by the time he landed it was gone, except for the loose end in his hand.

I wondered if it were silver.

Ryan has been out of prison for eleven months. Now, in July of 2020, amid a global pandemic, he and Abby are living mostly separate lives, he in San Diego, serving his probation and trying to navigate his new, tumultuous romance, and Abby here, "working on" her relationship with Eli—and herself. Ryan told me. Finally, she was able to say the words, "He raped me," to him. He told me that they talked through it, through lots of things, and that he would always be there for her. He said they talked often. I try to let that simply rest.

Once, during the whirlwind of the last three years, Abby tearfully asked me, "Mama, what's going to happen to us?"

I told her, "Love, I don't know. But, no matter how much it hurts, you are going to live, and so will he, for a long while if you're lucky. You might find new people to love. You might love each other, but even if you aren't together again, you will always remember. You'll always know this was real."

"But what about you?" she asked, leaving me confused.

"Sweetie, I'll always be your mother, and I will be here for you until I die.

Maybe after. I'm not sure how that works yet."

"Mom!" she said, playfully scolding. "I'm not four. I know you will be here for me, but what about Ry, you and Ry?" I knew what she hoped to hear, and I realized for the first time that she understood how I felt about him, but I found the strength for honesty.

"I will be here as long as he looks for me, if he needs me, but I know with time, he'll need me less, and one day, I'll just be the memory of a need that no longer exists. And that will be okay. I'll quietly let him go."

"But Mama, he'll always need you," she began, hearing the choked words, seeing my wet eyes. Then she asked, "What if I don't like that ending?"

"Well, then, I don't know," I got out, trying to control my emotion. "Maybe God knows a different one."

Even after all this time, whatever was or is between them seems to me to be akin to that force driving flowers through the green, or the green itself, or maybe I think of too many metaphors. They are still not together, but they talk often. I'm confused about what they have, and it isn't my business, but I wonder how long whatever it is will last. Will it change in ways I've hoped it would? Will they forget, with time, all the intensity held between them? Or will they carry it in memories of what was and might have been, recollections as checkered as a newly sodded lawn, into the rest of their lives? When love itself has been so alive, what connection remains? Will they always have it?

I think they will.

I think they know, even now, that their touch upon one another's lives is indelible.

I think they feel it in the ether.

Afterword

"Now, at the end of this ordeal, I can claim only that life continues to find new ways to teach us, to humble us, to expose us to what we do not think we can bear..."

Knowing I wrote that sentence slightly over a year ago baffles me. I thought I was writing a memoir about relationships: a mother and daughter, a strained romance, an adopted family—and I guess I was. I just didn't realize I was also writing the future, which is now present.

On July 4, 2021, I received a text from Ryan, several actually, but the last one was an article from *99 Percent Invisible* called "Grave Guns & Coffin Torpedoes: Vintage Defenses Aimed to Foil Grave Robbers." I guess he sent it because of its oddity, but I read it later in the day, when I had time, and I texted a response.

This is what it said:

> You know this sent me down a rabbit hole...so, these defense systems are great symbols of grief, for how sensitive people are to loss. A wrong word or sudden memory--like trip wires--can unleash a barrage of emotion poorly targeted. And 'mortsafes'—they're like attempting to keep grief contained, under constraint. And in doing that, never really dealing well with it, so it's all still sitting there, heavy after so long.

I sent it at 8:57 p.m., but moments before, at 8:52, this message came through Instagram:

Hey Colleen, I am a friend of Ryan Freeman's. There has been an accident and I spoke to his roommate and he said you are the closest thing to family. Could you please give me a call...?

I called immediately, but as I dialed, Ryan's roommate, Dion, called me. I answered and learned of the seriousness of the accident, but before I tell you the details, I'd like to clarify something: I am not the closest thing to family Ryan has. His siblings are his family, and he has two aunts, his mother's sisters. My name is simply the one Dion knew, mine and Abby's. I spoke to him, then called the young lady who sent the message. While we spoke, the other calls began coming in from San Diego, Iowa, Phoenix. When my phone lit up with Abby's name, I thanked the friend to whom I was speaking, assured her that we would be there as soon as possible, and answered Abby's call.

Abby had also spoken to Dion and reached Ryan's brother and aunt already. We made plans to go. She and I arrived in Phoenix the next evening and told the hospital staff that his family was on the way. The nurse allowed us to see him and explained his injuries. Words cannot convey what we felt.

Ryan's recent life had become the stuff of dreams. His record was expunged on May 14, 2021, and he took to Instagram to declare his truth: After a life of hardship, he was finally a truly "free man."

In the brief time he had after his arrest, he accomplished so much. He was inducted into an honor society at San Diego State. He had just acquired a fabulous job in sales. His military benefits were not only fully restored, but he also received a six-figure lump-sum of back-pay benefits. Additionally, he, Abby, and I were excited over this very book, and he and I had been texting about my up-coming meeting with a potential agent. Ryan was on the cusp of an incredible future, and he was supposed to be coming home to Louisiana for a friend's wedding on July eighth. Several weeks before this, Abby, who had eventually realized the futility of her relationship with Eli, had asked Ryan, newly single as well, if he would allow her to take him to dinner at Keith Young's, a local steakhouse. He happily accepted and asked if she preferred a Ferrari or Lamborghini: He'd rent whichever she liked best and pick her up in style. He would be in town through the weekend, and I was excited to see him.

The most consecutive time I ever spent with Ryan occurred over the week of July fourth through tenth, while he was on a ventilator in a level one trauma hospital. The details of that week are a haze of pain and helplessness. There are so many things I could tell you about it all—the presence of and outpouring of support from his friends from California, the inundation of texts and social media well-wishes from home; also, the barrage of misdirected emotion fired outside the hospital amid Covid restrictions in the 110° heat; the palliative care meetings I could not attend; and lastly, the miracle of consciousness—but none of it changes the outcome.

Ryan died on July 11, 2021, after being removed from the ventilator. His organs were procured, and he saved the lives of three more people.

I didn't know, when I began writing, that our story would encompass the totality of Ryan's life. I didn't know, as I wrote about the profound losses of my past, that another was waiting for me at the end. The pain of such loss is real and lasting, and coping with grief is very individual. But, grief teaches us when we search through it—when we feel it as love rather than as loss alone. The lessons grow within us and create beautiful, unimaginable futures, just as the loss of my brother made a place for Ryan in my life. Under the weight of this love, I cannot yet imagine what waits for me or Abby, but I trust it's there. I like to think all the synchronicities confirm that, that they attest to the hurt we carry, so humbled by love, and reach us with signs that say "yes, keep going," as mysteries circulate around us unseen.

Acknowledgements

Foremost, I am thankful to the people who love me and have supported me in this endeavor. Abby Hildebrand, without you and your wild, unprejudiced heart, this book would not exist. Ryan, there are no words to express my thanks to you; I hope your current vantage point allows clear sight into my heart. Scott, thank you for your constant love and patience when I am sure you were tired of hearing every thought that crossed my mind. Jenna, thank you for your beautiful spirit, reassuring words, and critical eye. Mom, Cindy, and especially Ryan, thank you for reading and remembering with me. Many others, from early readers such as Jessica Bietzel, Kevin Speakman, Hannah Estes, and Rebecca Pierce to my Instagram friends also deserve thanks for their feedback, advice, and continued support throughout this adventure. Lastly, I want to thank my brother and father for helping me weave your stories into my own and supporting me in spirit all these years, and Ryan, yet again, for your authenticity, trust, gratitude, and love. There is simply too much to say to you, but now more than ever, you already know.

About the Author

Colleen Hildebrand was born in New Orleans, Louisiana, in 1969. She has seldom left her home state, where she still resides. She received her BA in secondary English education from the University of New Orleans in 1990, raised her family, then earned her Master of Arts in English from Southeastern Louisiana University in 2016. She continues to teach in the public school system. This is her first book.